Classical American Recipes

Classical American Recipes

Margo Oliver

Enjoy America's most treasured recipes

GREAT POND PUBLISHING

Margo Oliver's Classical American Recipes
Copyright © 1993 Optimum Publishing Company, Stowe VT

This special deluxe edition is published for
Great Pond Publishing Ltd.
95 Glastonbury Blvd.
Glastonbury, CT 06033

Creative Direction
Yvan Bélisle

Computer Design and Layout
Martine Lamarche

Photography
Studio Michel Bodson inc.

Stylism
Muriel Bodson

Food Preparation
Chef Stéphane Drouin

Chef's Assistant
Isabelle Gagnon

Accessories
Pier 1 Imports; The Bay, Montreal; Stokes Ltd.

Index and Copy
Alison Baxendale

Editor and Publisher
Michael S. Baxendale

ISBN 0-88890-236-0

Book Deposit: 3rd Quarter 1993
Library of Congress, Washington

First Printing, September 1993

Published simultaneously in Canada by Optimum Publishing Company, Montreal.

Printed and bound in Canada.

A word from the publisher

After graduating from the *University of Minnesota*, Margo Oliver joined the culinary staff at *General Mills* where she became known as **Betty Crocker** to millions of Americans. Among her responsibilities as head of the test kitchens at General Mills was the reading of the gastronomic pulse of America and responding with appetizing new baking products.

Her second, and equally illustrious career, included twenty-five years as one of North America's most widely read cooking editors. Her famous column, *Good Food*, reached more than 6 million readers every week. Soon, families from coast to coast were looking forward to the latest recipe from Margo's kitchens.

By popular demand some of Margo's finest recipes were gathered in her first cook book. It went into ten printings. Five books were to follow, each containing tested recipes that readers had requested over and over. These books were an instant success. As a highly trained home economist Margo's recipes were not only mouth-watering to look at, delicious to taste, but also healthful and nutritiously sound.

The book you hold in your hands, **Margo Oliver's Classical American Recipes** is here by popular demand. It was because of thousands of requests made directly to the publisher and author that we decided to publish hundreds of Margo's most treasured recipes in this new book.

The easy-to-use format provides both conventional and metric measurements and the number of portions each recipe serves. In **Margo Oliver's Classical American Recipes** there are hundreds of color photographs so you can see how the mouth-watering dishes will look to your family and guests. Several step-by-step instructions provide for a realistic presentation of good cooking technique.

As you use this book, please let us know about recipes you particularly enjoy. That way you will have an important influence on the next collection of Margo's best loved recipes. Until then,

Bon appétit!

Foreword

What makes a recipe a classical recipe? Perhaps it is one that is loved because, though not simple to prepare, it can be counted on to be perfect for sophisticated entertaining, or, though easier to prepare but still extra special, it is just right for company. Or maybe it is loved because it is a tried and true family favorite. In any case, a treasured recipe is classical because it is one with which no cook would want to part.

That is what makes this book a special cookbook. Although it has the usual sections, it isn't an usual cookbook. The wide variety of dishes, from the delicious and very elegant to the very good but simple, were chosen by the readers of my column through their letters to me. My readers tell me these are their most treasured recipes and they have each survived the test of time and taste. To me that makes them classical recipes.

I have observed from the many letters I receive that cooks become more sophisticated each year. Many are willing to spend time experimenting with new and often rather glamorous dishes to please friends and family. So, although there are plenty of dishes for everyday use here, there are also many which take time and patience to prepare but give the kind of stunning results that can make your reputation as a cook.

Best Wishes

Margo Oliver

Table of Contents

Imperial and Metric Tables

Volume measure
(liquids)

Imperial		Metric
1/8 tsp		0.5 ml
1/4 tsp		1 ml
1/2 tsp		2 ml
3/4 tsp		3 ml
1 tsp		5 ml
2 tsp		10 ml
3 tsp		15 ml
1 tbsp		15 ml
4 tsp		20 ml
2 tbsp	1 oz	30 ml
3 tbsp		45 ml
4 tbsp	2 oz	60 ml
1/4 cup	2 oz	60 ml
5 tbsp		75 ml
1/3 cup		80 ml
1/2 cup	4 oz	125 ml
2/3 cup		160 ml
3/4 cup	6 oz	180 ml
1 cup	8 oz	250 ml
1 1/4 cups	10 oz	300 ml
1 1/2 cups	12 oz	375 ml
1 3/4 cups	14 oz	425 ml
2 cups	16 oz	500 ml
2 1/2 cups	20 oz	625 ml
3 cups	24 oz	750 ml
3 1/2 cups	28 oz	875 ml
4 cups	32 oz	1 L
5 cups		1.25 L
1 pint	40 oz	1.25 L
6 cups	48 oz	1.5 L
8 cups	64 oz	2 L
20 cups	160 oz	5 L
1 gallon	160 oz	5 L

Cans
(on the market in America)

Imperial	Metric
5 oz	142 ml
8 oz	227 ml
10 oz	284 ml
12 oz	341 ml
14 oz	398 ml
19 oz	540 ml
28 oz	796 ml

Weight measure

Imperial		Metric
1 oz		30 g
2 oz		60 g
3 oz		90 g
4 oz	1/4 lb	115 g
5 oz		140 g
6 oz		165 g
7 oz		190 g
8 oz	1/2 lb	225 g
9 oz		270 g
10 oz		280 g
12 oz	3/4 lb	350 g
16 oz	1 lb	450 g
	1 1/2 lb	675 g
32 oz	2 lb	900 g
	2 1/4 lb	1 kg
	3 lb	1.4 kg
	4 lb	1.8 kg
	4 1/2 lb	2 kg
	5 lb	2.2 kg
	10 lb	4.5 kg

Length measure

Imperial	Metric
1/8 inch	0.25 cm
1/4 inch	0.5 cm
1/2 inch	1.25 cm
1 inch	2.5 cm
1 1/2 inches	3.75 cm
2 inches	5 cm
3 inches	7.5 cm
4 inches	10 cm
5 inches	12.5 cm
6 inches	15 cm
7 inches	18 cm
8 inches	20.5 cm
9 inches	23 cm
10 inches	25 cm
11 inches	28 cm
12 inches	30.5 cm
13 inches	33 cm
14 inches	36 cm
15 inches	38 cm
16 inches	41 cm
17 inches	43 cm
18 inches	46 cm

Temperature

°F	°C
– 40°	– 40°
5°	– 15°
30°	– 1°
32°	0°
34°	1°
36°	2°
41°	5°
200°	95°
212°	100°
225°	105°
250°	120°
275°	135°
300°	150°
325°	160°
350°	175°
375°	190°
400°	205°
425°	220°
450°	230°
475°	245°
500°	260°
525°	275°
550°	290°

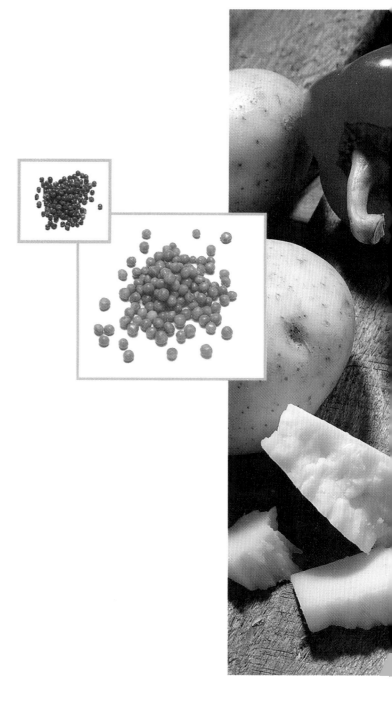

Soups

Soups

Good soups are part of good living. They can be the perfect appetizer or the backbone of a meal. And as soups satisfy the hunger of

those eating, they can also satisfy the creative instinct of the cook. They are fun and challenging to make because they are so different. Thin and light, a clear soup must be subtle yet enticing, while a robust chowder or potage may need more pronounced seasoning to be at its peak. Until you become an expert, experimenting and tasting is part of the pleasure of soup making.

Of course, a soup made with your own stock is a very special soup. On the other hand there are times when soup is called for and no stock is there to answer the call. Then perhaps a vegetable soup with a milk base or a fine chowder can be produced. Or maybe it is time to make use of the many canned, bottled and packaged ingredients that can result in extraordinary soup.

Here is a selection of some of my favorite recipes. Many are heart-of-the-meal soups that can be served as main courses. But there are also light soups, clear or creamy that are the perfect start to almost any meal. Finally, I have not forgotten to include some delightful cold soups – so refreshing on a hot day.

Barley Soup

8 cups	beef stock	2 L
3/4 cup	pearl barley	180 ml
4	carrots, cut in 1-inch (2.5-cm) pieces	4
2	onions, coarsely chopped	2
2 small	white turnips, cut in 1-inch (2.5-cm) cubes	2 small
2 stalks	celery, cut in 1-inch (2.5-cm) pieces	2 stalks
1	leek (white part only), chopped	1
1 cup	sliced mushrooms	250 ml
1/4 cup	butter	60 ml
1/4 tsp	pepper	1 ml
	salt to taste	
1/4 cup	chopped parsley	60 ml

Heat beef stock to boiling. Rinse barley under cold running water and add to boiling stock. Bring back to a boil, turn down heat, cover and simmer until barley is beginning to get tender, about 1 1/2 hours. Add vegetables and continue cooking about 30 minutes or until vegetables are just tender. Stir in butter and pepper. Taste and add salt if necessary. Stir in parsley.

SERVES 6

Bean and Macaroni Soup

1 cup	dried kidney beans	250 ml
4 cups	cold water	1 L
1 tbsp	olive or other cooking oil	15 ml
1 large	onion, chopped	1 large
1 clove	garlic, chopped finely	1 clove
1 1/2 cups	very finely shredded cabbage	375 ml
2 large	carrots, chopped	2 large
28-oz can	tomatoes	796-ml can
1 cube	beef bouillon	1 cube
1 1/2 tsp	salt	7 ml
1/4 tsp	pepper	1 ml
1/2 tsp	dried leaf basil	2 ml
1 cup	shell macaroni	250 ml
2 tbsp	chopped parsley	30 ml
	grated Parmesan cheese	

Soak beans in cold water overnight. Drain, measuring soaking water and adding enough to make 5 cups (1.25 L). Put beans in large saucepan and add the 5 cups (1.25 L) water. Bring to a boil, turn down heat, cover and simmer 1 hour or until beans are beginning to get tender.

Heat oil in small skillet and cook onion and garlic gently 5 minutes, stirring. Add to beans along with cabbage, carrots, tomatoes, bouillon cube, salt, pepper and basil. Cover and simmer 30 minutes.

Cook macaroni in plenty of boiling salted water 3 minutes. Drain. Add to soup along with parsley. Cook gently 10 minutes. Taste and adjust seasoning. Serve topped with a generous sprinkling of Parmesan cheese.

SERVES 6 TO 8

Cream of Asparagus Soup

Cream of Asparagus Soup

(blender recipe)

3/4 cup	water	180 ml
3/4 tsp	salt	3 ml
1 lb	asparagus, cut in 1/4-inch (0.5-cm) pieces on diagonal	450 g
1 cup	light cream	250 ml
1/8 tsp	pepper	0.5 ml
1/4 tsp	dill weed (optional)	1 ml
2 tbsp	butter	30 ml

Heat water and salt to boiling. Add asparagus pieces, cover and cook about 5 minutes or until asparagus is tender. Put asparagus and cooking water in blender, cover and blend until smooth. Blend in cream, pepper and dill weed. Return to saucepan and heat just to boiling point (do not boil). Stir in butter.

—————————— SERVES 4 ——————————

Corn Soup
(blender recipe)

3 tbsp	butter	45 ml
1 medium	onion, sliced thin	1 medium
1/2 cup	diced green pepper	125 ml
2 medium	potatoes, sliced thin	2 medium
2 cups	boiling water	500 ml
2 cups	milk	500 ml
1 tbsp	flour	15 ml
small piece	bay leaf	small piece
1 tsp	salt	5 ml
1/4 tsp	pepper	1 ml
19-oz can	cream-style corn	540-ml can

Heat butter in medium saucepan. Add onion and green pepper and cook gently 3 minutes, stirring. Add potatoes and water and bring to a boil. Turn down heat, cover and boil gently 15 minutes or until potatoes are tender. Mix about 1/4 cup (60 ml) of the milk with the flour until smooth and stir into the boiling mixture. Add remaining milk, bay leaf, salt, pepper and corn. Simmer 15 minutes. Discard bay leaf.

Whirl in blender (half at a time) until nearly smooth. Serve hot or chilled.

SERVES 6

Cabbage and Tomato Soup

2 tbsp	butter	30 ml
2 cups	coarsely cut cabbage	500 ml
2 cups	water	500 ml
1 tsp	salt	5 ml
2 tbsp	flour	30 ml
1/4 cup	cold water	60 ml
2 medium	tomatoes, peeled, seeded and coarsely chopped	2 medium
1 tbsp	dried parsley	15 ml
1/2 tsp	dried leaf basil	2 ml
1/4 tsp	celery salt	1 ml
1/8 tsp	garlic salt	0.5 ml
1/8 tsp	pepper	0.5 ml
3 cups	milk	750 ml

Heat butter in large saucepan. Add cabbage and cook gently 3 minutes, stirring. Add 2 cups (500 ml) water and salt, bring to a boil. Turn down heat and simmer 5 minutes. Bring back to a boil. Shake flour and 1/4 cup (60 ml) water together until blended in a small jar with a tight lid. Stir into boiling liquid gradually. Add tomatoes and seasonings. Bring to a boil, turn down heat and simmer gently 5 minutes, stirring often. Stir in milk. Heat to scalding. Serve immediately.

SERVES 6

Cauliflower Soup

1 medium	head cauliflower, broken into florets	1 medium
2	carrots, sliced	2
1/3 cup	butter	80 ml
5 tbsp	flour	75 ml
10-oz can	consommé	284-ml can
4 cups	liquid (vegetable cooking liquid plus water)	1 L
1 medium	green pepper, diced	1 medium
1 1/2 tsp	salt	7 ml
1 tsp	sugar	5 ml
2	eggs yolks, lightly beaten	2

Cook cauliflower and carrots separately in boiling salted water just until they are tender-crisp. Drain, saving cooking water.

Melt butter in large saucepan. Sprinkle in flour and stir to blend. Remove from heat. Add consommé. Add enough boiling water to vegetable cooking water to make the 4 cups (1 L) liquid called for and add this liquid to saucepan. Stir to blend. Return to high heat and bring to a boil, stirring constantly. Add green pepper, salt, pepper and sugar. Turn heat to low and boil gently 3 minutes.

Add about 1 cup (250 ml) of the boiling liquid to the egg yolks gradually, stirring constantly. Return mixture to saucepan, stirring constantly. Add cooked cauliflower and carrots and cook gently 2 minutes longer, stirring. Serve immediately.

SERVES 6

Lemon Consommé

2 10-oz cans	beef consommé	2 284-ml cans
2 1/2 cups	water	625 ml
1 tbsp	lemon juice	15 ml
2 tsp	grated lemon rind	10 ml
	paper thin slices lemon	

Heat consommé, water, lemon juice and lemon rind and simmer 5 minutes. Ladle into soup cups and float a slice of lemon on each.

SERVES 6

Lemon Consommé

Cold Cucumber Soup

2 medium	cucumbers	2 medium
4 cups	buttermilk	1 L
1 tbsp	finely chopped green onions	15 ml
1/4 cup	finely chopped parsley	60 ml
1 tsp	salt	5 ml
dash	pepper	dash
	paper thin slices unpeeled cucumber	

Peel cucumbers and scrape out seeds. Dice very finely. Combine with buttermilk, green onions, parsley, salt and pepper. Chill very well.

Stir and spoon into chilled soup cups at serving time. Top with a thin slice cucumber.

——————— SERVES 4 TO 6 ———————

Corn Chowder

1/4 lb	salt pork, diced	115 g
2 medium	onions, sliced thin	2 medium
4 cups	1/2-inch (1.25-cm) cubes raw potatoes	1 L
2 cups	water	500 ml
2 cups	fresh cooked corn, cut from cobs (2 large cobs)	500 ml
1 cup	milk	250 ml
1 cup	light cream	250 ml
1 1/2 tsp	salt	7 ml
1/4 tsp	pepper	1 ml
1 tbsp	butter	15 ml
1 tbsp	flour	15 ml
1/4 cup	minced parsley	60 ml
	crackers	

Fry salt pork gently in a large heavy saucepan until the pan is well greased. Add onions and cook gently 5 minutes, stirring. Add potatoes and water, bring to a boil, turn down heat, cover and simmer 10 minutes or until potatoes are just tender.

Add corn, milk, cream and seasonings and heat to scalding point. Cream butter and flour together and add to chowder, bit by bit, stirring well after each addition. Simmer for 1 minute. Sprinkle with parsley.

Ladle over crackers in bowls.

——————— SERVES 4 TO 6 ———————

Cold Cucumber Soup

Cream of Lettuce Soup

1/4 cup	butter	60 ml
4 cups	finely chopped lettuce	1 L
1 tbsp	finely chopped green onions	15 ml
2 tbsp	flour	30 ml
1 cup	light cream	250 ml
2 cups	chicken stock	500 ml
1/2 tsp	salt	2 ml
1/4 tsp	Worcestershire sauce	1 ml
2 tbsp	chopped chives	30 ml

Croûtons (recipe follows)

Heat butter in medium saucepan. Add lettuce and green onions and cook quickly, stirring constantly, just until lettuce is limp, about 1 minute. Sprinkle in flour and stir to blend. Remove from heat and add cream and chicken stock all at once. Stir to blend. Return to moderate heat and bring to a boil. Turn heat to low. Stir in salt and Worcestershire sauce. Simmer 3 minutes.

Stir in chives and ladle into soup cups. Sprinkle with croûtons and serve immediately.

SERVES 4 TO 6

Croûtons

3 slices	day old white bread	3 slices
2 tbsp	butter	30 ml

Cut crusts off bread slices and discard. Cut bread into 1/4-inch (0.5-cm) cubes. Heat butter in heavy skillet. Add bread cubes and heat until golden and crisp, stirring. Cool.

Curried Corn Soup

(blender recipe)

2 cups	raw corn (cut from cobs)	500 ml
1 tbsp	finely chopped onion	15 ml
1 cup	milk	250 ml
2 tbsp	butter	30 ml
1/2 tsp	curry powder	2 ml
1 cup	light cream	250 ml
1/2 tsp	salt	2 ml
1/8 tsp	pepper	0.5 ml

chopped parsley

Combine corn, onion and milk in medium saucepan. Bring to a boil. Turn down heat, cover and simmer 20 minutes. Pour into blender and buzz until nearly smooth.

Heat butter in same saucepan. Add curry powder and cook gently 3 minutes, stirring. Stir in corn mixture, cream, salt and pepper. Heat, stirring constantly. Taste and add more seasoning if needed. Serve sprinkled with parsley.

SERVES 3

Goddess of Spring Soup

(blender recipe)

3 large	diced peeled potatoes	3 large
1 cup	diced celery	250 ml
1 large	onion, sliced thin	1 large
1	leek, sliced thin (optional)	1
1 whole clove	garlic (optional)	1 whole clove
1 1/2 cups	boiling water	375 ml
1 1/2 cups	chicken stock	375 ml
2 tsp	salt	10 ml
1/4 tsp	pepper	1 ml
2 cups	spinach leaves, packed	500 ml
2 cups	torn up iceberg lettuce, lightly packed	500 ml
1 cup	watercress leaves, loosely packed	250 ml
2 cups	milk	500 ml

Croûtons (recipe p. 19)

Put potatoes, celery, onion, leek and garlic in large saucepan. Add water, chicken stock, salt and pepper and bring to a boil. Turn down heat, cover and simmer 10 minutes. Add spinach, lettuce and watercress, cover again and continue simmering 15 minutes. Whirl in blender, a little at a time, until smooth. Return to saucepan. Stir in milk, Heat to boiling point. Serve very hot topped with Croûtons.

———— SERVES 6 TO 8 ————

Cream of Parsley Soup

2 cups	finely chopped parsley	500 ml
3 cups	chicken stock	750 ml
3 cups	light cream	750 ml
2	egg yolks	2
1 tsp	salt	5 ml
dash	cayenne	dash
	salted whipped cream	
	chopped parsley	

Combine parsley and chicken stock in saucepan, bring to boil, turn down heat, cover and simmer 20 minutes.

Beat cream and egg yolks together lightly with a fork and stir into hot mixture gradually. Add salt and cayenne. Taste and add more seasoning if necessary. Cool quickly and chill.

Put an ice cube in each soup cup at serving time and ladle soup over. Top with a small spoonful of salted whipped cream and a sprinkling of parsley and serve.

———— SERVES 4 ————

Left: Goddess of Spring Soup
Right: Country Pea Soup

Country Pea Soup

1 lb	split green or yellow peas	450 g
8 cups	boiling water	2 L
4 cups	tomato juice	1 L
	ham bone, with a little meat (left over from cooked ham)	
1 1/2 cups	diced potato	375 ml
1 cup	diced celery	250 ml
1 cup	diced onion	250 ml
1 cup	diced carrot	250 ml
1 small	bay leaf	1 small
1 tsp	salt	5 ml
1/4 tsp	pepper	1 ml

Wash peas. Put in large kettle. Add water and tomato juice. Bring to a boil, turn down heat, cover tightly and simmer until peas are soft, about 45 minutes.

Add ham bone and all remaining ingredients. Cover again and simmer until vegetables are all tender, about 45 minutes. Lift out ham bone. Remove any pieces of meat from bone and return to soup. Discard bone. Taste and adjust seasoning (amount of salt depends on saltiness of ham).

Serve hot.

—————— MAKES 8 BIG SERVINGS ——————

Potato and Leek Soup

(blender recipe)

3 tbsp	butter	45 ml
4	leeks (white part only), chopped	4
1 medium	onion, chopped	1 medium
4 large	potatoes, diced	4 large
2 stalks	celery, chopped	2 stalks
6 large sprigs	parsley	6 large sprigs
5 cups	chicken stock	1.25 L
2 tsp	salt	10 ml
1/4 tsp	pepper	1 ml
1 tsp	dried leaf chervil	5 ml
1/4 tsp	dried leaf marjoram	1 ml
3 cups	milk, scalded	750 ml

Melt butter in large saucepan and add leeks and onion. Cook gently 5 minutes, stirring. Do not brown.

Add potatoes, celery, parsley, chicken stock, salt, pepper, chervil and marjoram. Cover and cook over moderate heat about 30 minutes or until vegetables are tender.

Whirl in the blender (or press through a sieve). Return to saucepan. Bring back to a boil and stir in hot milk. Taste and add more salt and pepper if necessary.

——————— SERVES 8 ———————

Vichyssoise

(blender recipe)

6 cups	chicken stock	1.5 L
4 medium	potatoes, peeled and sliced thin	4 medium
1 medium	onion, peeled and sliced thin (optional)	1 medium
3	leeks, sliced thin (white part only)	3
1 cup	heavy cream	250 ml
	salt and white pepper	
	milk (optional)	
	chopped chives	

Heat chicken stock to boiling. Add potatoes, onion and leeks, cover and cook gently until vegetables are very tender, about 45 minutes. Whirl in blender a little at a time until mixture is very smooth. Stir in cream. Taste and add salt and pepper if needed (oversalt slightly since salt loses some flavor on chilling). Chill very well.

Thin soup with a little milk if it is too thick for your taste. Ladle into chilled soup cups. Sprinkle each serving with chives.

——————— SERVES 6 TO 8 ———————

Potato-Cheese Chowder

Potato-Cheese Chowder

1 1/2 cups	diced raw potatoes	375 ml
2 cups	boiling water	500 ml
2 cubes	chicken bouillon	2 cubes
2 tbsp	butter	30 ml
1/4 cup	finely chopped onion	60 ml
1/4 cup	finely chopped green pepper	60 ml
2 tbsp	flour	30 ml
2 cups	milk	500 ml
1 tsp	salt	5 ml
1/8 tsp	pepper	0.5 ml
1 1/2 cups	finely grated strong cheddar cheese	375 ml
	chopped parsley	

Cook potatoes in boiling water until tender. Drain, saving cooking water. Add bouillon cubes to hot liquid and stir until dissolved.

Melt butter in saucepan. Add onion and green pepper and cook gently 3 minutes, stirring. Sprinkle in flour and let bubble. Remove from heat. Add milk and potato water all at once. Stir in salt and pepper. Return to moderate heat and cook until boiling and smooth, stirring constantly. Turn heat to low and simmer 2 minutes.

Add cheese and stir until cheese is melted. Stir in potatoes and heat well.

Serve very hot, sprinkled with chopped parsley.

SERVES 4 TO 6

Spicy Tomato Bouillon

48-oz can	tomato juice	1.36-L can
1	bay leaf	1
6	whole cloves	6
4 cubes	beef bouillon	4 cubes
3/4 tsp	salt	3 ml
2 tbsp	sugar	30 ml
1 cup	chili sauce	250 ml
4 cups	hot water	1 L
1/8 tsp	celery salt	0.5 ml
1/8 tsp	garlic salt	0.5 ml
1/2 tsp	dried leaf basil	2 ml
1/8 tsp	Tabasco	0.5 ml
1/4 cup	lemon juice	60 ml

Combine all ingredients except Tabasco and lemon juice in saucepan. Bring to a boil, turn down heat, cover and simmer 10 minutes. Strain. Return to saucepan, add Tabasco and lemon juice and heat just to boiling point. Serve in soup cups or mugs.

SERVES 12

Cold Tomato-Cottage Cheese Soup

(blender recipe)

19-oz can	tomato juice	540-ml can
1 cup	milk	250 ml
1 cup	cottage cheese	250 ml
2 tbsp	lemon juice	30 ml
2 tsp	prepared horseradish	10 ml
4	green onions, chopped coarsely	4
8 cubes	ice	8 cubes
1/2 tsp	salt (approx.)	2 ml
1/4 tsp	pepper (approx.)	1 ml

Combine tomato juice, milk, cottage cheese, lemon juice, horseradish, onions and ice cubes in the glass of the blender. Whirl just until blended (there should still be some little pieces of onions showing). Taste and add salt and pepper needed. Serve immediately in mugs.

SERVES 6

Peasant Soup

3 tbsp	butter or margarine	45 ml
1 clove	garlic, peeled and cut in half	1 clove
2 cups	1-inch (2.5-cm) cubes French bread (best if dry but not hard)	500 ml
2 tbsp	butter or margarine	30 ml
1 cup	chopped onion	250 ml
1 tsp	paprika	5 ml
4 cups	beef stock	1 L
2	eggs	2
1/2 tsp	salt (approx.)	2 ml
1/4 tsp	pepper (approx.)	1 ml
	chopped parsley	

Heat 3 tbsp (45 ml) butter or margarine in large saucepan with garlic pieces. Cook gently 5 minutes, stirring. Discard garlic. Add bread cubes and cook until golden, stirring. Lift out with a slotted spoon.

Add 2 tbsp (30 ml) butter or margarine to pan. Add onion and cook gently until onion is golden, stirring. Add paprika and stock, cover and simmer 20 minutes.

Beat eggs well at serving time. Remove simmering soup from heat. Add about 1 cup (250 ml) of the hot soup, a little at a time, to the eggs, beating constantly with a fork or whisk. Stir mixture back into soup and set over low heat. Heat just to boiling point, stirring. Do not boil. Add salt and pepper to taste. Put 1/4 of the bread cubes in each of four bowls, ladle the soup over and serve immediately. Sprinkle generously with parsley.

SERVES 4

Peasant Soup

Vegetable Chowder

1/4 cup	butter	60 ml
1 cup	diced celery	250 ml
1 cup	diced carrot	250 ml
1 cup	diced potato	250 ml
1/2 cup	diced turnip	125 ml
1/4 cup	finely chopped onion	60 ml
1/4 cup	thinly sliced leek	60 ml
1 cup	boiling water	250 ml
2 tsp	salt	10 ml
1/2 tsp	pepper	2 ml
1 tsp	sugar	5 ml
1 cup	frozen peas	250 ml
1 cup	slivered green pepper	250 ml
4 cups	milk, scalded	1 L
1/4 cup	chopped parsley	60 ml
1/2 cup	grated old cheddar cheese	125 ml

Melt butter in large saucepan. Add celery, carrot, potato, turnip, onion, leek, water, salt, pepper and sugar. Cover and simmer until vegetables are tender-crisp, about 10 minutes.

Add peas and green pepper and simmer 5 minutes more or until all vegetables are tender. Add hot milk. Sprinkle in parsley.

Ladle into soup bowls and sprinkle each with grated cheese.

——————— SERVES 6 ———————

Country Soup

2 tbsp	butter	30 ml
2 tbsp	water	30 ml
1/2 cup	fresh green beans, cut on diagonal	125 ml
2 medium	carrots, sliced thin	2 medium
2 cups	small thin slices turnip	500 ml
2	leeks, sliced paper thin (white part only)	2
1/2 cup	finely chopped celery	125 ml
1/2 cup	water	125 ml
1/2 cup	fresh or frozen peas	125 ml
2 cups	finely shredded green cabbage	500 ml
1 1/2 tsp	salt	7 ml
1/4 tsp	pepper	1 ml
1/2 tsp	paprika	2 ml
4 cups	milk	1 L
1/2 cup	shredded lettuce	125 ml
2 tsp	chopped fresh dill	10 ml

Heat butter in large saucepan. Add 2 tbsp (30 ml) water and beans. Cover and cook over high heat 3 minutes, shaking pan often. Add carrots, turnip, leeks, celery and 1/2 cup (125 ml) water. Cover and cook about 7 minutes or until vegetables are nearly tender. Add peas and simmer 5 minutes.

Add cabbage, salt, pepper, paprika and milk. Simmer 5 minutes. Stir in lettuce and heat. Ladle into bowls and sprinkle with dill.

——————— SERVES 6 ———————

Above: Vegetable Chowder
Below: Country Soup

Clam Chowder

48	hard shell clams	48
3 cups	liquid (clam broth plus water)	750 ml
1/4 lb	salt pork, diced	115 g
4 medium	onions, sliced thin	4 medium
1 1/2 cups	canned tomatoes	375 ml
2	leeks, chopped finely	2
2 stalks	celery (with leaves), chopped	2 stalks
2	carrots, chopped	2
1/4 cup	chopped parsley	60 ml
1/4 tsp	dried leaf thyme	1 ml
1	bay leaf	1
2 tsp	salt	10 ml
1/2 tsp	pepper	2 ml
pinch	nutmeg	pinch
4 large	potatoes, cut in 1/2-inch (1.25-cm) cubes	4 large
3 tbsp	butter	45 ml
3 tbsp	flour	45 ml
1 tbsp	Worcestershire sauce	15 ml
dash	Tabasco	dash
	hard crackers (optional)	

Scrub clams with a stiff brush under running water to remove all sand. Wash in several waters. Put 1/2 inch (1.25 cm) boiling water in extra-large kettle. Add the clams, cover tightly and steam about 10 minutes or until shells begin to open.

Lift clams out of kettle. Strain liquid left in pan through several thicknesses of fine cheesecloth. Measure, add water to make 3 cups (750 ml) liquid and set aside.

Loosen clams from shells (add any liquid left in shells to strained clam liquid) and chop half the clams coarsely.

Brown salt pork lightly in large heavy kettle. Add onions and cook gently until golden, stirring constantly. Add the 3 cups (750 ml) liquid, tomatoes, leeks, celery, carrots, parsley, thyme, bay leaf, salt, pepper and nutmeg. Bring to a boil.

Add potatoes, bring back to a boil. Turn down heat, cover and simmer until potatoes are just tender, about 15 minutes. Add chopped and whole clams.

Combine butter and flour in small heavy skillet, set over moderate heat and stir constantly until golden brown. Stir into chowder, bit by bit, stirring to blend after each addition. Stir in Worcestershire sauce and Tabasco. Simmer 2 minutes. Crumble hard crackers into chowder if desired and serve immediately.

SERVES 8

Lobster Chowder

1 2-lb	cooked lobster	1 1-kg
1 cup	cold water	250 ml
4 cups	milk	1 L
1 cup	cream	250 ml
1 small slice	onion	1 small slice
pinch	dried leaf thyme	pinch
1 small	bay leaf	1 small
1 whole	clove	1 whole
4	peppercorns	4
1 sprig	parsley	1 sprig
2 tbsp	butter	30 ml
4	square soda biscuits, crushed to fine crumbs	4
2 tsp	salt	10 ml
1/8 tsp	pepper	0.5 ml
1/2 tsp	paprika	2 ml
pinch	nutmeg	pinch
2	egg yolks	2
2 tbsp	dry sherry (optional)	30 ml

Lobster Chowder

Crack lobster and remove meat and liver (green), keeping liver separate. Dice lobster meat.

Put lobster shells in saucepan and add cold water. Bring to a boil, cover and boil 10 minutes. Strain off and save liquid. Discard shells.

Put milk, cream, onion, thyme, bay leaf, clove, peppercorns and parsley in saucepan and bring to scalding point. Strain and return to pan.

Cream butter, soda biscuit crumbs and lobster liver together in small bowl. Add a little of the hot mixture, blending well, then stir back into milk mixture. Add liquid from lobster shells. Bring to scalding again. Season with salt, pepper, paprika and nutmeg.

Beat egg yolks and sherry together. Add a little of the hot mixture gradually, stirring constantly. Stir back into saucepan. Bring to simmering. Add lobster meat and heat well but do not boil. Serve immediately.

—————— SERVES 4 TO 6 ——————

Curried Scallop Bisque

1 tbsp	butter	15 ml
1/2 tsp	curry powder	2 ml
1 1/2 tsp	grated onion	7 ml
10-oz can	tomato soup	284-ml can
2 cups	chicken stock	500 ml
1 lb	scallops, thawed if necessary	450 g
1 cup	milk	250 ml
1/2 cup	light cream	125 ml
1/2 tsp	salt	2 ml
1/8 tsp	pepper	0.5 ml
2 tbsp	chopped parsley	30 ml
	chopped parsley	

Easy Clam Chowder

4 5-oz cans	whole baby clams	4 142-ml cans
1/4 lb	salt pork, cut in small cubes	115 g
1 cup	chopped onion	250 ml
3 cups	liquid (clams liquid plus water)	750 ml
2 cups	diced potatoes	500 ml
1 1/2 tsp	salt	7 ml
1/2 tsp	pepper	2 ml
6 cups	milk	1.5 L
1/4 cup	butter	60 ml
1/4 cup	chopped parsley	60 ml

Drain clams, saving the liquid.

Put salt pork in heavy saucepan and fry until light brown, stirring constantly. Add onion and cook until tender but not brown. Measure clam liquid and add enough water to make the 3 cups (750 ml) liquid called for. Add to onion mixture along with potatoes, salt and pepper. Cover and cook gently 15 minutes or until potatoes are tender. Stir in milk and clams and bring just to a boil but do not boil. Stir in butter and parsley. Serve immediately.

SERVES 12

Oyster Chowder

Heat butter in medium saucepan. Add curry powder and onion and cook gently 3 minutes, stirring. Add tomato soup and chicken stock and bring to a boil. Add washed scallops (cut if they are large), turn down heat, cover and simmer 5 minutes. Stir in milk, cream, salt and pepper and heat but do not boil. Taste and add more salt and pepper if necessary. Stir in 2 tbsp (30 ml) parsley and serve immediately with more parsley sprinkled on each serving.

—————— SERVES 6 ——————

1 cup	*thinly sliced raw potatoes*	*250 ml*
1/2 cup	*thinly sliced carrots*	*125 ml*
1 cup	*chopped celery*	*250 ml*
1 tbsp	*grated onion*	*15 ml*
1/2 tsp	*salt*	*2 ml*
1/2 cup	*boiling water*	*125 ml*
4 cups	*milk, scalded*	*1 L*
1 tsp	*salt*	*5 ml*
1/4 tsp	*pepper*	*1 ml*
2 tbsp	*butter*	*30 ml*
2 tbsp	*flour*	*30 ml*
1/4 cup	*butter*	*60 ml*
2 cups	*shucked oysters (and their liquid)*	*500 ml*
1/4 cup	*chopped parsley*	*60 ml*

Combine potatoes, carrots, celery, onion, 1/2 tsp (2 ml) salt and boiling water in saucepan. Cover and boil until vegetables are tender, about 15 minutes. Add milk, 1 tsp (5 ml) salt and pepper and bring to simmering point.

Cream 2 tbsp (30 ml) butter and flour together and add to simmering liquid, bit by bit, stirring to blend after each addition. Simmer 2 minutes.

Heat 1/4 cup (60 ml) butter in heavy skillet and add oysters and their liquid. Cook gently just until edges of oysters begin to curl. Add to hot soup immediately. Sprinkle with parsley and serve immediately.

—————— SERVES 6 ——————

Left: Oyster Chowder
Right: Curried Scallop Bisque

31

Shrimp Creole Soup

2 tbsp	butter	30 ml
1/2 cup	chopped green pepper	125 ml
1/4 cup	chopped green onions	60 ml
6 medium	tomatoes, peeled and chopped	6 medium
1/2 cup	water	125 ml
1 1/2 tsp	salt	7 ml
1/4 tsp	pepper	1 ml
1/4 tsp	dried leaf thyme	1 ml
1/8 tsp	dried leaf basil	0.5 ml
1 cup	fresh or frozen peas	250 ml
2 tbsp	cornstarch	30 ml
1/4 cup	cold water	60 ml
4 1/2-oz can	shrimp	115-g can

Melt butter in saucepan. Add green pepper and onions. Cook gently 3 minutes, stirring.

Add tomatoes, 1/2 cup (125 ml) water, salt, pepper, thyme and basil. Bring to a boil, turn down heat, cover and simmer until tomatoes are soft. Add peas and simmer 5 minutes more.

Add cornstarch to cold water in a small jar with a tight lid. Shake until well blended and stir into hot mixture gradually. Simmer 2 minutes.

Drain shrimp and rinse under cold water. Add to soup and heat well. Serve immediately.

—————— SERVES 4 TO 6 ——————

Salmon Bisque

1 lb	canned pink salmon	450 g
1/4 cup	butter	60 ml
1/4 cup	chopped onion	60 ml
1/4 cup	chopped celery	60 ml
3 tbsp	flour	45 ml
1 1/2 tsp	salt	7 ml
1 cup	liquid (salmon liquid plus water)	250 ml
2 cups	milk	500 ml
1 cup	tomato juice	250 ml
2 tbsp	chopped parsley	30 ml

Drain salmon, saving liquid. Flake salmon.

Heat butter in large saucepan. Add onion and celery and cook gently 5 minutes, stirring. Sprinkle in flour and salt and stir to blend. Remove from heat.

Measure salmon liquid and add enough water to make the 1 cup (250 ml) liquid called for. Add, with milk, to butter-flour mixture. Stir to blend. Return to moderate heat and cook until thickened and smooth, stirring constantly. Stir in tomato juice and parsley. Heat to simmering (do not boil). Add salmon and heat well. Serve immediately.

—————— SERVES 6 ——————

Fish Chowder

4 slices	bacon, cut up	4 slices
1 large	onion, sliced thin	1 large
2 lb	haddock	900 g
4 cups	thinly sliced raw potatoes	1 L
	boiling water	
2 tbsp	butter	30 ml
1 tbsp	flour	15 ml
2 cups	milk, scalded	500 ml
1 1/2 tsp	salt	7 ml
1/4 tsp	pepper	1 ml
1/4 cup	chopped parsley	60 ml

Put bacon pieces in large heavy saucepan. Fry them until pan is well greased. Add onion and cook 3 minutes, stirring.

Remove skin and bones from haddock and cut into 1-inch (2.5-cm) pieces. Add to saucepan along with potato slices. Cover with boiling water.

Bring back to boil, turn down heat, cover and simmer gently just until potatoes are tender, about 15 minutes.

Blend butter and flour and add to chowder, bit by bit, stirring well after each addition. Add hot milk, salt and pepper. Taste and add more seasonings if desired. Cover and simmer 5 minutes.

Sprinkle with parsley and serve immediately.

——————— SERVES 6 TO 8 ———————

Fish Chowder

California Minestrone

1 cup	dry baby lima beans	250 ml
1/4 lb	salt pork, cut in 1/4-inch (0.5-cm) cubes	115 g
1 medium	onion, chopped	1 medium
1 clove	garlic, minced	1 clove
6 cups	boiling water	1.5 L
2 cubes	beef bouillon	2 cubes
2 tsp	salt	10 ml
1/4 tsp	pepper	1 ml
1 large	carrot, diced	1 large
2 cups	turnip, cut in 1/2-inch (1.25-cm) cubes	500 ml
2 stalks	celery, sliced	2 stalks
19-oz can	tomatoes	540-ml can
small piece	bay leaf	small piece
1/4 tsp	dried leaf basil	1 ml
2 cups	finely shredded cabbage	500 ml
1 cup	torn up spinach (pack in cup)	250 ml

Rinse lima beans under cold running water.

Put salt pork in large kettle and cook gently until pan is well greased. Add onion and garlic and cook gently 3 minutes, stirring. Add water, bouillon cubes, salt, pepper and lima beans. Bring to a boil. Turn down heat, cover tightly and simmer until Lima beans are beginning to get tender, about 1 hour.

Add carrot, turnip, celery, tomatoes, bay leaf and basil. Simmer until vegetables are just tender, about 30 minutes. Add cabbage and cook 5 minutes. Add spinach and cook 5 minutes more. Taste and correct seasoning if necessary. Serve very hot.

—————— MAKES 6 TO 8 LARGE SERVINGS ——————

Spanish Onion Soup

2 large	Spanish onions	2 large
1/2 cup	olive oil	125 ml
6 cups	beef stock	1.5 L
1 tsp	salt	5 ml
1/4 tsp	pepper	1 ml
pinch	mace	pinch
pinch	cloves	pinch
1 tsp	wine vinegar	5 ml
2 tbsp	chopped parsley	30 ml
6	eggs	6
6 slices	French bread, toasted	6 slices

grated Parmesan cheese
(optional)

Slice onions very thin. Heat oil in large saucepan and add onions. Cover and cook gently until very soft, about 30 minutes. Remove cover and cook until onions are very lightly browned. Add stock, salt, pepper, mace, cloves, vinegar and parsley. Bring to a boil, turn down heat, cover and simmer 20 minutes.

Soft poach the eggs (see note). Put a slice of toast in each of 6 soup bowls and top with a poached egg. Ladle hot soup over and sprinkle lightly with grated cheese.

Note: The Spanish way is to poach the eggs right in the simmering soup. It is difficult to get them out of the soup without breaking them so I prefer to poach them separately.

—————— SERVES 6 ——————

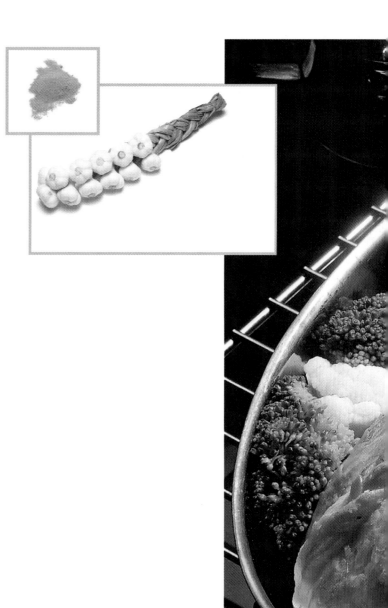

Beef

Beef

According to an old English saying, there are six requirements to make a good roast of beef, perfect. The meat must be choice and well hung; it must be roasted at a good fire; by a good cook; in a good temper; and the diner must have a good appetite.

Beef is the favorite meat of North America. Whatever the cut, a rib roast, a thick steak, a savory stew or a simple hamburger, the dark red, lean and fine grained meat gives both the diner and the cook good appetite and good temper.

Today, leaner beef is grown and made available to a health conscious market that has always had a taste for a good serving of beef. What aroma is more welcoming to the home-comer than a good roast in the oven or a well seasoned steak sizzling on the grill?

Beef yields a high level of protein in each serving. It is also a good source for vitamins B1 and B2. It is preferable to choose the most lean cuts of beef and the leanest hamburger. The color should be red, leaning slightly towards brown. Too clear a red signifies a cut of beef a bit too fresh. That brown tinge means that the beef is well hung and ready to use in these recipes.

BEEF

Beef and Broccoli Chinese Style	48
Beef Pie	57
Braised Short Ribs	58
Eye of the Round with Onion Gravy	47
Filet de Bœuf en Croûte	52
Freezer Steak Pies	70
Italian Pot Roast	43
Italian Stew, Hunter's Style	58
Italian Style Rump Roast	44
My Favorite Pot Roast	43
Red Wine London Broil	51
Savory Rolled Rib Roast	40
Spanish Style Pot Roast	44
Special Beef Stew	50
Stew and Dumplings	56
Stuffed Steak	48
Sweet and Sour Pot Roast	45
Swiss Steak	50

GROUND BEEF

Baked Beef Manicotti	64
Beef and Cabbage Turnovers	61
Beef Brioche	46
Cold Meat Loaf	63
Hamburgers with Green Onions	63
Meat Ball Sauce and Spaghetti	68
Mexican Style Chili	64
Paté Maison	66
Skillet Macaroni and Beef	67
Speedy Meat Loaf	61
Super Burgers with Asparagus	62

Savory Rolled Rib Roast

3 cloves	garlic, crushed	3 cloves
2 tsp	salt	10 ml
1 tsp	pepper	5 ml
1/2 tsp	dried leaf marjoram	2 ml
1/4 cup	flour	60 ml
5 to 6-lb	rolled rib roast of beef	2.2 to 2.6-kg
2	onions, chopped	2
6 slices	bacon	6 slices
1 cup	dry red table wine or consommé	250 ml
6 medium	potatoes, peeled and halved	6 medium
3	tomatoes, coarsely chopped	3
1/4 cup	chopped parsley	60 ml
	salt and pepper	

Heat oven to 500 °F (260 °C). Have roasting pan ready.

Combine garlic, 2 tsp (10 ml) salt, 1 tsp (5 ml) pepper, marjoram and flour. Rub into meat on all sides.

Put roast in roasting pan and put in hot oven. Turn heat down to 325 °F (160 °C) and cook until roast is brown on all sides. Remove roast from oven.

Sprinkle onions over roast. Lay strips of bacon over onions on top of roast and pour wine or consommé over all. Return to oven and roast 25 to 30 minutes per pounds for medium rare. (To be sure — use a meat thermometer: rare 140 °F (60 °C), medium 160 °F (70 °C), well done 176 °F (76 °C.) Baste often during roasting.

Add potatoes, tomatoes and parsley to roasting pan about 1 hour before roast should be done. Sprinkle vegetables with salt and pepper.

Lift meat and potatoes out on to hot platter when they are done. Strain drippings left in pan, pressing through as much of the tomato pulp as possible. Return to roasting pan and heat on top of stove, scraping up all browned bits from the bottom of the pan. Add wine or boiling water to make about 3 cups (750 ml) liquid in pan. Thicken by stirring in a little flour and water mixed together. Taste and season and serve as gravy with roast and potatoes.

SERVES 8 TO 10

Savory Rolled Rib Roast

Italian Pot Roast

4 slices	bacon, cut up	4 slices
4-lb	blade roast	1.8-kg
1 large	carrot, chopped	1 large
1 stalk	celery, chopped	1 stalk
1	onion, chopped	1
1/4 cup	chopped parsley	60 ml
2	strips lemon peel, about 2 inches (5 cm) long and 1/2 inch (1.25 cm) wide	2
1 cup	dry red wine	250 ml
1 1/2 tsp	salt	7 ml
1/4 tsp	pepper	1 ml
1 cube	beef bouillon dissolved in 1/2 cup (125 ml) boiling water	1 cube

Put bacon in large heavy saucepan or Dutch oven. Cook over low heat until pan is well greased. Add roast and brown well on all sides. Add all remaining ingredients, cover tightly, and simmer 3 hours or until very tender.

Lift meat out onto hot platter. Strain stock in pan, pressing as much of the vegetables as possible through the sieve. Return to saucepan, heat well and serve as gravy.

Note: If you want a thicker gravy use 1 1/2 tbsp (22 ml) flour per cup (250 ml) of liquid, mix it with cold water until smooth and stir into boiling liquid gradually. Cook until thick and smooth.

———— SERVES 6 TO 8 ————

My Favorite Pot Roast

2 tbsp	cooking oil	30 ml
4-lb	rump roast of beef	1.8-kg
1 medium	onion, halved	1 medium
1 clove	garlic, crushed (optional)	1 clove
1/4 cup	boiling water	60 ml
	salt and pepper	
3 tbsp	fat (see below)	45 ml
3 tbsp	flour	45 ml
2 cups	liquid (cooking liquid plus water)	500 ml
	salt and pepper	

Heat oil in large heavy saucepan or Dutch oven Add roast and brown very well on all sides over moderately high heat (this may take as long as 20 minutes).

Add onion, garlic and boiling water. Sprinkle meat generously with salt and pepper. Cover and simmer until meat is very tender, about 3 hours. Lift out meat. Drain all fat and liquid from the pan.

Return meat to pan and brown again until quite dark on the outside. Put meat on a hot platter and keep hot.

Skim fat off drippings from pan or chill drippings quickly by setting in ice water and lift off fat. Return 3 tbsp (45 ml) of this fat to the pan. Sprinkle in flour and let bubble up.

Measure liquid left from cooking after fat was removed and add boiling water to make 2 cups (500 ml) if necessary.

Remove pan from heat and add liquid all at once, stirring to blend well. Return to moderate heat and cook until thick and smooth, stirring constantly. Taste and season if necessary. Serve with roast.

———— SERVES 6 TO 8 ————

Italian Pot Roast

Spanish Style Pot Roast

1	green pepper	1
1 small	onion	1 small
1 clove	garlic, crushed	1 clove
1	bay leaf, crumbled	1
1/4 tsp	dried leaf marjoram	1 ml
1/2 tsp	salt	2 ml
2 tbsp	olive oil	30 ml
4-lb	chuck roast	1.8-kg
2 tbsp	olive oil	30 ml
19-oz can	tomatoes	540-ml can
1/4 tsp	cinnamon	1 ml
1/8 tsp	cloves	0.5 ml
2 tsp	salt	10 ml
1/4 tsp	pepper	1 ml
2 cups	dry red wine	250 ml
1 tbsp	cornstarch	15 ml
1/4 cup	cold water	60 ml

Cut green pepper into strips, discarding stem, seeds and membrane. Peel and quarter onion. Chop pepper and onion fine in food processor or food chopper; be careful not to purée. Add garlic, bay leaf, marjoram, 1/2 tsp (2 ml) salt and 2 tbsp (30 ml) olive oil, blending well. Rub this mixture into both sides of the roast. Let stand 1 hour.

Scrape any of the green pepper mixture that is loose off the roast and save. Heat 2 tbsp (30 ml) olive oil in large heavy saucepan or Dutch oven and brown the meat well on all sides. Add tomatoes, green pepper mixture, cinnamon, cloves, 2 tsp (10 ml) salt, pepper and wine. Bring to a boil, turn down heat, cover and simmer 3 to 4 hours or until meat is very tender, turning the roast occasionally.

Lift meat out onto hot platter. Add cornstarch to cold water and stir until smooth and blended. Bring liquid in pan to a boil and stir in cornstarch mixture gradually. Cook until boiling and slightly thickened. Taste and add salt and pepper if necessary. Serve as gravy with sliced meat.

SERVES 6 TO 8

Italian Style Rump Roast

2 tbsp	cooking oil	30 ml
4 to 5-lb	rump roast of beef	1.8 to 2.2-kg
1 tsp	salt	5 ml
1/2 cup	chopped carrots	125 ml
1 1/2 cup	chopped celery	375 ml
1/2 cup	chopped onion	125 ml
1 cup	dry red table wine	250 ml
10-oz can	consommé	284-ml can
5 1/2-oz can	tomato paste	156-ml can
6	anchovy fillets, finely copped	6
small piece	bay leaf	small piece
2 cloves	garlic, crushed	2 cloves
2 tbsp	butter	30 ml
1/2 lb	mushrooms, sliced	225 ml
	hot cooked spaghetti	

Heat oil in large heavy saucepan or Dutch oven. Add roast and brown slowly and well on all sides. Sprinkle with salt. Drop carrots, celery and onion into hot fat and cook and stir until they are lightly browned. Add wine, consommé, tomato paste, anchovies, bay leaf and garlic. Cover and simmer until meat is tender, about 3 hours.

Heat butter in heavy skillet. Add mushrooms and cook gently 3 minutes, stirring. Add to roast and sauce and continue cooking gently, covered, about 30 minutes more or until roast is very tender. Lift roast out onto hot platter and keep warm.

Cook sauce over moderate heat, uncovered, until it thickens like a spaghetti sauce. Slice meat and put on serving plates. Add spaghetti to each plate and spoon sauce over all.

SERVES 6 TO 8

Spanish Style Pot Roast

Sweet and Sour Pot Roast

2 tbsp	cooking oil	30 ml
4-lb	chuck roast	1.8-kg
1 cup	chopped onion	250 ml
1 tsp	salt	5 ml
1/4 tsp	pepper	1 ml
1/2 tsp	dried leaf thyme	2 ml
1/2 cup	beef bouillon	125 ml
1/3 cup	cider vinegar	80 ml
1/3 cup	liquid honey	80 ml
1 tbsp	cornstarch	15 ml
1/4 cup	water	60 ml

Heat oil in large heavy saucepan or Dutch oven. Add meat and brown well on all sides. Lift out meat and add onion to fat in pan. Cook 3 minutes, stirring. Return meat to pan. Sprinkle with salt, pepper and thyme. Add bouillon and vinegar, cover and simmer about 2 hours or until beginning to get tender. Add honey and continue simmering, turning the roast occasionally, until tender, about 1 hour more.

Put meat on hot serving platter and keep hot. Bring liquid left in pan to a full boil. Add cornstarch to water and stir to blend well. Stir into boiling liquid gradually. Cook until thickened and clear, stirring. Turn heat to low and simmer 3 minutes. Serve over slices of roast.

——————— SERVES 6 TO 8 ———————

Beef Brioche

Brioche Dough (recipe p. 53)		
50 oz	fresh spinach (5 bags)	1.4 kg
2 lb	ground beef chuck	900 g
1/2 cup	chopped onion	125 ml
3 cloves	garlic, crushed	3 cloves
2	eggs, lightly beaten	2
3 tsp	salt	15 ml
1/2 tsp	pepper	5 ml
1/8 tsp	nutmeg	0.5 ml
1 cup	soft bread crumbs	250 ml
1 cup	crumbled blue cheese	250 ml
2 tbsp	light cream (approx.)	30 ml
2 tbsp	chopped chives	30 ml
1	egg yolk	1
1 tbsp	light cream	15 ml

Make the Brioche Dough the day before you complete the rolls — it must be chilled overnight.

Cook spinach in a large kettle just until wilted. Drain it very well. Chop it quite finely (kitchen shears make the job easy) then put in a large sieve and press hard with the back of a large spoon to get out as much water as possible.

Heat oven to 450 °F (230 °C). Grease a large baking sheet (one with sides is a good idea in case dough breaks during baking and meat juices leak out).

Combine meat, cooked spinach, onion, garlic, eggs, salt, pepper, nutmeg and bread crumbs, blending well with a fork. Shape into 2 rolls, 12 inches (30.5 cm) long, on waxed paper.

Divide Brioche Dough into 2 equal parts. Roll 1/2 into an oblong 14 x 12 inches (30 X 30.5 cm). Beat cheese, 2 tbsp (30 ml) cream and chives together until smooth, using enough cream to make the mixture of spreading consistency. Spread 1/2 of the mixture on the rolled-out dough, spreading it to within 1/2 inch (1.25 cm) of the edges. Lay a meat roll in the middle of the dough. Wrap dough around meat, over-lapping and sealing together well. Turn in ends and seal well. Lift carefully onto prepared baking sheet, putting sealed side down. Prick in several places with the tines of a fork. Repeat with second half of dough and remaining meat roll.

Beat egg yolk and 1 tbsp (15 ml) cream together with a fork and brush outside of rolls with mixture.

Bake 10 minutes at 450 °F (230 °C). Reduce oven temperature to 350 °F (175 °C) and continue baking 50 minutes or until crust is golden brown (meat will still be a little pink). Cool, wrap in foil and refrigerate until shortly before serving time. Cut each roll in 12 slices and serve cold.

Note: Don't worry if the dough splits a little during baking — it won't affect the goodness of the rolls. If they have split, fasten the foil tightly around the rolls during chilling and the dough will seal itself to the meat again. The rolls can be made ahead of time. They can be refrigerated 2 or 3 days or frozen.

MAKES 24 PORTIONS

Eye of the Round with Onion Gravy

1 cup	chopped onion	250 ml
2 tsp	salt	10 ml
1/4 tsp	pepper	1 ml
1/2 tsp	dried leaf thyme	2 ml
1/2 tsp	paprika	2 ml
1/8 tsp	nutmeg	0.5 ml
3-lb	eye of the round roast	1.4-kg
6 strips	bacon	6 strips

Onion Gravy
(recipe follows)

Eye of the Round with Onion Gravy

Heat oven to 325 °F (160 °C).

Sprinkle bottom of shallow roasting pan with onion.

Combine salt, pepper, thyme, paprika and nutmeg and rub all over outside of roast. Lay it on top of onion (not on rack). Lay slices of bacon close together over the top of roast.

Roast 1 1/2 to 2 hours — 140 to 160 °F (60 to 70 °C) on meat thermometer (see note) — Serve sliced very thin with Onion Gravy.

Note: This roast is best cooked only until rare or medium — it is likely to be tough if well done.

— SERVES 6 —

Onion Gravy

	drippings from roast	
1 large	onion, chopped	1 large
3 tbsp	flour	45 ml
1 cup	water	250 ml
1 cup	milk	250 ml

salt and pepper

Pour drippings from roasting pan into medium saucepan (most of the drippings will be from the bacon and will give the gravy a different and good taste). Add onion to drippings and cook gently 3 minutes, stirring. Sprinkle in flour and let bubble. Remove from heat and stir in water and cook until boiling, thickened and smooth, stirring constantly. Taste and add salt and pepper if necessary.

Beef and Broccoli Chinese Style

1 lb	round steak, cut 1 inch (2.5 cm) thick	450 gr
1 1/2 lb	fresh broccoli (1 bunch)	675 g
1/4 cup	water	60 ml
1 tbsp	cornstarch	15 ml
2 tbsp	soya sauce	30 ml
1/4 tsp	ginger	1 ml
1/4 cup	peanut oil	60 ml
1/2 lb	fresh mushrooms, sliced	225 g
2 tbsp	peanut oil	30 ml
1 tsp	salt	5 ml
1/4 cup	water	60 ml

Cut steak into very thin slices across the grain, then cut slices into 2-inch (5-cm) lengths. Trim broccoli and cut off florets. Cut florets into bite-size pieces. Combine 1/4 cup (60 ml) water, cornstarch, soya sauce and ginger, blending well.

Heat 1/4 cup (60 ml) oil to smoking in wok or large heavy skillet. Add meat and cook and stir over high heat just until lightly browned, about 1 minute. Add mushrooms and continue cooking and stirring 30 seconds. Lift meat and mushrooms out of pan with a slotted spoon and set aside.

Add 2 tbsp (30 ml) oil, broccoli stems and salt to pan and cook over high heat 30 seconds, stirring. Add broccoli florets and cook 1 minute, stirring. Add 1/4 cup (60 ml) water, turn heat to medium, cover and cook 3 minutes. Turn heat back to high. Return meat and mushrooms to pan and heat 1 minute, stirring. Push meat and vegetables to one side of pan and stir cornstarch mixture gradually into boiling liquid. Cook until thick and clear, stirring. Stir meat and vegetables into sauce and serve immediately.

—————— SERVES 6 ——————

Stuffed Steak

2 1/2 lb	top round steak, cut 1 1/2 inches (3.75 cm) thick	1.1 kg
1 tsp	salt	5 ml
	pepper	
3 tbsp	butter or cooking oil	45 ml
2 large	onions, chopped	2 large
1 clove	garlic, minced	1 clove
1/2 lb	fresh mushrooms, chopped	225 ml
1/2 tsp	dried leaf tarragon	2 ml
4	egg yolks	4
1 cup	soft bread crumbs	250 ml
1/2 cup	grated Parmesan cheese	125 ml
1/2 lb	ready-to-serve or leftover cooked ham	225 ml

Have butcher split the steak nearly in half horizontally to make a thin piece of meat twice the size of the original steak, or do it yourself with a very sharp knife. (This is called butterflied steak.) Pound along the centre of the steak where it is slightly thicker with the edge of heavy plate to make it as thin as the rest of the meat. Lay the steak open on a counter top. Sprinkle with salt and freshly ground pepper.

→

Beef and Broccoli Chinese Style

Heat butter or oil in large heavy skillet. Add onions and garlic and cook gently until onions are limp, stirring. Add mushrooms and cook over high heat about 2 minutes. Remove from heat and sprinkle in tarragon.

Beat egg yolks 2 minutes at high speed on the mixer. Stir in bread crumbs and cheese. Add onion-mushroom mixture and blend lightly.

Spread the butterflied steak with the onion-mushroom mixture and lay the ham strips on top of it close together and parallel to the shorter sides of the piece of meat. Roll the meat up from one of the short sides and tie it securely in several places down the length of the roll.

Heat oven to 425 °F (220 °C).

Put the roll in a shallow baking pan and bake for 15 minutes at 425 °F (220 °C). Reduce oven temperature to 375 °F (190 °C) and continue baking 30 minutes longer for medium rare. Cool and then chill well.

Slice thin to serve.

SERVES 8 TO 10

Swiss Steak

3/4 cup	flour	180 ml
1 1/2 tbsp	dry mustard	22 ml
1 1/2 tsp	salt	7 ml
1/4 tsp	pepper	1 ml
2 1/2 lb	round steak, cut 1 inch (2.5 cm) thick	1.1 kg
3 tbsp	cooking oil	45 ml
1 1/2 cups	sliced onion	375 ml
1 clove	garlic, chopped fine	1 clove
2 large	carrots, diced	2 large
4 cups	coarsely chopped peeled tomatoes	1 L
2 tbsp	Worcestershire sauce	30 ml
2 tsp	brown sugar	10 ml
	mashed or boiled potatoes	

Combine flour, mustard, salt and pepper. Pound as much of the mixture as possible into the steak with a meat pounder or the edge of a heavy plate. Cut meat into serving-size pieces.

Heat oil in large heavy skillet or Dutch oven. Brown meat well on both sides. Sprinkle onion, garlic and carrots over meat. Add tomatoes, Worcestershire sauce and brown sugar. Cover and heat gently until tomatoes begin to break up. Stir sauce to blend, turn meat pieces over, cover tightly and simmer about 2 hours or until meat is very tender. Stir often and add a little water if necessary to keep the sauce from sticking. Serve with potatoes.

SERVES 6

Special Beef Stew

4 lb	cubed stewing beef	1.8 kg
1/2 cup	flour	125 ml
6 tbsp	cooking oil	90 ml
1 large	onion, sliced	1 large
2 tsp	salt	10 ml
1/4 tsp	pepper	1 ml
1 tsp	curry powder	5 ml
1 clove	garlic, minced	1 clove
2 cups	water	500 ml
3 tbsp	chili sauce	45 ml
1	bay leaf	1
	hot cooked noodles	

→

Roll pieces of meat in the flour to coat on all sides. Heat oil in large heavy saucepan or Dutch oven. Add meat and brown well on all sides. Part way through the browning add the onion, salt, pepper and curry powder. Continue the browning, stirring constantly.

Add garlic, water, chili sauce and bay leaf. Bring to a boil. Turn down heat, cover tightly and simmer until meat is tender, about 2 hours. Serve with noodles.

—————— SERVES 8 ——————

Red Wine London Broil

1 3/4 lb	flank steak	800 g
1 clove	garlic, finely chopped	1 clove
1/2 cup	dry red table wine	125 ml
	salt and pepper	

Remove all fat and membrane from steak. Put steak in a large glass, pottery or enamel baking dish. Sprinkle with garlic. Pour wine over. Cover and let marinate several hours, turning often.

Heat broiler. Lift steak out of marinade (save marinade), drain well and brush off garlic. Put on rack in broiler pan and put under hot broiler. Broil 4 minutes on first side. Sprinkle with salt and pepper and turn. Broil 4 minutes on second side. Sprinkle with salt and pepper. Put on board or platter.

Pour pan juices into small saucepan. Add saved marinade and heat to boiling.

Cut meat in thin slices on the diagonal across the grain. Spoon some of pan juices-wine mixture over each serving.

—————— SERVES 4 ——————

Left: Special Beef Stew
Right: Swiss Steak

51

Filet de Bœuf en Croûte

1/2 lb	back bacon, in 1 piece	225 g
	boiling water	
sprig	celery leaves	sprig
sprig	parsley	sprig
1 small slice	onion	1 small slice
4	peppercorns	4
1/4 cup	butter	60 ml
1 lb	mushrooms, finely chopped	450 g
1	Spanish onion, finely chopped	1
1/2 cup	chopped parsley	125 ml
1/2 tsp	salt	2 ml
1 pinch	pepper	1 pinch
1/2 cup	brandy	125 ml
4-lb	filet of beef	1.8-kg
	brandy	
2 tbsp	soft butter	30 ml
2 tbsp	soft butter	30 ml
	salt and pepper	
	Brioche Dough (recipe follows)	
1	egg yolk	1
1 tbsp	light cream	15 ml
	Horseradish Cream (recipe follows)	
	Béarnaise Sauce (recipe follows)	

Prepare Brioche Dough the day before you plan to make this recipe.

Put bacon in saucepan. Add boiling water to nearly cover. Add sprig celery leaves, sprig parsley, slice of onion and peppercorns. Cover and simmer until tender, about 1 1/2 hours. Lift out of water and cool.

Heat 1/4 cup (60 ml) butter in large heavy skillet. Add mushrooms, chopped onion, chopped parsley, salt, pinch pepper and brandy and cook until liquid has evaporated. Remove from heat.

Trim filet of beef well. Cut it into 1-inch (2.5-cm) slices down to but not through the bottom. Slice bacon thin and put a slice between each slice of beef. Add about 1 tbsp (15 ml) mushroom mixture between each slice, spreading it evenly. Tie filet back together securely, running strings lengthwise.

Heat oven to 425 °F (220 °C). Brush filet with a little brandy and spread with 2 tbsp (30 ml) soft butter. Put on rack in roasting pan and roast 20 minutes. Cool well and remove strings.

Spread filet with another 2 tbsp (30 ml) butter and sprinkle generously with salt and pepper.

Roll Brioche Dough thin — a little less than 1/4 inch (0.5 cm) — into an oblong about 18 x 16 inches (46 x 41 cm). Trim dough to make oblong even and save bits to make a decoration on top.

Heat oven to 425 °F (220 °C).

Dry the cooled filet with paper towelling and put it, top side down, in the centre of the dough. Spread with remaining mushroom mixture (be sure there is no moisture in the mixture — if there is the dough is likely to become soft and break during baking). Wrap dough around filet overlapping and sealing together well. Turn in ends and seal well.

Put on greased baking sheet (one that has sides is a good idea in case pastry leaks) seam side down. Braid strips of dough trimmed from the oblong of dough or cut bits into leaves and flowers. Beat egg yolk and cream together lightly with a fork and use mixture to stick decorations on top of the roll.

Bake 15 minutes. Brush whole surface of pastry with the egg yolk-cream mixture and continue baking until crust is dark golden brown, about 30 minutes more. (If any spots start browning too much, cover them with aluminum foil.)

Slice into 1-inch (2.5-cm) slices where meat is already cut so each person gets a slice of bacon with the slice of meat. Serve hot with Horseradish Cream or Béarnaise Sauce.

—————— SERVES 8 ——————

Brioche Dough

1/2 cup	warm water	125 ml
2 tsp	sugar	10 ml
2 pkg	dry yeast	2 pkg
1 cup	sifted all-purpose flour	250 ml
3 cups	sifted all-purpose flour	750 ml
1 tsp	salt	5 ml
2 tsp	sugar	10 ml
6	eggs	6
1/2 lb	cold butter	225 g

Measure water into small bowl. Add 2 tsp (10 ml) sugar and stir to dissolve. Sprinkle yeast over water and let stand 10 minutes. Stir well. Stir in 1 cup (25 ml) flour. Beat hard with a wooden spoon then turn out on floured board and knead until smooth and elastic. Shape into a ball and cut a deep cross in the top with a sharp knife or kitchen shears. Drop ball of dough into a bowl of warm water and let stand until it rises to the surface and opens up like a flower.

Combine 3 cups (750 ml) flour, salt, and 2 tsp (10 ml) sugar in a large bowl. Make a well in the centre and add the eggs. Mix with a spoon then with hands, beating dough against side of bowl, picking it up and slapping it down into bowl and kneading until dough is smooth and elastic.

Wash butter under cold running water, kneading it with hands, until it is very pliable. Hold it in one hand and hit it hard with other hand until all water is beaten out. Add to second dough and work it in with hands.

Lift ball of risen dough out of water and hold in hand until water drains off. Add to mixture in large bowl and beat in with hand (dough will be soft). Put combined dough in greased bowl, sprinkle lightly with flour, cover with damp towel and let rise in a warm place until double, about 1 hour. Cover with transparent wrap and chill overnight. Punch down and roll to wrap meat as directed.

Trim filet of beef well.

Cut in into 1-inch (2.5-cm) slices down to but not through the bottom.

Add about 1 tbsp (15 ml) mushroom mixture between each slice, spreading it evenly.

Dry the cooled filet with paper towelling and put it, top side down, in the centre of the dough. Wrap dough around filet overlapping and sealing together well.

Béarnaise Sauce

3	green onions (with tops), cut up	3
large sprig	parsley, chopped	large sprig
1/2 tsp	dried leaf tarragon	2 ml
1/2 tsp	dried leaf chervil	2 ml
1/4 cup	wine vinegar	60 ml
2 tbsp	water	30 ml
4	egg yolks	4
1/4 cup	soft butter	60 ml
1/4 tsp	salt	1 ml
1 dash	cayenne	1 dash

Combine onions, parsley, tarragon, chervil, vinegar and water in small saucepan. Set over low heat and simmer 5 minutes. Strain, saving liquid and discarding remainder.

Put egg yolks in top of double boiler. Add vinegar mixture to yolks a little at a time, beating constantly with a wire whip or rotary beater. Set over simmering (it must not be boiling) water and cook until mixture thickens, stirring constantly.

Add butter a little at a time, stirring until butter is blended after each addition. (Mixture should look like mayonnaise.) Season with salt and cayenne. Serve slightly warm.

Note: The secret of success with this sauce is not to let it get too hot (water should be simmering in bottom of double boiler — not boiling) and to stir well after each addition of butter. If sauce should separate, a few drops of cold water should put it back together again. It is usually made with fresh herbs but I find this method very satisfactory when fresh herbs are not available.

Horseradish Cream

Fold 3 tbsp (45 ml) well drained commercial horseradish and 1/2 tsp (2 ml) salt into 1/2 cup (125 ml) whipping cream, whipped.

Filet de Bœuf en Croûte

Stew and Dumplings

1/4 cup	flour	60 ml
1/2 tsp	salt	2 ml
1/4 tsp	pepper	1 ml
2 lb	stewing beef, cubed	900 g
2 tbsp	cooking oil	30 ml
4 medium	onions, sliced	4 medium
1/2 cup	tomato juice	125 ml
3 cups	boiling water	750 ml
1 tsp	salt	5 ml
3 dashes	Tabasco	3 dashes
6 medium	carrots	6 medium
1/2 cup	leftover coffee	125 ml
12-oz pkg	frozen lima beans	350-g pkg
1 tsp	sugar	5 ml

Savory Dumplings (recipe follows)

Combine flour, 1/2 tsp (2 ml) salt and 1/4 tsp (1 ml) pepper in a flat dish. Roll cubes of beef in this mixture to coat all sides.

Heat oil in large heavy saucepan or Dutch oven. Add meat cubes and brown well on all sides. Add onions, tomato juice, water, 1 tsp (5 ml) salt and Tabasco. Cover tightly and simmer 1 hour.

Cut carrots diagonally into pieces about 1 inch (2.5 cm) long. Add to meat and simmer about 45 minutes.

Add coffee, lima beans and sugar and simmer for 30 minutes or until everything is tender.

Drop Savory Dumplings on top of meat and vegetables and cook as directed in recipe. Put dumplings around outside of a large serving dish and spoon meat and vegetables into centre of dish. Thicken gravy slightly by shaking 2 tbsp (30 ml) flour with 1/4 cup (60 ml) cold water in a small jar and gradually stirring into boiling gravy. Pour gravy over meat and vegetables.

SERVES 6

Savory Dumplings

1 1/3 cups	sifted all-purpose flour	330 ml
2 1/2 tsp	baking powder	12 ml
3/4 tsp	salt	3 ml
1/4 tsp	dried leaf marjoram	1 ml
1/4 tsp	dried leaf savory	1 ml
1 1/2 tbsp	shortening	22 ml
2/3 cup	milk	160 ml

Sift flour, baking powder and salt into bowl. Add marjoram and savory and mix lightly with a fork. Add shortening and cut in finely. Add milk and mix lightly and quickly with a fork. Drop by large spoonfuls on top meat and vegetables (not in liquid). Cover tightly and simmer 15 minutes. Do not lift cover during cooking.

Beef Pie

2 lb	stewing beef, cut in 1 1/2-inch (3.75-cm) cubes	900 g
2 whole	cloves	2 whole
16 small	onions or 8 medium onions, cut in half	16 small
2 tbsp	sugar	30 ml
1 cup	boiling water	250 ml
1 1/2 tsp	salt	7 ml
1/4 tsp	pepper	1 ml
1 tsp	steak sauce	5 ml
1 tbsp	red wine vinegar	15 ml
1 small	bay leaf	1 small
1/8 tsp	dried leaf thyme	0.5 ml

2 tbsp	butter	30 ml
2 tbsp	flour	30 ml
1 cup	water	250 ml
	pastry for 2 crust 9-inch (23-cm) pie	
1	egg yolk	1
1 tbsp	water	15 ml

Heat oven to 325 °F (160 °C). Grease a 2-qt (2.5-L) casserole.

Put meat in casserole. Stick cloves in 2 of the onions and add all of the onions to casserole.

Heat sugar in large heavy skillet until it melts and turns dark golden brown. Remove from heat and stir in 1 cup (250 ml) boiling water. Return to heat and stir in salt, pepper, steak sauce, vinegar, bay leaf, thyme and butter. Shake flour and remaining 1 cup (250 ml) water together and stir into hot mixture gradually. Pour over meat and onions.

Roll pastry 1 inch (2.5 cm) larger than the top of the casserole (it will be thicker than you usually roll it) and lay it over mixture in casserole. Turn under edge and crimp it against the side of the casserole to seal well. Cut a large vent in pastry to let the steam escape. Beat egg yolk and water together with a fork and brush over pastry (not on crimped edge).

Bake 2 to 3 hours or until meat is tender. Serve hot.

— SERVES 6 —

Beef Pie

Italian Stew, Hunter's Style

3 tbsp	olive oil	45 ml
2 lb	stewing beef, cubed	900 g
6 small	onions, peeled and cut in half	6 small
2 cloves	garlic, crushed	2 cloves
5 1/2-oz can	tomato paste	156-ml can
1 tbsp	flour	15 ml
1 tsp	chili powder	5 ml
1 tsp	dried leaf oregano	5 ml
1 tsp	dried leaf rosemary	5 ml
1 1/2 tsp	seasoned salt	7 ml
1 tsp	salt	5 ml
28-oz can	tomatoes	796-ml can
1/2 cup	parsley, finely chopped	125 ml
1 cup	water	250 ml
3 large	carrots, cut into 1-inch (2.5-cm) pieces	3 large
8 oz	elbow macaroni	225 g
1/3 cup	grated Parmesan cheese	80 ml

Heat olive oil in large heavy saucepan or Dutch oven. Add beef and cook until lightly browned on all sides, stirring. Add onions and garlic and continue cooking and stirring 5 minutes.

Combine tomato paste, flour, chili powder, oregano, rosemary, seasoned salt and salt. Stir into mixture in pan along with tomatoes, parsley and water. Bring to a boil, turn down heat, cover and simmer 1 hour and 15 minutes. Add carrots and continue simmering 45 minutes or until meat is tender.

Cook macaroni in boiling salted water while stew is cooking. Rinse under cold running water. Stir into stew and heat. Stir in Parmesan cheese and serve immediately with lots of crusty bread.

SERVES 6

Braised Short Ribs

2 lb	beef short ribs	900 g
large clove	garlic, cut in half	large clove
1/4 cup	flour	60 ml
1 tsp	salt	5 ml
1/4 tsp	pepper	1 ml
1 tsp	paprika	5 ml
1/4 cup	cooking oil	60 ml
19-oz can	tomatoes	540-ml can
1 cup	hot water	250 ml
1 large	carrot, peeled and diced	1 large
1 medium	onion, sliced	1 medium
1 tsp	salt	5 ml
1/4 tsp	pepper	1 ml
1 small	bay leaf	1 small

Heat oven to 325 °F (160 °C).

Cut short ribs into pieces and trim off all excess fat. Rub all over with cut sides of garlic. Combine flour, 1 tsp (5 ml) salt, 1/4 tsp (1 ml) pepper and paprika in flat dish and roll meat pieces in mixture.

Heat oil in Dutch oven or other heavy saucepan that can go in the oven. Add ribs and brown well on all sides. Lift out pieces as they brown.

Drain all except 2 tbsp (30 ml) of the fat from the pan. Sprinkle in any flour that was left from coating the pieces of meat and let bubble, stirring constantly. Remove from heat and add tomatoes and hot water all at once, stirring to blend. Return to heat and bring to boil, stirring constantly. Add carrot, onion, 1 tsp (5 ml) salt, 1/4 tsp (1 ml) pepper, bay leaf and short ribs. Cover tightly, put in oven and cook until tender, 2 to 2 1/2 hours

SERVES 4

Braised Short Ribs

Speedy Meat Loaf

1 cup	paper-thin slices onion	250 ml
1 tbsp	cooking oil	15 ml
2 lb	ground beef	900 g
1 cup	commercial sour cream	250 ml
2	eggs	2
1 envelope	onion soup mix	1 envelope
dash	nutmeg	dash
1 cup	soft bread crumbs	250 ml
	cooked mixed vegetables	

Heat oven to 500 °F (260 °C).

Grease a 9-inch (23-cm) ring mould very well. Separate the onion slices into rings and spread them evenly in the bottom of the ring mould. Cover the mould with aluminum foil and put in oven for 10 minutes.

Heat oil in large heavy skillet while onions are cooking. Add ground beef and cook, stirring often, until meat has lost all its pink color and is lightly browned. Remove from heat.

Beat sour cream and eggs together lightly with a fork to blend. Stir in onion soup mix, nutmeg and bread crumbs. Add browned beef and blend well.

Remove ring mould from oven and discard aluminum foil. Pack meat mixture into mould on top of onions. Return pan to oven and bake 15 minutes. Turn on broiler and continue cooking 5 minutes more or until well browned on top. Drain off any juices in pan and unmould meat loaf on serving platter. Fill centre with hot mixed vegetables. Serve immediately.

—————— SERVES 6 ——————

Beef and Cabbage Turnovers

3 tbsp	butter	45 ml
3/4 cup	finely chopped onion	180 ml
1 1/2 lb	lean ground beef	675 g
4 cups	grated cabbage (use medium grater)	1 L
3/4 cup	grated raw carrot (use medium grater)	180 ml
2 tsp	salt	10 ml
1/4 tsp	pepper	1 ml
1/4 tsp	mace	1 ml
1/4 tsp	Worcestershire sauce	1 ml
2 tbsp	water	30 ml
	double recipe Basic Pastry (p. 302)	
1	egg yolk	1
1 tbsp	water	15 ml

Heat butter in large saucepan. Add onion and cook gently until tender, about 5 minutes. Add meat and cook and stir until all redness disappears. Add cabbage, carrot, salt, pepper, mace, Worcestershire sauce and water. Cover and simmer 15 minutes. Uncover and continue cooking until all excess liquid cooks away. Meat should be moist but not wet. Cool.

Heat oven to 425 °F (220 °C).

Roll pastry very thin into oblongs or squares (roll 1/2 at a time) and cut into 6-inch (15-cm) squares. You should be able to make 18 squares so be sure to roll very thin.

Lay the pastry squares out on the counter and top each one with 1/4 cup (60 ml) of the meat mixture. Moisten 2 adjacent edges of the squares with water and fold pastry over to form a triangle, pressing together along edges with the tines of a fork to seal. Prick tops of turnovers in a few places with the tines of the fork. Put on large cookie sheets. Beat egg yolk and water together and brush over tops of turnovers (not on edges).

Bake 25 to 30 minutes or until very well browned. Serve hot.

—————— MAKES 18 ——————

Beef and Cabbage Turnovers

Super Burgers with Asparagus

2 lb	ground round steak	900 g
1 1/2 tsp	coarse-cracked pepper (see note)	7 ml
1/4 cup	butter	60 ml
2 lb	fresh asparagus	900 g
1/4 cup	butter, melted	60 ml
1/3 cup	grated Parmesan cheese	80 ml
	salt and pepper	
2 tbsp	soft butter	30 ml
1 tbsp	chopped parsley	15 ml
	salt	
1 cup	red wine	250 ml
1/2 cup	water	125 ml
1 tbsp	soft butter	15 ml
1 tbsp	flour	15 ml

Divide meat into 4 equal parts and shape each part into a large thick patty. Sprinkle both sides of each patty with some of the cracked pepper, patting lightly so the pepper sticks.

Heat 1/4 cup (60 ml) butter in large heavy skillet. Add meat patties and cook quickly until well browned and done to your taste (about 5 minutes a side for rare).

Cook asparagus while meat is cooking. Drain and add 1/4 cup (60 ml) melted butter. Shake pan gently so butter coats asparagus. Sprinkle with Parmesan cheese and then lightly with salt and pepper.

Cream 2 tbsp (30 ml) butter and parsley together. Put meat patties on hot platter and sprinkle generously with salt. Add a dab of the parsley butter to the top of each. Keep hot. Pour wine and water into the pan the meat was cooked in and bring to a boil. Blend 1 tbsp (15 ml) butter and flour and add this mixture a little at a time to the boiling liquid, stirring to blend well after each addition. Cook until slightly thickened and pour over meat. Add asparagus to platter and serve immediately.

Note: You can buy commercially packed coarse cracked pepper or crush black peppercorns.

SERVES 4

Super Burgers with Asparagus

Hamburgers with Green Onions

1 lb	ground chuck	450 ml
1 tsp	salt	5 ml
1/8 tsp	pepper	0.5 ml
1 tbsp	sweet butter	15 ml
3 tbsp	sweet butter	45 ml
1 1/2 cups	1-inch (2.5-cm) pieces green onions	375 ml
1/2 cup	chopped parsley	125 ml
3/4 cup	sliced mushrooms	180 ml
	salt and pepper	
4	toasted hamburger buns	4

Combine meat, 1 tsp (5 ml) salt and 1/8 tsp (0.5 ml) pepper, mixing lightly with a fork. Shape into 4 patties about 1/2 inch (1.25 cm) thick.

Heat oven to 205 °F (400 °C). Put 1 tbsp (15 ml) sweet butter in baking dish just large enough to hold the patties in a single layer. Put pan in oven to melt butter.

Heat a heavy iron skillet to very hot. Add meat patties and cook very fast until well browned on both sides (if they stick add a little cooking oil). Lift patties out of a pan as soon as they are brown (they should still be quite pink inside) and put them in the hot baking dish. Put in oven to keep warm.

Add 3 tbsp (45 ml) sweet butter to skillet. Add green onions, parsley and mushrooms, and cook quickly 2 minutes.

Sprinkle generously with salt and pepper. Put meat patties into hamburger buns and spoon some of the green onion mixture into each. Serve immediately.

MAKES 4

Cold Meat Loaf

1 lb	ground beef	450 g
1/2 lb	ground lean pork	225 g
2 cups	soft bread cubes	500 ml
1 cup	milk	250 ml
1	egg	1
1/4 cup	finely chopped onion	60 ml
1 clove	garlic, crushed	1 clove
1 1/4 tsp	salt	6 ml
1/4 tsp	pepper	1 ml
1/4 tsp	dry mustard	1 ml
1/4 tsp	sage	1 ml
1 tbsp	Worcestershire sauce	15 ml
1 tbsp	prepared horseradish	15 ml
1 tbsp	ketchup	15 ml

Heat oven to 350 °F (160 °C). Have ready a glass or metal loaf pan about 9 x 5 x 3 inches (23 x 12.5 x 7.5 cm).

Combine meat and bread cubes in large bowl. Beat milk and egg together with a fork and add to meat mixture along with all remaining ingredients. Blend well with a fork. Pack into loaf pan.

Bake 1 1/2 hours. Drain off any liquid in pan and cool meat loaf. Cover with foil or transparent wrap and chill. Good with potato salad or on buttered French bread as a sandwich.

SERVES 6

Mexican Style Chili

14-oz pkg	dry kidney beans	398-ml pkg
1/4 lb	salt pork, diced	115 g
3 cloves	garlic, minced	3 cloves
2 large	onions, chopped	2 large
1 lb	lean beef, diced	450 g
1 lb	lean pork, diced (shoulder is good)	450 g
14-oz can	tomato sauce	398-ml can
3 tbsp	chili powder	45 ml
2 tsp	salt	10 ml
1/4 tsp	pepper	1 ml
1/2 tsp	dried leaf oregano	2 ml
pinch	cumin	pinch
	tomato juice	

Wash and look over beans. Soak in 6 cups (1.5 L) cold water overnight (or follow package directions). Drain.

Cook salt pork until very crisp in a large skillet or Dutch oven. Add garlic and onions and cook and stir until limp. Add beef and pork bits and cook gently until lightly browned, stirring. Stir in all remaining ingredients except tomato juice. Cover tightly and simmer 1 1/2 hours or until meat and beans are tender. Add tomato juice a bit at a time if the pan appears to be going dry (chili should be moist but not wet when cooking is finished). Taste and adjust seasoning if necessary.

Note: I like to make my chili in a large buffet-size electric skillet. When I use it, I find I have to add quite a bit of liquid during cooking — up to a full 19-oz (540-ml) can tomato juice.

SERVES 6 TO 8

Baked Meat Manicotti

1 tbsp	olive oil	15 ml
1 large	onion, chopped	1 large
2 cloves	garlic, minced	2 cloves
28-oz can	tomatoes	796-ml can
5 1/2-oz can	tomato paste	156-ml can
1 envelope	spaghetti sauce mix	1 envelope
1/2 cup	water	125 ml
8	manicotti shells (see note)	8
1/2 lb	spinach (approx.)	250 g
1 tbsp	olive oil	15 ml
3/4 lb	ground beef	350 g
1/4 cup	finely chopped green pepper	60 ml
4 oz	Mozzarella cheese, cut in very small cubes	115 g
1	egg, lightly beaten	1
1/4 cup	grated Parmesan cheese	60 ml

Heat 1 tbsp (15 ml) olive oil in medium saucepan. Add onion and garlic and cook gently 5 minutes, stirring. Add tomatoes, tomato paste, spaghetti sauce mix and water. Break up any large pieces of tomato. Bring to a boil, turn down heat, cover and simmer 20 minutes.

→

Baked Meat Manicotti

Cook manicotti shells in boiling salted water 7 minutes. Drain.

Remove stems from spinach and wash enough leaves to make 2 cups (500 ml) when packed. Cook spinach in the water clinging to its leaves just until it wilts. Drain and chop finely with kitchen shears.

Heat 1 tbsp (15 ml) oil in skillet. Add ground beef and green pepper and fry until meat is lightly browned, stirring constantly. Remove from heat, drain off any excess fat and cool. Toss meat, chopped spinach, cheese cubes and egg together with a fork. Use to stuff the manicotti shells.

Heat oven to 375 °F (190 °C). Have ready a 12- x 8- x 2-inch (30.5- x 20.5- x 5-cm) glass baking dish.

Put about 3/4 of the tomato mixture in the baking dish. Lay the stuffed manicotti in the sauce and pour remaining sauce over all. Sprinkle with Parmesan cheese.

Bake 30 minutes or until very hot.

—————— SERVES 4 ——————

Pâté Maison

1/2 lb	bacon	225 g
1 lb	ground beef	450 g
1 lb	ground pork	450 g
2 cloves	garlic, crushed	2 cloves
1/2 cup	finely chopped parsley	125 ml
1/2 tsp	dried leaf tarragon	2 ml
1/2 tsp	dried leaf thyme	2 ml
1/2 tsp	paprika	2 ml
1 1/2 tsp	salt	7 ml
1/4 tsp	pepper	1 ml
2	eggs, lightly beaten	2
1/2 cup	brandy	125 ml
1 lb	ground cooked ham	450 g
1 1/2 tsp	dry mustard	7 ml
1/2 tsp	nutmeg	2 ml
1/4 cup	dry sherry	60 ml
1 cup	finely chopped green onions	250 ml
1 cup	finely chopped parsley	250 ml
1/2 cup	dry sherry	125 ml

Heat oven to 325 °F (160 °C). Line the bottom of two glass loaf pans, 8 1/2 x 4 1/2 x 2 1/2 inches (20.5 x 10 x 5 cm), with 3 strips of bacon each.

Combine beef, pork, garlic, 1/2 cup (125 ml) parsley, tarragon, thyme, paprika, salt, pepper, eggs and brandy, blending very well.

Combine ham, mustard, nutmeg and 1/4 cup (60 ml) sherry, blending very well.

Put 1/4 of the beef mixture in each of the prepared pans, packing it firmly. Sprinkle each with 1/4 cup (60 ml) of green onions and 1/4 cup (60 ml) of parsley. Top each with half the ham mixture then another 1/4 cup (60 ml) green onions and 1/4 cup (60 ml) parsley. Add a layer of the beef mixture, dividing it evenly between the two pans. Pack firmly. Lay remaining bacon strips on top. Pour 1/2 cup (125 ml) sherry over all.

Cover pans tightly with aluminum foil and bake 3 hours.

Take pans from oven, set on rack, remove foil and weight down the meat while it cools. (To do this I put a layer of aluminum foil on top of each pâté then top it with a layer of heavy cardboard cut so it goes down into the pan and rests on top of the foil. On this I set the heaviest cans I can find in my cupboard.)

Remove weights from pâtés when they are cool and cover pans. Chill very well before serving. Serve with crackers or melba toast for hors-d'œuvre or serve a slice as the appetizer for dinner.

4 TO 6 PORTIONS

Skillet Macaroni and Beef

1/3 cup	cooking oil	80 ml
1 lb	ground beef	450 g
1/2 cup	chopped onion	125 ml
1 clove	garlic, minced	1 clove
2 cups	uncooked elbow macaroni	500 ml
1 cup	slivered green pepper	250 ml
1/2 cup	sliced celery	125 ml
1 cup	frozen green beans, thawed enough to measure	250 ml
28-oz can	tomatoes	796-ml can
2 tsp	salt	10 ml
1/4 tsp	pepper	1 ml
2 tbsp	Worcestershire sauce	30 ml
1/2 cup	slivered ripe olives	125 ml

Skillet Macaroni and Beef

Heat oil in large heavy skillet. Add beef, cook and stir until lightly browned. Add onion, garlic and macaroni and cook until macaroni is lightly browned, stirring.

Add green pepper, celery, beans, tomatoes, salt, pepper and Worcestershire sauce. Bring to a boil, turn down heat, cover and simmer until macaroni is tender, about 20 minutes. Stir several times during cooking and add a little water if necessary to keep from sticking.

Stir in olives and serve.

SERVES 6

Meat Ball Sauce and Spaghetti

1 lb	ground beef	450 g
1/2 lb	ground lean pork	225 g
1/2 lb	ground veal	225 g
1/2 cup	finely chopped parsley	125 ml
1/2 cup	grated Parmesan cheese	125 ml
2 cloves	garlic, crushed	2 cloves
1 cup	fine dry bread crumbs	250 ml
2 tsp	salt	10 ml
1/4 tsp	pepper	1 ml
1	egg	1
1/4 cup	milk	60 ml
2 tbsp	cooking oil	30 ml
2 tbsp	cooking oil	30 ml
2 medium	onions, chopped	2 medium
10 cups	canned Italian-style tomatoes	2.5 L
2 7 1/2-oz cans	tomato sauce	2 213-ml cans
2 5 1/2-oz cans	tomato paste	2 156-ml cans
1 clove	garlic, crushed	1 clove
	hot cooked spaghetti	
	grated Parmesan cheese	

Combine beef, pork, veal, parsley, 1/2 cup (125 ml) Parmesan cheese, 2 cloves garlic, bread crumbs, salt and pepper in a large bowl. Beat egg and milk together lightly with a fork and add. Blend mixture well with a fork and shape into small meat balls, about 1 1/2 inches (3.75 cm) in diameter.

Heat 2 tbsp (30 ml) oil in large heavy saucepan or Dutch oven. Brown meat balls in oil, removing them as they brown and adding more oil if necessary.

Add another 2 tbsp (30 ml) oil to same pan when all meat balls have been removed and add onions. Cook gently 3 minutes, stirring. Add tomatoes, tomato sauce, tomato paste and 1 clove garlic. Bring to a boil, turn down heat, cover and simmer 2 hours.

Drop in browned meat balls and continue simmering, uncovered, 1 hour more or until sauce is thick. Taste and add salt and pepper if necessary.

Serve over hot spaghetti and pass the Parmesan cheese.

———————— SERVES 8 TO 10 ————————

Meat Ball Sauce and Spaghetti

Freezer Steak Pie

3 lb	round steak, 1 inch (2.5 cm) thick	1.4 kg
1/2 cup	flour	125 ml
3/4 tsp	salt	3 ml
1/4 tsp	pepper	1 ml
3 tbsp	butter	45 ml
3 tbsp	cooking oil	45 ml
2 tbsp	cooking oil	30 ml
1/2 cup	chopped onions	125 ml
1 lb	fresh mushrooms, sliced	450 g
2 cups	beef stock (see note)	500 ml
1/2 cup	chopped parsley	125 ml
1 tsp	Worcestershire sauce	5 ml
1 tsp	salt	5 ml
1/2 tsp	pepper	2 ml
1/4 tsp	nutmeg	1 ml
1	bay leaf	1
	pastry (see note)	
1	egg yolk	1
1 tbsp	water	15 ml

Trim fat from steak and cut meat into 1-inch (2.5-cm) cubes. Combine flour, 3/4 tsp (3 ml) salt and 1/4 tsp (1 ml) pepper in a flat dish. Roll beef cubes in the mixture to coat all sides.

Heat butter and 3 tbsp (45 ml) oil in a large heavy saucepan or Dutch oven. Add meat cubes and brown well on all sides. Remove meat with a slotted spoon and set aside.

Add remaining 2 tbsp (30 ml) oil to same pan and add the onions and mushrooms. Cook gently, stirring, until onion is limp but not brown, about 5 minutes. Stir in all remaining

ingredients except pastry, egg yolk and water. Add browned meat cubes. Cover and simmer until meat is just tender, about 1 hour. Chill quickly by setting pan in ice water.

Divide the meat mixture evenly among 8 small aluminum foil pie pans.

Roll pastry thin and cut 8 rounds slightly larger in diameter than the tops of the pans. If you don't have a cutter the right size cut around a small bowl. Top the meat mixture with pastry, sealing it well to the edges of the pans. Beat egg yolk and water together with a fork and brush over tops of pies. Do not cut vents in tops.

Wrap each pie in heavy-duty aluminum foil and freeze immediately.

To serve, heat oven to 350 °F (175 °C). Unwrap frozen pie and cut vents in the tops. Set on baking sheet. Bake about 1 hour or until pastry is well browned and filling is hot and bubbling.

If you wish to serve the pies immediately rather than freezing them, omit chilling step and cut vents in the pastry after brushing with egg yolk mixture. Set on baking sheet and bake at 350 °F (175 °C) about 35 minutes or until brown and bubbling.

Note: You can use homemade beef stock, canned beef bouillon or 2 bouillon cubes dissolved in boiling water for the stock in this recipe.

Pastry for a 2 crust 9-inch (23-cm) pie should be enough if your pie pans are the smaller size. If you are using the larger pans you will need to make a quantity using 3 cups (750 ml) flour or 1 1/2 envelopes or sticks of pie crust mix.

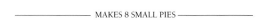

MAKES 8 SMALL PIES

Veal

Veal

It is hard to believe that delicate, light colored veal is related to husky red beef. When this very young beef is handled properly no other meat can rival its juicy tenderness. And what other meat lends itself so well to so many delectable sauces and garnishes.

Veal comes from young animals of from 3 to 10 months. There are several kinds and qualities of veal. Young veal is a pinky-white but grows darker as the animal ages. That is why we should look for the lightest cuts — the sign of tenderness. One can also tell the difference between milk fed, grain, or range fed veal by the color of the flesh. Meat will generally take on the color of the animals feed.

Veal is a lean meat, low in fat, that will sometimes require larding to avoid dryness. The choicest pieces of veal are the filet, the loin, the leg and the shoulder. Less costly but very tasty are the breast and brisket meat which makes wonderful braised dishes and is excellent in classical stews such as the delectable Veal Blanquette.

Veal bones are full of nutritious marrow and gelatine and every good cook is well aware of the richness of bouillon made with veal bones. This is the bouillon that is so vital in the preparation of the tastiest pâté.

Properly prepared veal deserves our full attention as a meat for fine entertaining or delicious everyday fare. This section provides you with veal recipes which are easily followed and result in rich culinary rewards.

Barbecued Veal Roast

2 tbsp	cooking oil	30 ml
4-lb	veal roast	1.8-kg
2 tbsp	brown sugar	30 ml
1 tbsp	paprika	15 ml
1 tsp	salt	5 ml
1 tsp	dry mustard	5 ml
1/4 tsp	chili powder	1 ml
1/8 tsp	cayenne	0.5 ml
2 tbsp	Worcestershire sauce	30 ml
1/4 cup	white vinegar	60 ml
1 cup	tomato juice	250 ml
1/4 cup	ketchup	60 ml
1/2 cup	water	125 ml
1/4 cup	finely chopped celery	60 ml
1 small	onion, chopped	1 small
	potatoes, peeled and halved	
	carrots, peeled and cut in large pieces	
	small onions, peeled	

Heat oil in large Dutch oven. Add meat and brown well on all sides. Combine all remaining ingredients except potatoes, carrots and whole onions in a saucepan. Heat to boiling. Pour over meat. Bring to a boil, cover tightly, turn down heat and simmer 1 1/2 hours. Turn meat occasionally. Add potatoes, carrots and whole onions, cover again and continue simmering until everything is tender, about 1 hour. Spoon mixture in pan over sliced meat and vegetables to serve.

———— SERVES 6 TO 8 ————

Piquant Veal

3 tbsp	sweet pickle juice	45 ml
1 tbsp	dry mustard	15 ml
1 tbsp	salt	15 ml
1 tsp	sage	15 ml
1/2 tsp	dried leaf rosemary	2 ml
4-lb	rump roast of veal	1.8-kg
6 slices	bacon	6 slices

Heat oven to 325 °F (160 °C).

Combine pickle juice, mustard, salt, sage and rosemary and spread over roast. Set on rack in roasting pan and lay bacon slices over.

Roast, uncovered, about 35 minutes a pound (450 g) or until very tender.

———— SERVES 6 TO 8 ————

Barbecued Veal Roast

Top-of-the-Stove Veal Roast

2 tbsp	flour	30 ml
1 tbsp	dry mustard	15 ml
1 tbsp	sugar	15 ml
2 tsp	salt	30 ml
1/4 tsp	pepper	1 ml
1/2 tsp	dried leaf thyme	2 ml
1/2 tsp	dried leaf savory	2 ml
4 to 5-lb	rump roast of veal	1.8 to 2.2-kg
1/4 cup	cooking oil	60 ml
1/4 cup	white vinegar	60 ml
1/2 cup	chicken bouillon or water	125 ml
1 cup	chopped onion	250 ml
1/4 cup	chopped parsley	60 ml
1/4 cup	chopped celery leaves	60 ml

Combine flour, mustard, sugar, salt, pepper, thyme and savory and rub into meat well. (Save any left-over flour mixture and use to thicken gravy).

Heat oil in large heavy saucepan or Dutch oven. Add meat and brown well on all sides. Add remaining ingredients, cover and simmer until meat is very tender, about 2 hours. Lift meat out to a warm platter.

Strain liquid left in pan, return to pan. Bring to a boil. Shake a little cold water and the flour mixture left from coating roast together in a small jar with a tight lid until smooth. Stir into boiling liquid gradually. Boil gently 5 minutes, stirring constantly. Serve with roast.

—————— SERVES 8 TO 10 ——————

Veal Chops with Tomato Sauce

1 envelope	dry onion soup mix	1 envelope
1 cup	fine dry bread crumbs	250 ml
2	eggs	2
2 tbsp	water	30 ml
6	loin veal chops, cut 3/4 inch (2 cm) thick	6
2 tbsp	butter or margarine	30 ml
2 tbsp	cooking oil	30 ml
1/2 cup	chicken stock	125 ml

Tomato Sauce
(recipe follows)

Crush onion soup mix with fingers and add to bread crumbs in shallow dish (a pie pan is fine). Mix well. Put eggs and water in another shallow dish and beat together with a fork. Dip chops into crumb mixture, then into egg mixture and finally into crumb mixture again.

Heat oven to 350 °F (175 °C). Butter a shallow baking dish just large enough to hold chops in a single layer.

Heat butter or margarine and oil in large heavy skillet. Brown chops slowly on both sides and put them in baking dish as they brown. Add chicken stock. Cover tightly and bake 15 minutes.

Turn chops, cover again and bake 15 minutes. Remove cover and bake about 10 minutes more or until very tender. Serve with Tomato Sauce.

——————— SERVES 6 ———————

Tomato Sauce

2 tbsp	olive oil	30 ml
1 small clove	garlic, peeled and cut in half	1 small clove
1/4 cup	chopped onion	60 ml
1/4 cup	chopped celery	60 ml
1 cup	slices mushrooms	250 ml
1/2 cup	finely chopped cooked ham	125 ml
14-oz can	tomato sauce	398-ml can
1/4 cup	water	60 ml
1/4 cup	finely grated carrot	60 ml
1/2 tsp	salt	2 ml
1/4 tsp	pepper	1 ml

Heat oil in medium saucepan. Add garlic and cook gently 3 minutes. Remove and discard garlic. Add onion, celery, mushrooms and ham to oil left in pan and cook gently 3 minutes, stirring. Add remaining ingredients and bring to a boil. Turn down heat, cover and simmer 20 minutes. Keep hot to serve with veal.

Veal Shoulder Chops with Onions

8	veal shoulder chops	8
	flour	
2 tbsp	butter	30 ml
2 tbsp	cooking oil	30 ml
	salt and pepper to taste	
4 large	onions, chopped finely	4 large
1/2 cup	water	125 ml
3 tbsp	butter or margarine	45 ml
2 tbsp	flour	30 ml
1 1/2 cups	milk	375 ml
1/2 tsp	salt	2 ml
1/8 tsp	black pepper	0.5 ml
1/3 cup	grated Parmesan cheese	80 ml
1/4 cup	grated Parmesan cheese	60 ml

Trim membrane from veal shoulder chops and cut meat into serving-size pieces. Dip in flour to coat both sides. Heat 2 tbsp (30 ml) butter and oil in large heavy skillet and brown meat lightly on both sides.

Heat oven to 350 °F (175 °C). Have ready a baking dish that will just hold the meat in a single layer.

Sprinkle meat generously with salt and pepper and put in baking dish.

Add onions to drippings left in pan. Add 1/2 cup (125 ml) water, cover and simmer until onions are transparent but not brown. Remove cover and cook gently until liquid cooks away, about 5 minutes. Add 3 tbsp (45 ml) butter or margarine to onions and stir to blend. Sprinkle in 2 tbsp (30 ml) flour and stir to blend. Cook and stir gently 3 minutes.

Remove from heat and stir in milk. Return to moderate heat and cook and stir until boiling, thickened and smooth. Remove from heat and stir in salt, pepper and 1/3 cup (80 ml) cheese. Pour over veal. Cover and bake about 1 hour or until meat is very tender. Remove cover and sprinkle with 1/4 cup (60 ml) cheese. Slip low under hot broiler to brown top. Serve immediately.

—————— SERVES 4 ——————

Veal Chops with Tomato Sauce

Veal Rolls

12	veal cutlets, cut very thin	12
6 to 12	thin slices prosciutto or cooked ham (amount depends on size of cutlets)	6 to 12
1 tbsp	butter or margarine	15 ml
1 tbsp	olive oil	15 ml
1 clove	garlic, peeled	1 clove
1/2 cup	chicken stock or water	125 ml
1/4 cup	dry white wine	60 ml
24 oz	cooked fresh spinach, drained	675 g
1/2 tsp	salt	2 ml

Pound veal cutlets with a rolling pin or mallet between 2 sheets of waxed paper until as thin as possible. Put a piece of prosciutto or ham, trimmed to a size slightly smaller than the veal piece, on top of each piece of veal and roll up, fastening each roll with a skewer or toothpick.

Heat butter or margarine, oil and clove of garlic in large skillet. Add veal rolls and brown lightly on all sides. Add chicken stock or water and wine. Cover tightly and simmer 15 minutes. Remove rolls from pan and keep hot. Discard garlic.

Heat oven to 350 °F (175 °C). Butter a 10- x 6- x 2-inch (25- x 15- x 5-cm) baking dish.

Boil the liquid left in the skillet hard until only the fat remains. Add the spinach and salt and stir until spinach is hot, about 1 minute. Spoon spinach into prepared baking dish. Put veal rolls on top and pour any pan juices over all. Cover baking dish and bake 15 minutes or until veal is very tender.

———————— SERVES 4 OR 6 ————————

Breaded Veal Cutlets

1 1/2 lb	thin veal cutlets	675 g
1/2 cup	milk	125 ml
2	eggs	2
1/3 cup	flour	80 ml
1 cup	fine dry bread crumbs (approx.)	250 ml
3 tbsp	butter or margarine	45 ml
3 tbsp	cooking oil	45 ml
	salt and pepper	

Put cutlets in a shallow baking dish and pour milk over. Let stand at room temperature 1 hour, turning often.

Put eggs in a flat dish (a pie pan is fine). Drain milk from cutlets into eggs and beat them together with a fork. Put some flour in another flat dish — about 1/3 cup (80 ml) — and bread crumbs in a third dish.

Dip cutlets into flour, then in egg mixture and finally in bread crumbs.

Heat butter or margarine and oil in large heavy skillet. Add cutlets and cook fairly quickly until well browned and tender, about 3 minutes a side. Sprinkle with salt and pepper. Serve immediately.

———————— SERVES 4 ————————

Above: Breaded Veal Cutlets
Below: Veal Rolls

Veal Marengo

1/3 cup	olive oil	80 ml
3 lb	stewing veal (shoulder or shank), cubed	1.4 kg
1/2 cup	chopped onion	125 ml
19-oz can	tomatoes	540-ml can
2 tsp	salt	10 ml
1/2 tsp	sugar	2 ml
1/4 tsp	pepper	1 ml
1/2 tsp	dried leaf basil	2 ml
1/2 tsp	paprika	2 ml
2 tbsp	flour	30 ml
3 cups	chicken stock or 3 chicken bouillon cubes dissolved in 3 cups (750 ml) boiling water	750 ml
1 cup	dry white table wine	250 ml
16 small	onions or 8 medium onions cut in half	16 small
8 medium	carrots	8 medium
1/2 lb	whole fresh mushrooms	225 g
12 oz	frozen peas	350 g

Heat oil in large heavy saucepan or Dutch oven. Add veal and cook over high heat until lightly browned. Add chopped onion, tomatoes, salt, sugar, pepper, basil and paprika.

Add flour to 1/2 cup (125 ml) cold chicken stock and blend until smooth. Add remaining chicken stock and wine to veal mixture. Bring to a boil. Stir in flour and chicken stock mixture gradually. Turn down heat, cover and simmer 45 minutes or until meat is beginning to get tender. Add onions and simmer 15 minutes. Cut carrots into 1-inch (2.5-cm) pieces diagonally. Add to stew and continue simmering 15 minutes more. Add mushrooms and simmer 10 minutes or until meat is fork-tender. Add peas and simmer 5 minutes. Serve immediately.

———————— SERVES 6 TO 8 ————————

Veal Marsala

1 tbsp	flour	15 ml
1/4 tsp	salt	1 ml
dash	pepper	dash
1/4 tsp	paprika	1 ml
3/4 lb	veal steak, cut 1/4 inch (0.5 cm) thick	350 g
2 tbsp	butter	30 ml
1 tbsp	olive oil	15 ml
1 cup	thickly sliced fresh mushrooms	250 ml
1/3 cup	Marsala	80 ml
	salt and pepper	
1 tbsp	chopped parsley	15 ml
4	paper thin slices lemon	4

Combine flour, 1/4 tsp (1 ml) salt, dash pepper and paprika in a flat dish. Cut veal into two pieces of equal size. Dip pieces in flour mixture to coat both sides.

Heat 1 tbsp (15 ml) of the butter and olive oil to very hot in large heavy skillet. Add mushrooms and cook quickly 2 minutes, stirring. Lift out with slotted spoon and set aside. Add remaining 1 tbsp (15 ml) butter to drippings in skillet and heat well. Add veal pieces and brown quickly on both sides. Lift pan off heat and let cool for a minute then add Marsala. Sprinkle each piece of veal lightly with salt and pepper. Cover pan tightly. Return to low heat and simmer about 10 minutes or until veal is tender.

Lift veal out onto hot platter. Add parsley and mushrooms to drippings in pan (add a little hot water if Marsala has nearly cooked away). Heat well and pour over veal. Garnish with lemon slices. Serve immediately.

———————— SERVES 2 ————————

Veal Marengo

Cream Schnitzel

2 tbsp	flour	30 ml
1/4 tsp	salt	1 ml
dash	pepper	dash
1 lb	veal steak, cut 1/4 inch (0.5 cm) thick	450 g
4 slices	bacon	4 slices
1 tbsp	butter	15 ml
1 tbsp	finely chopped onion	15 ml
1 tbsp	paprika	15 ml
1 cup	tomato sauce	250 ml
1/2 cup	water	125 ml
10 oz	frozen French-style green beans	280 g
19-oz can	whole potatoes, drained and sliced	540-ml can
1/2 cup	commercial sour cream	125 ml

Combine flour, salt and pepper. Cut meat into serving-size pieces and dip in flour mixture to coat both sides.

Fry bacon in heavy skillet until crisp. Lift out of pan, drain and crumble. Set aside.

Add butter to bacon drippings in pan and turn heat to high. Fry veal quickly until golden on both sides. Turn heat to low. Add onion, paprika, tomato sauce, water, beans and potato slices. Cover tightly and simmer about 20 minutes or until everything is tender, uncovering and breaking up beans as necessary and adding more water if liquid has cooked away. Stir sour cream into liquid in pan. Heat but do not boil. Sprinkle in bacon bits.

SERVES 2 OR 3

Veal and Ham Pie

1 1/2 lb	boneless veal shoulder	675 ml
1 1/2 lb	uncooked ham	675 ml
2 tsp	salt	10 ml
1/2 tsp	pepper	2 ml
1/2 tsp	dried leaf savory	2 ml
1/4 tsp	allspice	1 ml
1/8 tsp	nutmeg	0.5 ml
1 tsp	grated lemon rind	5 ml
2	eggs, beaten	2
	Hot Water Pastry (recipe follows)	
4	hard-cooked eggs	4
1	egg yolk	1
1 tbsp	cold water	15 ml
1 envelope	unflavored gelatin	1 envelope
2 cups	chicken stock	500 ml

Grind 1/2 lb (225 g) of the veal and 1/2 lb (225 g) of the ham through the fine blade of the food chopper. Cut remaining meat into 1/2-inch (1.25-cm) cubes. Mix ground meat, meat cubes, salt, pepper, savory, allspice, nutmeg, lemon rind and beaten eggs.

Have ready two 8- x 4 1/4- x 2 1/4-inch (20.5- x 10.5- x 5.5-cm) aluminum foil loaf pans.

Divide chilled Hot Water Pastry into 3 equal parts. Roll 1 part into an oblong about 13 x 9 inches (33 x 23 cm). Put carefully into one of loaf pans, fitting it into the corners and being careful not to stretch. Trim pastry so that it hangs about 1/2 inch (1.25 cm) over the sides of the pan. Repeat for other loaf pans.

Pack each pan about 1/3 full of the meat mixture — about 1 cup (250 ml) each. Top each meat layer with 2 of the hard-cooked eggs, laying them lengthwise. Pack remaining meat mixture — about 2 cups (500 ml) per pan — into the pans around and on top of the eggs to enclose them completely.

Divide remaining pastry into two and roll each piece slightly larger than the tops of the pans. Moisten edges of bottom pastry, lay pastry on top and seal together by pressing firmly. Trim top pastry to same size as lower pastry and roll edges under. Crimp.

Heat oven to 425 °F (220 °C).

Beat egg yolk and water together lightly with a fork and brush over top crust. Decorate with flowers and leaves cut from left-over pastry if desired. Cut a small round hole in the centre of the top crust so steam can escape. Bake at 425 °F (220 °C) for 40 minutes. Reduce oven temperature to 350 °F (175 °C) and continue baking 1 1/2 hours more. Cool to lukewarm in pan.

Soak gelatin in 1/4 cup (60 ml) of the chicken stock 5 minutes. Heat remaining chicken stock to boiling. Add gelatin mixture and stir until gelatin is dissolved. Cool but do not chill. Pour mixture very slowly into holes in tops of partly cooled pies to fill up the spaces. (If you have a small funnel it will make the job easier. Pour the gelatin mixture a little at a time into the hole, letting pies sit between additions until the gelatin runs into any spaces. Keep adding the

gelatin until the pies won't hold any more. You will probably have some of the gelatin mixture left over. It can be
chilled as an aspic or you can add some leftover vegetables
and chill as a salad.) Cool pies completely, then chill very
well.

Unmould by loosening pan all around at serving time. Set on
greens on serving plate. Cut away and discard end pastry,
then cut in thick slices to serve.

——————— SERVES 10 TO 12 ———————

Hot Water Pastry

1/2 lb	lard	225 g
1/2 cup	boiling water	125 ml
2 3/4 cups	sifted all-purpose flour	685 ml
1 tsp	baking powder	5 ml
1 tsp	salt	5 ml
1 tsp	paprika	5 ml

Cut lard into small pieces into a bowl. Add boiling water
and beat with electric mixer or rotary beater until cold and
creamy (don't worry if mixture doesn't completely blend).

Sift remaining ingredients together into lard mixture. Stir
with a wooden spoon until smooth and dough leaves the
sides of the bowl. Wrap in waxed paper and chill well.

Put dough carefully into one
of loaf pans, fitting it into the
corners and being careful not to
stretch. Trim pastry so that it
hangs about 1/2 inch (1.25 cm)
over the sides of the pan.

Pack each pan about 1/3 full
of the meat mixture — about
1 cup (250 ml) each. Top each
meat layer with 2 of the hard-
cooked eggs, laying them
lengthwise.

Moisten edges of bottom
pastry, lay pastry on top and
seal together by pressing
firmly. Trim top pastry to
same size as lower pastry and
roll edges under. Crimp.

Pour mixture very slowly into
holes in tops of partly cooled
pies to fill up the spaces. If
you have a small funnel it will
make the job easier. Pour the
gelatin mixture a little at a
time into the hole, letting pies
sit between additions until the
gelatin runs into any spaces.
Keep adding the gelatin until
the pies won't hold any more.

Broiled Liver and Bacon

1 1/2 lb	calf's or baby beef (veal) liver, cut 1/2 inch (1.25 cm) thick	675 g
	salt and pepper	
	garlic salt	
8 slices	bacon	8 slices
2 large	onions, sliced paper thin	2 large
	cooking oil	
12	mushroom caps	12
1/4 cup	boiling water	60 ml
1/4 tsp	Worcestershire sauce	1 ml

Heat broiler.

Remove skin and tubes from liver and dry well on paper towelling. Sprinkle lightly on both sides with salt, pepper and garlic salt.

Put slices of bacon on shallow broiler pan (not on rack). Put low under broiler (just below the middle of the oven) and broil until done, turning once. Remove pan from oven, lift off bacon and set aside. Leave bacon drippings in pan.

→

Add onions to broiler pan and return pan to oven. Broil onions (low under the broiler), stirring several times, about 3 minutes. Remove pan from oven. Push onions to one end of pan. Put liver pieces on other end of pan. Drizzle each piece with a few drops of oil. Raise oven rack to just under broiler and return pan to oven. Broil liver about 3 minutes a side or until done the way you like it. Spoon pan juices over liver twice during broiling. Stir onions at the same time.

Put a drop of cooking oil in each mushroom cap. About 1 minute before the liver is ready, return the bacon to the broiler pan and add the mushroom caps. Continue broiling watching carefully, until bacon is hot and liver is ready.

Put liver on a hot platter, pile onions on top and garnish platter with bacon strips. Spoon pan drippings over mushrooms and return to oven for 1 minute. Add mushrooms to platter.

Add boiling water and Worcestershire sauce to drippings in pan and stir to blend. Pour over liver and onions. Serve immediately.

———————— SERVES 6 ————————

Broiled Liver and Bacon

Veal Terrine

1/2 lb	side bacon	225 g
2 lb	veal steak, cut 1/4 inch (0.5 cm) thick	900 g
3/4 cup	finely chopped green onions	180 ml
3/4 cup	finely chopped parsley	180 ml
	freshly ground pepper	
	dried leaf savory	
	dried leaf basil	
1	bay leaf	1
1 lb	back bacon, sliced very thin	450 g
1/2 cup	dry vermouth	125 ml

Heat oven to 300 °F (150 °C). Have ready a 9- x 5- x 3-inch (23- x 12.5- x 7.5-cm) glass loaf pan.

Line bottom and sides of loaf pan with some of the side bacon.

Cut veal steak apart along its natural divisions and remove all fat, bone and membrane. Put a single layer of veal pieces on top of bacon in bottom of loaf pan. Sprinkle with about 1/4 of the onion and parsley. Grate a little pepper over and sprinkle with a pinch each of savory and basil. Break off a small piece of bay leaf and crumble it over all. Add a single layer of back bacon slices. Repeat the layers of meat and the seasonings until everything is used. Top with remaining side bacon. Pour in the vermouth.

Cover the pan tightly with a double thickness of aluminum foil. Bake 3 hours.

Remove the terrine from the oven. Fold several layers of heavy aluminum foil so it just fits inside the top of the loaf pan. Put this foil on top of terrine. Cut a piece of heavy cardboard to just the size of the inside of the top of the pan. Wrap it with foil and lay it on top of terrine. Put weights on this cardboard (you can use heavy cans of food, an iron or brick, if you have one handy) and let the terrine stand at room temperature until cool.

Chill very well (leave weights on if you can). Turn out on platter and slice thinly to serve.

———————— SERVES 8 TO 10 ————————

Blanquette of Veal

2 lb	shoulder of veal, cubed	1.8 kg
3 cups	boiling water	750 ml
4 medium	carrots	4 medium
12 small	onions or 6 medium onions, halved	12 small
1	leek (white part only), chopped	1
1 cup	chopped celery	250 ml
2 tsp	salt	10 ml
1/4 tsp	dried leaf thyme	1 ml
1 large	bay leaf	1 large
1 clove	garlic	1 clove
3 sprigs	parsley	3 sprigs
3 tbsp	butter	45 ml
3/4 lb	fresh mushrooms, sliced	350 g
1/4 cup	lemon juice	60 ml
2 tbsp	flour	30 ml
1/2 cup	cold water	125 ml
2	egg yolks	2
1 cup	heavy cream	250 ml
1/4 cup	chopped parsley	60 ml

Put veal in large heavy saucepan or Dutch oven. Add 3 cups (750 ml) boiling water. Bring to a boil, turn down heat, cover and simmer 30 minutes.

Cut carrots into 4, lengthwise, then cut into 1-inch (2.5-cm) lengths. Add to veal along with onions, leek, celery, salt and thyme. Tie bay leaf, garlic and parsley in a small cloth bag and add. Bring back to boiling, turn down heat, cover and continue simmering until veal and vegetables are tender, about 1 hour.

Lift out and discard bag of herbs.

Heat butter in large heavy skillet and add mushrooms. Cook over high heat 3 minutes, stirring. Add to veal along with lemon juice, Bring to a boil, turn down heat and simmer 5 minutes.

Add flour to cold water and blend until smooth. Stir into boiling mixture and simmer 5 minutes. Beat egg yolks and cream together with a fork. Stir in a little of the hot liquid, then return the mixture to the pan. Heat but do not boil. Sprinkle with parsley. Serve immediately.

—————— SERVES 6 ——————

Pork

P*ork*

Pork is very popular and for good reason. Pork is now grown much leaner and the lower fat cuts of pork have an abundance of protein, high in minerals and B vitamins. The result is fewer calories, less fat and less cholesterol. Thus a versatile meat in its many forms returns to delight the palate of the most vitality conscious — at any meal time.

Pork is eaten fresh, or cured as ham. The preferred cooking method for fresh pork is well done but not overdone. The method is up to you, roasted rapidly at high heat or more gently for a longer time. The cut will suggest the method. Make sure grilled chops or cutlets are cooked throughout. Browning and finishing in an oven casserole is a good way to ensure tenderness without flavor loss.

Cured pork in the form of hams and bacon are standbys of the versatile cook. Hams can fill the bill on both festive and everyday occasions. The flavor of ham, while distinctive, can be enhanced in a good kitchen. I have included several rather special ham recipes in this section. They should earn raves from even the most critical of ham lovers.

Herbs and spices and garnishes complement the rich flavor of pork. In the recipes that follow, anise, cloves, garlic, chervil, cinnamon, ginger, mustard, nutmeg, oregano, paprika, sage, savory, and thyme are used to flavor. Garnishes include apples, oranges, ginger, pineapple, honey, brown sugar and cranberries — so versatile is this diners delight.

Stuffed Roast Pork

1/4 cup	butter or margarine	60 ml
1 lb	fresh mushrooms, chopped finely	450 g
1 cup	thinly sliced celery	250 ml
2 tbsp	chopped parsley	30 ml
1/2 tsp	dried leaf savory	2 ml
1/2 tsp	dried leaf marjoram	2 ml
1/4 tsp	dried leaf thyme	1 ml
1 tsp	salt	5 ml
1/8 tsp	pepper	0.5 ml
1	egg, lightly beaten	1
2 cups	coarsely crushed unsalted soda biscuits	500 ml
6-lb	loin of pork	2.6-kg

Heat butter (or margarine) in large heavy skillet. Add mushrooms and celery and cook gently 5 minutes, stirring constantly. Remove from heat. Stir in parsley, herbs, salt and pepper. Cool for a few minutes. stir in egg and soda biscuit crumbs.

Heat oven to 325 °F (160 °C). Have ready a roasting pan just large enough to hold the roast.

Cut down from top of roast just to but not through backbone (you will end up with 8 to 10 thick chops still joined along the bottom). Spoon the stuffing into these cuts, packing it in quite well (the stuffing should be moist and will stay in place). Start at the middle and work out towards each end to make it easiest. Push short skewers through the fat at each end of the roast to hold the roast together until you tie it. Tie it from end to end.

Set roast in roasting pan on bones. Cover loosely with a tent of aluminum foil.

Roast 2 hours. Uncover, slash fat in a few places and continue roasting about 1 hour and 15 minutes more or until very tender and cooked through — 185 °F (85 °C) on the meat thermometer.

SERVES 8 TO 10

Roast Loin of Pork

4-lb	loin of pork	1.8-kg
	olive oil	
	salt and pepper	
1/2 tsp	dried leaf thyme	2 ml
1/2 tsp	dried leaf oregano	2 ml
1/4 tsp	anise seeds	1 ml
2 tbsp	flour	30 ml
1	onion, sliced paper-thin	1
1 cup	chicken stock	250 ml
1 cup	dry white wine	250 ml
1 clove	garlic, crushed	1 clove
dash	nutmeg	dash

Rub roast all over with olive oil. Sprinkle generously with salt and pepper.

Combine thyme, oregano, anise seeds and flour and rub mixture over roast (not on ends). Attach onion slices with toothpicks to fat side of roast. Set in roasting pan bone side down (bones will serve as a rack), cover with transparent wrap and let stand in refrigerator at least 8 hours. Let stand at room temperature 2 hours before roasting.

Heat oven to 375 °F (190 °C). Remove transparent wrap from roast and put in oven for 30 minutes. Remove from oven. Reduce oven temperature to 325 °F (160 °C).

While roast is cooking the first 30 minutes, combine chicken stock, wine, garlic and nutmeg in a small saucepan. Simmer 10 minutes. Pour this mixture over meat after first 30 minutes cooking. Return meat to oven and roast to 185 °F (85 °C) on meat thermometer — 45 minutes per lb (450 g) or about 3 hours. Baste often during cooking.

SERVES 6 TO 8

Braised Pork Tenderloin with Orange Sauce

1/4 cup	flour	60 ml
1 tsp	salt	5 ml
1/4 tsp	pepper	1 ml
1/2 tsp	paprika	2 ml
1/4 tsp	allspice	1 ml
1 lb	pork tenderloin, sliced and Frenched	450 g
2 tbsp	cooking oil	30 ml
1/4 cup	chicken stock	60 ml
1/2 cup	commercial sour cream	125 ml
2 tbsp	orange juice	30 ml
1 tbsp	grated orange rind	15 ml
1/4 tsp	salt	1 ml
1/2 tsp	Worcestershire sauce	2 ml

Combine flour, 1 tsp (5 ml) salt, pepper, paprika and all-spice in a flat dish. Dip slices of tenderloin in this mixture to coat both sides.

Heat 2 tbsp (30 ml) oil in heavy skillet. Add pork slices and brown well on both sides. Add chicken stock, cover tightly and simmer until very tender, about 30 minutes.

Combine sour cream, orange juice, orange rind, 1/4 tsp (1 ml) salt and Worcestershire sauce in small pan and heat but do not boil. Spoon over pork tenderloin at serving time.

——— SERVES 4 ———

Pork Chop Packages
(for the barbecue)

4	pork chops	4
4 thick slices	unpeeled apple	4 thick slices
4 thick slices	peeled sweet potato	4 thick slices
4 thick slices	Spanish onion	4 thick slices
	savory	
	nutmeg	
	salt and pepper	
	butter	

Trim excess fat from pork chops. Heat some of this fat in a heavy skillet until skillet is well greased. Discard fat. Brown chops lightly on both sides.

→

Fruited Pork Chops

Tear off four 13-inch (33-cm) lengths of heavy-duty aluminum foil. Place a pork chop on each. Top each with a slice of apple, potato and onion. Add a pinch of savory, a dash of nutmeg, a generous sprinkling of salt and pepper and a little dab of butter to each. Wrap tightly, making double folds at all joins in the foil. Roast over moderate coals until chops are very tender and cooked through, about 1 hour.

Note: Cook in 400 °F (205 °C) oven about 1 hour if desired.

SERVES 4

1 tsp	salt	5 ml
1/4 tsp	pepper	1 ml
1/4 tsp	paprika	1 ml
1 tsp	sugar	5 ml
1/8 tsp	cinnamon	0.5 ml
1/8 tsp	cloves	0.5 ml
2 tbsp	cooking oil	30 ml
6	loin pork chops	6
1/2 cup	orange juice	125 ml
1/2 cup	water	125 ml
2 tbsp	lemon juice	30 ml
6 slices	canned pineapple	6 slices
6 thin slices	orange	6 thin slices
	pepper	

Mix salt, 1/4 tsp (1 ml) pepper, paprika, sugar, cinnamon and cloves in a small dish. Sprinkle a little of the mixture on each side of each pork chop and rub it in well.

Heat oil in heavy skillet. Add chops and brown slowly. Add orange juice, water and lemon juice. Cover tightly and simmer about 40 minutes or until cooked through. Lay a slice of pineapple and an orange slice on each chop. Cover again and simmer 10 minutes. Sprinkle lightly with pepper.

Note: If you want extra sauce, add 1 cup (250 ml) orange juice or pineapple juice to skillet after chops have been removed. Let boil and thicken slightly with 1 tsp (5 ml) cornstarch stirred into 2 tbsp (30 ml) cold water.

SERVES 6

Left: Fruited Pork Chops
Right: Pork Chop Packages

Cottage Pork Chops

6	pork chops	6
	flour	
1 clove	garlic, chopped	1 clove
1 tsp	salt	5 ml
1/4 tsp	pepper	1 ml
1 tbsp	chopped parsley	15 ml
2 tbsp	flour	30 ml
6 medium	potatoes, sliced thin	6 medium
2 medium	onions, sliced	2 medium
2 cups	hot milk	500 ml
1 1/2 tsp	salt	7 ml
1 tsp	dry mustard	5 ml

Heat oven to 350 °F (175 °C).

Cut fat from chops and grease hot skillet with a piece of it.

Roll chops in flour and brown in skillet along with garlic. Season with 1 tsp (5 ml) salt and pepper.

Combine parsley and 2 tbsp (30 ml) flour.

Butter a 2-qt (2.5-L) casserole and put 3 of the chops in it in a single layer. Sprinkle with half of flour-parsley mixture and top with half of potato and onion slices. Repeat layers.

Mix milk, 1 1/2 tsp (7 ml) salt and mustard. Pour over all. Cover tightly and bake 1 1/2 hours. Remove cover last 30 minutes to brown.

———————— SERVES 6 ————————

Barbecued Pork Chops

1/3 cup	cooking oil	80 ml
1/4 cup	vinegar or lemon juice	60 ml
2 tbsp	chopped onion	30 ml
1 clove	garlic, crushed	1 clove
1/2 tsp	salt	2 ml
1/8 tsp	pepper	0.5 ml
1/2 tsp	sage	2 ml
1/4 tsp	dry mustard	1 ml
2 tbsp	soya sauce	30 ml
1 tbsp	Worcestershire sauce	15 ml
4	pork chops	4

Combine all ingredients except chops in a small jar with a tight lid. Shake to blend well. Trim excess fat from chops, put them in a shallow glass dish in a single layer and pour oil mixture over. Let stand 1 hour at room temperature or in refrigerator several hours. Turn occasionally.

Heat oven to 350 °F (175 °C). Bake chops in marinade about 1 hour or until very tender. Turn once during baking.

———————— SERVES 4 ————————

Sauerkraut Alsatian Style

1 lb	bacon sliced 1/4 inch (0.5 cm) thick	450 g
8	thin pork chops	8
2 lb	spareribs, cut in 2 or 3 rib pieces	900 g
84 oz	sauerkraut (3 large cans)	2.4 L
2 tsp	salt	10 ml
1/2 tsp	pepper	2 ml
2 tbsp	fat (left from browning meat — see directions below)	30 ml
2 cloves	garlic, peeled	2 cloves
1 large	bay leaf	1 large
12	juniper berries (optional — see note)	12
1 large	onion	1 large
6	cloves	6
1 cup	dry white table wine (preferably Alsatian)	250 ml
8 medium	potatoes, cut in half	8 medium
1 lb	wieners	450 g

Fry bacon in a large skillet just until pan is well greased. Remove bacon. Fry pork chops in pan until lightly browned. Remove. Brown spareribs lightly in fat in pan. Remove. Measure out 2 tbsp (30 ml) of the fat left from browning the meat and set aside. Discard remaining fat.

Put 1 1/2 cans of the sauerkraut in a very large kettle. Add bacon slices, chops and ribs. Sprinkle with salt and pepper. Cover with remaining sauerkraut. Drizzle the 2 tbsp (30 ml) cooking fat over the sauerkraut. Add whole cloves garlic, bay leaf, juniper berries and the onion stuck with the whole cloves, pushing them down into the sauerkraut. Pour wine over all.

Cover tightly and simmer 1 hour. Add potatoes and wieners and continue cooking 1 hour or until all meat is tender and potatoes are cooked.

Lift meat out of the kettle. Pile the sauerkraut in the middle of a large platter and stand the meat up around it. Surround the meat and sauerkraut with the potatoes.

Note: Juniper berries can be purchased at food specialty stores.

———— SERVES 8 ————

Sauerkraut Alsatian Style

Oven Barbecued Spareribs

4 lb	spareribs	1.8 kg
1 tsp	salt	5 ml
1/2 cup	chopped onion	125 ml
2 cloves	garlic, crushed	2 cloves
1 cup	ketchup	250 ml
1/2 cup	chili sauce	125 ml
2 tbsp	vinegar	30 ml
1 tsp	salt	5 ml
1 tbsp	prepared mustard	15 ml
1/2 tsp	pepper	2 ml
2 tbsp	steak sauce	30 ml
1 cup	liquid honey	250 ml

Cut spareribs into serving-size pieces. Put in large saucepan. Add 1 tsp (5 ml) salt and enough boiling water to cover. Bring to a boil. Turn down heat, cover and simmer 30 minutes.

Combine all remaining ingredients in a saucepan. Bring to a boil, turn down heat and simmer 10 minutes.

Heat oven to 400 °F (205 °C).

Lift spareribs out of cooking water and put them into a large shallow roasting pan in a single layer. Pour the honey mixture over all.

Bake about 45 minutes or until ribs are very tender. Baste often with the honey mixture and turn ribs occasionally.

——————— SERVES 4 TO 6 ———————

Apple Glazed Spareribs

(for the barbecue)

2 lb	spareribs	900 g
	boiling water	
1	bay leaf	1
4	peppercorns	4
1 tsp	salt	5 ml
small bunch	parsley sprigs	small bunch
small slice	onion	small slice
1 tsp	salt	5 ml
1/4 tsp	pepper	1 ml
3/4 cup	apple jelly	180 ml
1 tbsp	lemon juice	15 ml
1 1/2 tsp	Worcestershire sauce	7 ml
dash	Tabasco	dash
1 tsp	dry mustard	5 ml

Cut ribs into 3-rib sections. Put them in a large kettle and cover with boiling water. Add bay leaf, peppercorns, 1 tsp (5 ml) salt, parsley and slice of onion. Bring to a boil, turn down heat, cover and simmer 30 minutes. Lift out of water and drain well.

Sprinkle ribs with 1 tsp (5 ml) salt and 1/4 tsp (1 ml) pepper at cooking time.

Combine apple jelly, lemon juice, Worcestershire sauce, Tabasco and mustard in a small pan and set on back of barbecue to heat and blend. Brush ribs with apple jelly mixture and set over hot coals. Cook 10 minutes. Brush well with apple jelly mixture, turn and cook about 10 minutes. Continue cooking, brushing with jelly mixture and turning often until very well browned and crisp, about 10 minutes longer.

——————— SERVES 4 ———————

Above: Oven Barbecued Spareribs
Below: Apple Glazed Spareribs

Sweet-Sour Pork Balls and Vegetables

1 1/2 lb	ground lean pork	675 g
1/2 cup	thinly sliced green onions	125 ml
1 cup	soft bread cubes	250 ml
1/4 cup	chopped water chestnuts	60 ml
1	egg	1
3 tbsp	water	45 ml
1 tsp	salt	5 ml
1/4 tsp	pepper	1 ml
1/4 tsp	ginger	1 ml
2 tbsp	cooking oil	30 ml

2 cups	chicken stock	500 ml
1/4 cup	brown sugar	60 ml
1/4 cup	white vinegar	60 ml
1 tbsp	paprika	15 ml
2 cups	thinly sliced carrots	500 ml
1 cup	thin diagonal slices celery	250 ml
	salt and pepper	
2	small zucchini, sliced	2
2 tbsp	cold water	30 ml
1 tbsp	cornstarch	15 ml

→

Tourtière

makes two 9-inch (23-cm) pies

2 lb	ground pork	900 g
1/2 lb	ground veal	225 g
1 1/2 cups	hot water	375 ml
1 1/2 tsp	salt	7 ml
1/4 tsp	pepper	1 ml
1 large	onion, chopped	1 large
1 sprig	celery leaves	1 sprig
1/2 tsp	allspice	2 ml
dash	cloves	dash
1 large	potato, peeled	1 large

**double Basic Pastry recipe
(p. 302)**

Combine pork, onions, bread cubes, water chestnuts, egg, 3 tbsp (45 ml) water, 1 tsp (5 ml) salt, 1/4 tsp (1 ml) pepper and ginger, blending well. Shape into 1-inch (2.5-cm) balls. Heat oil in heavy skillet. Add pork balls and brown well on all sides. Cover and cook gently 10 minutes.

Combine chicken stock, sugar, vinegar and paprika and add to skillet. Stir to blend. Add carrots and celery, sprinkle with salt and pepper, cover and simmer 10 to 15 minutes or until vegetables are beginning to get tender. Add zucchini, cover again and simmer about 5 minutes or until vegetables are tender-crisp. Push meat and vegetables to one side of skillet. Combine 2 tbsp (30 ml) cold water and cornstarch and stir into boiling liquid in skillet gradually. Cook until thick and clear.

—————— SERVES 4 ——————

Combine pork, veal, hot water, salt, pepper, onion, celery leaves, allspice and cloves in a large heavy saucepan. Bring to a boil, turn down heat, cover and cook gently 30 minutes, stirring occasionally. Add whole potato and continue cooking gently 1 hour (potato will absorb excess fat). Lift out and discard potato and celery leaves. Cool meat mixture (it should be thick but still moist).

Heat oven to 375 °F (190 °C).

Line two 9-inch (23-cm) pie pans with pastry. Fill with meat mixture. Cover with remaining pastry, seal edges well and flute. Cut slits in tops to let steam escape.

Bake pies about 1 hour or until pastry is very well browned. Serve hot.

—————— SERVES 12 ——————

Sweet-Sour Pork Balls and Vegetables

Pork Pie

3-lb	shoulder of pork	1.4-kg
1 1/2 to 2 lb	pig's feet	675 to 900 g
1 medium	onion, sliced	1 medium
1/4 tsp	dried leaf thyme	1 ml
1 large	bay leaf	1 large
3 whole	cloves	3 whole
2 tsp	salt	10 ml
6	peppercorns	6
	boiling water	
	Lard Pastry (recipe follows)	
3/4 cup	chopped onion	180 ml
1/2 tsp	sage	2 ml
1 tsp	salt	5 ml
1/4 tsp	pepper	1 ml
2 tbsp	butter	30 ml
1/2 cup	water	125 ml
1	egg yolk	1
1 tbsp	milk	15 ml

Remove bone and all fat from pork. Discard fat. Cut meat into 1 1/2-inch (3.75-cm) cubes and store in refrigerator for use later.

Combine pork bones, pig's feet, slices onion, thyme, bay leaf, cloves, 2 tsp (10 ml) salt and peppercorns in kettle. Add boiling water to just cover. Bring to a boil. Turn down heat, cover and simmer 3 hours.

Strain broth from pork bones and pig's feet. Remove any pieces of lean meat from pig's feet and add to raw pork. Discard all bones. Chill broth and lift off and discard fat. Boil broth hard until reduced to about 2 cups (500 ml) if necessary. Set aside for use later.

Heat oven to 325 °F (160 °C). Have ready a 9-inch (23-cm) spring-form pan, 3 inches (7.5 cm) deep.

Roll 2/3 of the Lard Pastry into a round big enough to line the bottom and sides of the spring-form pan. Ease it into the pan, anchoring it by pressing firmly against the sides of the pan.

Put the cubed raw pork and the bits of meat from the pig's feet into the pastry-lined pan. Sprinkle with chopped onion, sage, 1 tsp (5 ml) salt and pepper. Dot with the butter.

Roll the remaining dough into a round a little larger than the top of the pan. Lay it over the meat, moisten the under edge and seal it to the under crust by pressing and crimping firmly.

Cut a small round hole (about the size of a quarter) in the centre of the top crust. Pour in 1/2 cup (125 ml) water.

Bake about 4 hours or until pork is completely cooked through and pastry is well browned. Beat egg yolk and milk together with a fork and brush this over top crust after baking 3 hours.

Remove pie from oven. Heat the 2 cups (500 ml) broth saved from cooking pig's feet and pour as much of the broth into the hole in the top as the pie will take.

Cool then chill for a least 12 hours. Serve cold cut in wedges or thick slices.

SERVES 12 TO 16

Lard Pastry

2/3 cup	boiling water	160 ml
1 1/2 cups	lard	330 ml
4 cups	sifted all-purpose flour	1 L
1 1/2 tsp	salt	7 ml

Add boiling water to lard and beat with wooden spoon or rotary beater until creamy. Cool. Stir in flour and salt, mixing with a fork. Gather into a ball, wrap in waxed paper and chill. Roll and use for pork pie as directed in recipe.

Pork Pie

Ham Loaf

2 cups	ground cooked ham	500 ml
1 1/2 lb	ground pork	675 g
1 cup	fine dry bread crumbs	250 ml
1 tbsp	prepared mustard	15 ml
1/2 tsp	salt	2 ml
1/4 tsp	pepper	1 ml
2	eggs, beaten	2
1 cup	milk	250 ml

Raisin Sauce (recipe follows)

Heat oven to 350 °F (175 °C). Have ready a 9- x 5- x 3-inch (23- x 12.5- x 7.5-cm) loaf pan.

Combine all ingredients except Raisin Sauce and pack into loaf pan. Bake 1 1/2 hours. Cut in thick slices and serve with Raisin Sauce.

SERVES 6

Raisin Sauce

1/2 cup	brown sugar, packed	125 ml
1/4 cup	water	60 ml
1/2 cup	raisins	125 ml
2 tbsp	vinegar	30 ml
1 tbsp	butter	15 ml
3/4 tsp	Worcestershire sauce	3 ml
1/4 tsp	salt	1 ml
dash	pepper	dash
dash	cloves	dash
dash	mace	dash
1/2 cup	cranberry jelly	125 ml

Simmer brown sugar, water and raisins 10 minutes. Add remaining ingredients and heat gently until jelly melts. Serve warm.

Glazed Cottage Roll

3-lb	cottage roll (boneless cured ham)	1.4-kg
3 cups	boiling water	750 ml
1	bay leaf	1
6 whole	cloves	6 whole
1 clove	garlic, crushed	1 clove
3 large	cooking apples	3 large
1/2 cup	red currant jelly	125 ml
2 tbsp	horseradish	30 ml

Put cottage roll in kettle and add boiling water, bay leaf, cloves and garlic. Cover and simmer gently until meat is tender, about 1 1/2 hours. Turn occasionally during cooking.

→

Heat oven to 425 °F (220 °C).

Lift meat out of water and remove casing if necessary. Put meat in greased baking dish about 13 x 9 x 2 inches (33 x 23 x 5 cm).

Core apples (do not peel) and cut into thick rings. Put them in a single layer around the meat. Combine red currant jelly and horseradish and spread over meat and apples.

Bake about 15 minutes or until apples are tender. Baste occasionally during baking.

SERVES 6

Currant Glazed Baked Ham

6 to 8-lb	ready-to-serve half ham (shank end)	2.7 to 3.6-kg
1/2 cup	port	125 ml
1/2 cup	raisins	125 ml
6	green onions	6
1 medium	orange	1 medium
1	lemon	1
10-oz jar	red currant jelly	284-ml jar
2 tbsp	port	30 ml
1 tsp	prepared mustard	5 ml
1/16 tsp	ginger	0.25 ml
	whole cloves	

Roast ham according to wrapper directions — or 15 minutes a pound (450 g) in 325 °F (160 °C) oven. Remove it from the oven 30 minutes before it should be done.

Do the following steps while the ham is cooking.

Boil 1/2 cup (125 ml) port and raisins in a small saucepan until all the port is absorbed and raisins are plump. Set aside.

Chop green onions very finely. Grate the rind from the orange and lemon. Put the onions and rinds in a small saucepan and add boiling water just to cover. Bring to a boil and boil 2 minutes. Drain well. Put in bowl. Squeeze the orange and half the lemon and add this juice to the onion mixture — you should have about 1/3 cup (80 ml) orange juice and 1 tbsp (15 ml) lemon juice.

Heat red currant jelly and 2 tbsp (60 ml) port gently just until jelly is melted. Add it to orange mixture along with mustard and ginger. Blend well.

Remove ham from oven 30 minutes before end of cooking time as directed above. Remove rind and score fat. Stud all over with cloves.

Press the plumped raisins into the cuts in the ham fat. Brush all over the ham lightly with the orange-red currant jelly mixture. Return to oven and bake 30 minutes more. Serve remaining orange-red currant jelly mixture with ham.

SERVES 8 TO 10

Glazed Cottage Roll

Ham Stuffed Cabbage Rolls

3 tbsp	cooking oil	45 ml
1 medium	onion, chopped	1 medium
1 medium	green pepper, chopped	1 medium
14-oz can	tomato sauce	398-ml can
1 cup	water	250 ml
1/2 tsp	powdered ginger	2 ml
2 tsp	brown sugar	10 ml
1/4 cup	lemon juice	60 ml
small piece	bay leaf	small piece
1/2 tsp	salt	2 ml
1/8 tsp	pepper	0.5 ml
8 large	cabbage leaves (see note)	8 large
2 cups	ground cooked ham	500 ml

1 cup	grated raw potato	250 ml
1 small	onion, chopped	1 small
1/2 tsp	dry mustard	2 ml
dash	cloves	dash
1	egg	1
4 medium	carrots, cut into sticks	4 medium
2 large	green peppers, cut into strips	2 large

Heat oil in heavy skillet. Add 1 chopped medium onion and 1 chopped green pepper and cook gently 3 minutes, stirring. Add tomato sauce, water, ginger, sugar, lemon juice, bay leaf, salt and pepper. Bring to a boil, turn down heat, cover and simmer 15 minutes.

Put cabbage leaves in a large saucepan and cover with boiling water. Boil 2 minutes. Lift out cabbage leaves and drain. Cut away the tough vein at the bottom of each leaf. Combine ham, potato, 1 chopped small onion, mustard, cloves and egg, blending well.

Put a scant 1/3 cup (80 ml) of this mixture on each cabbage leaf. Roll leaves up around ham filling, starting at side of leaf where vein was cut away. Tuck in the ends of the cabbage leaves so the meat is tightly wrapped. Add the cabbage rolls to the sauce after it has simmered for the first 15 minutes. Cover the pan and simmer 30 minutes.

Add carrots and simmer 15 minutes. Add green peppers and simmer 10 minutes more. Add water to sauce if liquid has evaporated.

Note: To loosen the cabbage leaves without breaking them, cut away some of the core of the cabbage. Set cabbage in a bowl, with the hole made by cutting out the core facing up. Pour boiling water into the hole and carefully loosen the outside leaves. Pour more boiling water into the cabbage, taking off the leaves as they become limp enough to remove easily, until you have 8 perfect leaves.

SERVES 4

Ham Stuffed Cabbage Rolls

Sausage and Cabbage

1 lb	pork sausages	450 ml
1 large	firm cabbage, cut into quarters	1 large
	boiling water	
3 tbsp	butter	45 ml
3 tbsp	flour	45 ml
1 tsp	salt	5 ml
1/8 tsp	pepper	0.5 ml
2 cups	milk	500 ml
1 1/2 cups	soft bread crumbs	375 ml
3 tbsp	butter, melted	45 ml

Heat oven to 350 °F (175 °C). Grease a glass baking dish about 13 x 9 x 2 inches (33 x 23 x 5 cm).

Put sausages in heavy skillet and add a little boiling water. Simmer until water evaporates, then fry sausages until well browned and cooked through. Cut each sausage in 3 pieces.

Put cabbage in a single layer in a large saucepan while sausages are cooking. Add enough boiling water to about half cover cabbage pieces. Cover pan and cook gently just until tender, about 20 minutes. Lift out cabbage pieces and chop the cabbage coarsely. Put a layer of cabbage in the prepared baking dish, top with the sausage pieces and then the rest of the cabbage.

Melt 3 tbsp (45 ml) butter in saucepan. Sprinkle in flour, salt and pepper and let bubble. Remove from heat and add milk all at once. Stir to blend and return to moderate heat and cook until boiling, thickened and smooth, stirring constantly.

Pour over cabbage-sausage mixture slowly so it runs all through the meat and vegetable. Combine bread crumbs and 3 tbsp (45 ml) melted butter and sprinkle over top. Bake 30 minutes or until crumbs are brown and sauce is bubbling well. Serve immediately.

———— SERVES 4 ————

Ham and Egg Scallop

6 tbsp	butter	90 ml
20 oz	mushroom pieces, drained (2 cans)	568 ml
1/2 cup	flour	125 ml
1 tsp	salt	5 ml
1/4 tsp	pepper	1 ml
1/4 tsp	dried leaf chervil	1 ml
4 cups	milk	1 L
12	hard-cooked eggs, sliced	12
2 cups	1-inch (2.5-cm) cubes cooked ham	500 ml
1 cup	fine dry bread crumbs	250 ml
1/4 cup	butter, melted	60 ml

Heat oven to 350 °F (175 °C). Butter a 3-qt (4-L) casserole.

Melt 6 tbsp (90 ml) butter in medium saucepan. Add mushroom pieces and cook gently until lightly browned, stirring. Sprinkle in flour, salt, pepper and chervil and stir to blend. Remove from heat and add milk all at once. Stir to blend. Return to heat and cook until boiling, thickened and smooth, stirring constantly.

Put 1/3 of the egg slices in the bottom of prepared casserole. Add 1/3 of the ham cubes and 1/3 of the sauce. Repeat these layers twice more.

Combine bread crumbs and 1/4 cup (60 ml) melted butter. Sprinkle over top.

Bake about 30 minutes or until bubbling well.

———— SERVES 8 ————

My Favorite Pizza

	Pizza Dough	
	(recipe follows)	
2 tbsp	olive oil	30 ml
1 1/2 lb	pepperoni (approx.), sliced thin	450 g
1/2 cup	grated Parmesan cheese	125 ml
2 7 1/2-oz cans	tomato sauce	2 213-ml cans
2 tsp	dried leaf oregano	10 ml
1 tsp	anise seeds	5 ml
4 cloves	garlic, crushed	4 cloves
12 oz	Mozzarella cheese slices	350 g
1/2 cup	grated Parmesan cheese	125 ml
2 tbsp	olive oil	30 ml

Heat oven to 450 °F (230 °C). Line two 14-inch (36-cm) pizza pans with dough as directed in Pizza Dough recipe.

Drizzle each dough with 1 tbsp (15 ml) olive oil. Set aside about 24 of the pepperoni slices to use later as garnish. Sprinkle the remaining pepperoni slices evenly over the two doughs. Sprinkle about half of 1/2 cup (125 ml) Parmesan cheese over each pie.

Combine tomato sauce, oregano, anise seeds and garlic and pour about half of this mixture over each pie, spreading it evenly. Cut Mozzarella cheese slices into strips about 1 inch (2.5 cm) wide. Put half of these strips on each pie and sprinkle each with about half of the remaining 1/2 cup (125 ml) Parmesan cheese. Drizzle each pie with 1 tbsp (15 ml) olive oil and trim edges with the slices of pepperoni you set aside.

Bake about 25 minutes or until crust is well browned and filling is bubbling well. Serve hot.

—————— MAKES TWO 14-INCH (36-CM) PIZZAS ——————

Pizza Dough

1 1/3 cups	warm water	330 ml
1/2 tsp	sugar	2 ml
1 pkg	dry yeast	1 pkg
2 tbsp	olive oil	30 ml
2 tsp	salt	10 ml
3 1/2 to 4 cups	sifted all-purpose flour	875 ml to 1 L

Measure water into bowl. Add sugar and stir until sugar is dissolved. Sprinkle yeast over water and let stand 10 minutes. Stir well. Add oil, salt, and 3 1/2 cups (875 ml) flour. Mix well with a wooden spoon.

Turn dough out on floured board and knead in more flour, enough to make a stiff dough. Knead until smooth, about 10 minutes. Gather dough into a round, put in a greased bowl, cover with a damp cloth and let rise in a warm place until more than double (about 2 hours). Punch down.

Divide dough into 2 equal pieces and roll and stretch each piece to fit a 14-inch (36-cm) pizza pan. If dough is very bouncy, let it rest a few minutes until it will roll more easily. If dough isn't quite the right size when you get it in the pan, press and stretch it until you can seal it firmly to the sides of the pan. If you don't have pizza pans, roll the dough into 14-inch (36-cm) rounds, put them on large cookie sheets and roll edges under a little to make a raised edge to hold the filling.

Top crust with filling and bake immediately (no more rising) as directed in recipe.

Mustardy Back Bacon

2 1/2-lb piece	*back bacon*	1.1-kg piece
	whole cloves	
2 tbsp	*Dijon mustard (see note)*	30 ml
2 tbsp	*molasses*	30 ml
2 tsp	*grated orange rind*	10 ml

Heat oven to 350 °F (175 °C). Remove casing from bacon if necessary and score fat. Stick fat with about 12 whole cloves. Wrap bacon in heavy-duty aluminum foil, set in a baking dish and roast in oven 1 hour.

Combine mustard, molasses and orange rind. Open foil and spread mustard mixture over the bacon. Return to oven (leave foil open) and continue roasting until meat is very tender, 45 to 60 minutes. Baste often. Serve hot or cold.

Note: Any prepared mustard is fine for this recipe but Dijon gives it a special flavor.

———————— SERVES 6 TO 8 ————————

Sauerkraut and Wieners

(for the barbecue)

1 lb	*wieners*	450 g
1 cup	*canned sauerkraut, drained*	250 ml
1/4 cup	*chili sauce*	60 ml
1 tsp	*caraway seeds*	5 ml
12	*bacon slices*	12

Slit wieners lengthwise almost through. Combine sauerkraut, chili sauce and caraway seeds and use a spoonful of this mixture to stuff each wiener. Wrap each wiener with a strip of bacon. Fasten bacon in place with small metal skewers or toothpicks.

Cook over hot coals, turning often, until bacon is crisp. Serve hot.

———————— MAKES 10 TO 12 ————————

Lamb

*L*amb

Lamb has a tantalizing flavor that adds welcome variety to the cooks repertoire. Like other meats, it brings essential body building proteins, iron and B vitamins to the table.

The flavors of many herbs and spices blend well with lamb's subtle flavor to give it glamour and distinction. Thus, mint, curry, dill, rosemary, tarragon, oregano or nutmeg are fine accompaniments.

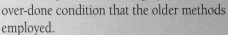

Because fresh spring lamb can become a classical if not regal dish we are fortunate that it is so widely available. Fresh lamb can be bought in food markets from coast to coast and New Zealand and Australia provide an abundance of the frozen variety the year round.

The flesh of young lamb is pink and the grains of fat creamy white. It is soft to the touch. When a lamb reaches a year of age its meat is known as mutton and its color darkens. Mutton is firmer to the touch, the fat takes on a yellow tinge, the taste is stronger and the flesh less tender.

One can cook lamb to many tastes but I recommend a level of cooking that permits the delicate flavor of this meat to be enhanced. Today we lean toward roasting and grilling that leaves the meat rosé, certainly not bloody but much less grey than the

over-done condition that the older methods employed.

Stuffed Leg of Lamb

6 to 7-lb	leg of lamb, boned	2.7 to 3.2-kg
12 oz	frozen spinach	350 g
1/4 cup	butter	60 ml
1 1/2 cups	soft bread crumbs	375 ml
1/2 cup	chopped fresh mint	125 ml
1 tsp	salt	5 ml
1/4 tsp	pepper	1 ml
1/8 tsp	nutmeg	0.5 ml
1 tbsp	butter	15 ml
2 medium	tomatoes, peeled and diced	2 medium
2 small	onions, chopped coarsely	2 small
2 small	carrots, chopped coarsely	2 small
2 stalks	celery, chopped	2 stalks
small piece	bay leaf	small piece
2 tbsp	flour	30 ml
2 cups	water	500 ml
	salt and pepper	

Have the butcher bone the leg of lamb and open it so it can be laid flat to spread with stuffing, rolled back into shape and tied.

Heat oven to 325 °F (160 °C). Have ready a shallow roasting pan.

Cook spinach. Drain very well and chop.

Heat 1/4 cup (60 ml) butter in skillet. Add bread crumbs and cook gently until they are lightly browned, stirring. Remove from heat. Add spinach, mint, 1 tsp (5 ml) salt, 1/4 tsp (1 ml) pepper and nutmeg and toss all together with a fork. Lay lamb out flat and spread spinach mixture over.

Add 1 tbsp (15 ml) butter to same skillet. Add tomatoes and cook gently just until hot. about 2 minutes. Spread over spinach. Roll the lamb up around the stuffing and tie it securely in several places.

Put onions, carrots, celery and bay leaf in the bottom of the roasting pan. Set the roast on them. Roast 3 to 3 1/2 hours or until done the way you like it — 170 °F (76 °C) on meat thermometer for medium, 180 °F (82 °C) for well done.

Remove roast from oven and put on hot platter.

Chill drippings in roasting pan quickly by setting in ice water. Remove and discard all but 2 tbsp (30 ml) of the fat. Heat the 2 tbsp (30 ml) fat in a saucepan, sprinkle in flour and stir to blend. Remove from heat and add any cooking liquid left in roasting pan and 2 cups (500 ml) water. Return to heat and bring to a boil stirring constantly. Turn down heat and cook gently 5 minutes, stirring. Taste and add salt and pepper if necessary. Serve with roast.

Note: A 5-lb (2.2-kg) boned shoulder of lamb is fine for this recipe, too.

SERVES 8 TO 10

Leg of Lamb, Spanish Style

Leg of Lamb, Spanish Style

6 to 7-lb	leg of lamb	2.7 to 3.2-kg
2 tbsp	olive oil	30 ml
2 cloves	garlic, crushed	2 cloves
1 tsp	salt	5 ml
1/2 tsp	coarse-cracked pepper	2 ml
1 tbsp	finely chopped parsley	15 ml
2 thin slices	cooked ham	2 thin slices

Heat oven to 350 °F (160 °C).

Put leg of lamb on rack in roasting pan. Combine olive oil, garlic, salt, pepper and parsley. Spread some of this mixture on the slices of ham. Cut the ham into thin strips.

Cut deep gashes all over the leg of lamb with the point of a sharp knife and force one of ham strips down into each gash with a finger. Rub meat all over with remaining oil mixture.

Roast to 170 °F (76 °C) on meat thermometer for pink — 25 minutes a lb (450 g) — or 180 °F (82 °C) for well done — 30 minutes a lb (450 g).

SERVES 8

119

Lamb Riblets in Barbecue Sauce

4 lb	lamb riblets	1.8 kg
2 tbsp	cooking oil	30 ml
14-oz can	pineapple tidbits	398-ml can
1	lemon, sliced thin	1
3/4 cup	chili sauce	180 ml
1/3 cup	finely chopped onion	80 ml
2 tbsp	brown sugar	30 ml
2 tbsp	vinegar	30 ml
2 tsp	Worcestershire sauce	10 ml
1 tsp	salt	5 ml
1/4 tsp	ginger	1 ml
1/8 tsp	crushed chilies	0.5 ml

Trim as much fat as possible from riblets. Heat oil in large heavy skillet or Dutch oven. Add riblets and brown well.

Drain pineapple, saving juice. Add pineapple and lemon to riblets. Combine all remaining ingredients and pineapple juice. Pour over riblets. Cover and simmer 1 1/2 hours or until meat is very tender. Turn riblets often.

——————— SERVES 6 ———————

Apricot-Prune Stuffed Lamb

1/2 cup	chopped dried apricots (uncooked)	125 ml
1/2 cup	chopped prunes (uncooked)	125 ml
3/4 cup	regular long grain rice	180 ml
1/2 cup	finely chopped celery	125 ml
1/2 cup	finely chopped onion	125 ml
1/4 cup	slivered blanched almonds	60 ml
1/2 tsp	dried leaf savory	2 ml
1/2 tsp	salt	2 ml
1 1/2 cups	boiling water	375 ml
4-lb	rolled boned lamb shoulder	1.8-kg
1/2 tsp	salt	2 ml

mint sauce

Combine apricots, prunes, rice, celery, onion, almonds, savory and 1/2 tsp (5 ml) salt in medium saucepan. Add boiling water. Bring to a boil. Turn down heat, cover and simmer 20 minutes or until water is absorbed.

Heat oven to 325 °F (160 °C).

Unroll lamb shoulder and sprinkle inside with 1/2 tsp (5 ml) salt. Spread rice mixture over meat, roll it up again and tie. (If some of the stuffing squeezes out of the roast, put it in foil and heat it for 30 minutes.)

Put roast, fat side up, on a rack in a roasting pan. Roast until meat thermometer registers 180 °F (82 °C), about 3 hours.

Serve with mint sauce if desired.

——————— SERVES 6 ———————

Apricot-Prune Stuffed Lamb

Lamb Chops and Green Peppers

1/4 cup	flour	60 ml
1/2 tsp	garlic powder	2 ml
6	shoulder lamb chops	6
2 tbsp	cooking oil	30 ml
1 cup	commercial chili sauce	250 ml
1/2 cup	wine vinegar	125 ml
1/4 cup	brown sugar, packed	60 ml
2 tbsp	Worcestershire sauce	30 ml
2 tsp	salt	10 ml
2 tsp	prepared mustard	10 ml
6 thick slices	onion	6 thick slices
4	green peppers, cut in 1/2-inch (1.25-cm) squares	4
	hot cooked rice	

Combine flour and garlic powder in a flat dish. Dip chops in mixture to coat both sides.

Heat oil in large heavy skillet (an electric skillet is good for this recipe). Add chops and brown well on both sides. Drain off any excess fat.

Combine chili sauce, vinegar, sugar, Worcestershire sauce, salt and mustard and pour over chops. Cover and simmer 45 minutes.

Lay an onion slice on each chop and sprinkle green pepper pieces over all. Cover and continue cooking until chops are very tender, about 15 minutes. Serve with rice.

———————— SERVES 6 ————————

Skillet Lamb Chops

4	shoulder lamb chops	4
	salt and pepper	
1/4 cup	cooking oil	60 ml
1 clove	garlic, cut in half	1 clove
1/2 cup	dry white wine	125 ml
1 cup	boiling water	250 ml
1 cube	chicken bouillon	1 cube
2 strips	lemon rind, cut the length of the lemon with a vegetable peeler	2 strips
8 small	onions	8 small
8	carrots, cut in thick slices on diagonal	8
4 medium	potatoes, peeled	4 medium
	chopped parsley	

Sprinkle chops generously with salt and pepper. Heat oil and garlic pieces in heavy skillet. Lift out and discard garlic. Add chops and brown well on both sides. Add wine, water, chicken bouillon cube and lemon rind, cover tightly and simmer until chops are beginning to get tender, about 30 minutes.

Add onions, carrots and potatoes. Sprinkle generously with salt and pepper, cover again and continue simmering about 30 minutes or until vegetables are tender. Sprinkle with parsley.

———————— SERVES 4 ————————

Lamb Chops and Green Peppers

Lamb and Chicken Stew

2 lb	shoulder of lamb, cut in large cubes	900 g
1/4 cup	cooking oil	60 ml
3 lb	chicken, cut in 8 pieces	1.4 kg
3 cups	chopped onions	750 ml
2 medium	green peppers, chopped	2 medium
3 large	carrots, sliced	3 large
2 cups	diced turnip	500 ml
2	leeks (white part), sliced thin	2
1/2 cup	diced celery	125 ml
19-oz can	tomatoes	540-ml can
	boiling water	
4 tsp	salt	20 ml
1/2 tsp	pepper	2 ml
1 small	bay leaf, crumbled	1 small
4 whole	cloves	4 whole
1 small	onion	1 small
19-oz can	chick peas	540-ml can
2 tsp	cumin seeds	10 ml
1/2 tsp	crushed chili peppers	2 ml
	hot cooked rice	

Trim excess fat from lamb. Heat oil in large heavy saucepan or Dutch oven. Add lamb and brown well, lifting out pieces as they brown. Add chicken pieces and brown well, lifting out pieces as they brown. Add a little more oil if necessary.

Add chopped onion, green peppers, carrots, turnip, leeks and celery and cook and stir until onion is yellow. Return lamb and chicken to pan.

Add tomatoes and enough water to cover the meat. Add salt, pepper and bay leaf. Stick cloves in small onion and add. Bring to a boil, turn down heat, cover pan tightly and simmer until meat is tender, about 1 1/2 hours.

Drain chick peas and add to stew.

Dip about 3/4 cup (180 ml) of the liquid out of the stew and put in a small saucepan. Add the cumin seeds and crushed chili peppers. Set over high heat and boil until about half the liquid is cooked away. Add this mixture to the stew, a little at a time, tasting after each addition, until the flavor is as you like it.

Serve with hot rice and pass any of the chili pepper mixture that is left for those who like more seasoning.

SERVES 8

124

Lamb Cakes

Lamb Cakes

2 large	carrots	2 large
1 large	potato	1 large
1 medium	onion	1 medium
1 clove	garlic	1 clove
1 lb	shoulder of lamb, ground	450 g
1 1/2 tsp	salt	7 ml
1/4 tsp	dried leaf rosemary	1 ml
1/4 tsp	pepper	1 ml
1	egg, beaten	1
	flour	
2 tbsp	cooking oil	30 ml
1/4 cup	chicken stock	60 ml
3/4 cup	chicken stock (optional)	180 ml

Heat oven to 350 °F (175 °C).

Grind carrots, potato, onion and garlic through the fine blade of the food chopper. Add to ground lamb along with salt, rosemary, pepper and egg, and blend. Shape mixture into 8 large thick cakes. Dip cakes into flour to coat all sides.

Heat oil in large heavy skillet that can go in the oven. Brown lamb cakes slowly in oil. Drain off all fat when cakes are well browned. Add 1/4 cup (60 ml) chicken stock to skillet.

Cover tightly and put in oven for 45 minutes, turning once.

Serve immediately with remaining 3/4 cup (180 ml) stock thickened slightly for gravy.

SERVES 4 OR 8

Lamb and Brown Rice

1 to 1 1/2 lb	cubed lean lamb	450 to 675 g
2 tbsp	cooking oil	30 ml
1 small	onion, sliced thin	1 small
1 small clove	garlic, crushed	1 small clove
1 1/2 cups	chicken stock	375 ml
3/4 cup	brown rice	180 ml
1 1/2 cups	sliced carrots	375 ml
1 cup	boiling water	250 ml
1/4 tsp	dried leaf thyme	1 ml
1 tsp	salt	5 ml
1/8 tsp	pepper	0.5 ml
1 1/2 cups	fresh or frozen peas	375 ml
1/4 cup	chopped parsley	60 ml

Trim excess fat from lamb. Heat oil in large heavy skillet. Add onion and garlic and cook gently 3 minutes, stirring. Add meat cubes and continue cooking until meat is lightly browned. Add chicken stock and cover tightly. Simmer 30 to 45 minutes or until lamb is beginning to get tender. Add all remaining ingredients except peas and parsley. Cover again and continue cooking gently, stirring occasionally, until rice is cooked and meat is tender, 45 minutes to 1 hour. Add peas and parsley for last 10 minutes of cooking.

—————— SERVES 3 ——————

Island Lamb Stew

(leftover lamb)

1/4 cup	butter or margarine	60 ml
1 cup	sliced onions	250 ml
1 cup	sliced celery	250 ml
3/4 cup	chopped green pepper	180 ml
1 tbsp	curry powder	15 ml
3 cups	diced cooked lamb	750 ml
1/8 tsp	crushed dry chili peppers	0.5 ml
1 tsp	salt	5 ml
2 tsp	sugar	10 ml
28-oz can	tomatoes	796-ml can
	hot cooked rice	
	chutney (optional)	

Heat butter or margarine in large heavy saucepan. Add onions, celery, green pepper and curry powder. Cook until onions are transparent, stirring constantly. Add all remaining ingredients except rice and chutney. Simmer about 45 minutes. Serve over rice. Pass the chutney.

—————— SERVES 4 ——————

Herbed Lamb Loaf

Herbed Lamb Loaf

2	eggs	2
1 1/2 lb	ground lamb	675 g
1/4 lb	ground pork	115 g
1 cube	chicken bouillon	1 cube
3/4 cup	boiling water	180 ml
1 cup	quick-cooking rolled oats	250 ml
1/4 cup	finely chopped onion	60 ml
1 1/2 tsp	salt	7 ml
1/4 tsp	pepper	1 ml
1/2 tsp	dried leaf marjoram	2 ml
1/4 tsp	dried leaf basil	1 ml
1/4 tsp	dried leaf rosemary	1 ml

Heat oven to 350 °F (175 °C). Have ready a 9- x 5- x 3-inch (23- x 12.5- x 7.5-cm) loaf pan.

Beat eggs lightly with a fork in a mixing bowl. Add meat and blend together lightly with a fork. Dissolve bouillon cube in boiling water and add along with all remaining ingredients. Blend lightly with a fork.

Put into loaf pan. Bake 1 1/2 hours.

——————— SERVES 4 ———————

127

Lamb and Eggplant

1 medium	eggplant	1 medium
1/2 tsp	salt	2 ml
1/4 cup	fine dry bread crumbs	60 ml
1/4 cup	flour	60 ml
1/4 cup	cooking oil	60 ml
1 1/2 lb	ground lamb	675 g
1/2 cup	finely chopped onion	125 ml
1/4 cup	dry red wine	60 ml
1/2 cup	tomato sauce	125 ml
1 tbsp	chopped parsley	15 ml
1/2 tsp	dried leaf thyme	2 ml
1 tsp	salt	5 ml
1/8 tsp	pepper	0.5 ml
2	tomatoes, peeled and sliced	2
1 cup	plain yogurt	250 ml
2	egg yolks	2
1/4 cup	flour	60 ml
1/4 cup	grated Parmesan cheese	60 ml
1/4 cup	fine dry bread crumbs	60 ml

Slice unpeeled eggplant about 1/4 inch (0.5 cm) thick. Spread out in glass baking pan about 13 x 9 x 2 inches (33 x 23 x 5 cm) and sprinkle with 1/2 tsp (2 ml) salt. Let stand 1 hour.

Heat oven to 375 °F (190 °C). Lift eggplant slices out of baking pan and lay them on paper towelling. Dry and grease baking pan. Sprinkle bottom of pan with 1/4 cup (60 ml) bread crumbs. Dry eggplant slices with paper towelling.

Put 1/4 cup (60 ml) flour in flat dish and dip eggplant slices in it to coat both sides. Heat oil in large heavy skillet and brown eggplant slices lightly on both sides. Put eggplant in prepared baking pan as it browns. Add more oil to skillet as needed to brown eggplant.

→

Lamb Curry

(leftover lamb)

Add a little more oil to skillet, if necessary, after all eggplant is browned. Add lamb and onion and cook over moderate heat until lamb is lightly browned, stirring. Add wine, tomato sauce, parsley, thyme, 1 tsp (5 ml) salt and pepper. Cook gently 5 minutes, stirring occasionally. Spread mixture over eggplant slices.

Put tomato slices on top of meat. Beat yogurt, egg yolks and 1/4 cup (60 ml) flour together with a fork and pour over all, spreading evenly. Combine cheese and 1/4 cup (60 ml) bread crumbs and sprinkle over all.

Bake 40 minutes.

———————— SERVES 4 TO 6 ————————

2 tbsp	butter or cooking oil	30 ml
1 tbsp	curry powder	15 ml
2	tart apples, peeled, cored and chopped	2
1 medium	onion, chopped	1 medium
1/2 medium	green pepper, chopped	1/2 medium
1/2 cup	chopped celery	125 ml
1/2 clove	garlic, minced	1/2 clove
2 tbsp	flour	30 ml
2 cups	liquid (leftover lamb gravy plus water)	500 ml
1 tbsp	lemon juice	15 ml
	grated rind of 1/2 lemon	
1/2 cup	raisins	125 ml
pinch	cloves	pinch
2 cups	1/2-inch (1.25-cm) cubes leftover lamb roast	500 ml
	hot cooked rice	
	chutney	

Heat butter or oil in large saucepan. Add curry powder and cook gently 3 minutes, stirring. Add apples, onion, green pepper, celery and garlic and cook 3 minutes, stirring. Sprinkle in flour. Stir to blend. Remove from heat.

Add liquid, lemon juice, lemon rind, raisins and cloves and stir to blend. Return to moderate heat and cook until boiling, thickened and smooth, stirring. Turn heat to low, cover and simmer 20 minutes, stirring often. Add lamb cubes and simmer 15 minutes more.

Serve over rice and pass the chutney.

———————— SERVES 4 ————————

Left: Lamb and Eggplant
Right: Lamb Curry

Lamb Pie

2 tbsp	cooking oil	30 ml
2 lb	2-inch (5-cm) cubes boneless stewing lamb	900 g
1/3 cup	flour	80 ml
3 tsp	salt	45 ml
1/2 tsp	pepper	2 ml
1 tsp	dried leaf thyme	5 ml
1/4 cup	chopped parsley	60 ml
3 1/2 cups	tomato juice	875 ml
6 small	onions	6 small
6 medium	carrots, cut in large pieces	6 medium
6 medium	potatoes, cut in large pieces	6 medium
1 small	turnip, cut in large pieces	1 small
12 oz	frozen peas	350 g

*Herb Biscuits
(recipe follows)*

Heat oven to 325 °F (160 °C).

Heat oil in Dutch oven or large heavy saucepan that can go into the oven. Brown meat quickly on all sides in hot oil. Sprinkle meat with flour and brown again lightly. Add all remaining ingredients except peas and herb biscuits. Cover tightly and cook in oven until meat and vegetables are tender, about 2 hours. Add peas, cover and cook 10 minutes longer.

Remove pan from oven and increase oven temperature to 450 °F (230 °C). Top meat and vegetables with herb biscuits and bake 15 minutes, uncovered, or until biscuits are well browned.

SERVES 6

Herb Biscuits

2 cups	sifted all-purpose flour	500 ml
4 tsp	baking powder	20 ml
1 tsp	salt	5 ml
2 tsp	celery seeds	10 ml
1 tsp	paprika	5 ml
1 tbsp	chopped parsley	15 ml
1/4 tsp	dried leaf thyme	1 ml
1/2 tsp	dried leaf marjoram	2 ml
1/4 cup	shortening	60 ml
3/4 to 1 cup	milk	180 to 250 ml

Sift flour, baking powder, salt, celery seeds and paprika into a bowl. Add parsley, thyme and marjoram and stir lightly with a fork. Add shortening and cut in finely. Stir in enough milk with a fork to make a soft puffy dough that is easy to handle, mixing lightly. Turn dough out on floured board and knead lightly 12 times to round up. Roll into a round 1/2 inch (1.25 cm) thick. Cut round into 6 wedges. Use to top lamb pie.

Poultry

*P*oultry

No matter what the dimensions, from the biggest turkey that ever crowded an oven, to the tiniest edible bird, the poultry family is a culinary favorite. The member of the family that is most abundant and most popular, is the chicken. However, do not lose sight of the versatile turkey that, while still a distant second, is making immense strides in popularity and not just for the Thanksgiving or Christmas table.

Chicken is a bird of many moods. It will appear at the table simply as a whole roasted bird or it can be dressed up to be elegant enough for a white-tie dinner. Indeed, so versatile is this meat, that you could probably serve chicken every day of the year without repeating a recipe.

Almost every country in the world has a classical chicken dish. I have included dishes here that have a foreign flair. But the reason you find them in this book is because they are delectable in any language.

Turkey and chicken with low fat, protein-rich meat are the staples of the calorie conscious. But remember, other very special birds share these healthful attributes. For the holiday's and other important occasions, goose or game hens can be perfect. Whose mouth will not water when told you will serve Duckling à l'Orange or Pheasants with Wild Rice. These recipes are in this section along with several more that my readers consider classical.

Roast Chickens with Mushrooms

2 5-lb	roasting chickens	2 2.2-kg
	salt	
	poultry seasoning	
2 medium	onions	2 medium
4 large sprigs	parsley	4 large sprigs
2 large sprigs	celery leaves	2 large sprigs
1/4 cup	olive oil	60 ml
2 cloves	garlic, peeled and cut in half	2 cloves
8 whole	peppercorns	8 whole
1	bay leaf	1
1/4 tsp	dried leaf thyme	1 ml
4 medium	carrots, sliced	4 medium
2	leeks, sliced thin (white part only)	2
2 large stalks	celery, sliced	2 large stalks
1 medium	onion, chopped	1 medium
1/2 cup	dry red table wine	125 ml
1/2 cup	butter or margarine	125 ml
1 large clove	garlic, crushed	1 large clove
1 1/2 lb	fresh mushrooms, sliced	675 g
1/4 tsp	dried leaf tarragon	1 ml
1/4 tsp	dried leaf chervil	1 ml
1/4 cup	finely chopped parsley	60 ml
3 tbsp	flour	45 ml
1 cup	chicken stock or 1 cube chicken bouillon, dissolved in 1 cup (250 ml) boiling water	250 ml
1/2 cup	dry red table wine	125 ml

Heat oven to 400 °F (205 °C).

Dry chickens well inside and out with paper towelling. Sprinkle inside lightly with salt and poultry seasoning. Put a whole onion, 2 sprigs parsley and 1 sprig celery leaves inside each chicken. Fasten neck skin to body with a skewer and fold wing tops under. Tie wings and legs close to bodies. Rub each chicken all over with 2 tbsp (30 ml) olive oil.

Put chickens in a large roasting pan (not on rack). Roast about 30 minutes or until lightly browned. Turn heat down to 375 °F (190 °C).

Tie 2 cloves garlic, peppercorns, bay leaf and thyme together in a small cheesecloth bag and add to roasting pan. Add carrots, leeks, celery and chopped onion to pan and pour in 1/2 cup (125 ml) wine. Continue roasting, uncovered, about 1 1/2 hours or until chickens are tender. Baste often.

Lift out chickens, put on large hot platter and keep warm. Lift out and discard cheesecloth bag. Spoon vegetables and liquid in roasting pan into blender and blend until smooth (do half at a time if necessary). Press vegetables through a sieve if you don't have a blender. Set vegetable purée aside to use in sauce.

Melt butter in large heavy skillet. Add crushed garlic and cook gently 2 minutes, stirring. Add mushrooms and sprinkle in tarragon, chervil and chopped parsley. Cook 3 minutes, stirring. Lift mushrooms out of pan with slotted spoon and add to chickens on platter.

Stir flour into drippings left in skillet. Add puréed vegetables, a little at a time, stirring until smooth after each addition. Stir in chicken stock (or chicken bouillon cube dissolved in boiling water). Cook until boiling, thickened and smooth, stirring. Stir in 1/2 cup (125 ml) wine and bring back to a boil. Serve very hot with carved chickens.

SERVES 8 TO 10

Roast Chicken with Mushrooms

Orange Glazed Capons

2 6-lb	capons (see note)	2 2.8-kg
6 cups	water	1.5 L
1 small	carrot, cut up	1 small
2 stalks	celery with leaves, cut up	2 stalks
1 slice	onion	1 slice
1 1/2 tsp	salt	7 ml
6	peppercorns	6
2 sprigs	parsley	2 sprigs
1/2 tsp	dried leaf marjoram	2 ml
1/2 tsp	dried leaf thyme	2 ml
1/4 cup	butter or margarine	60 ml
1 lb	mushrooms, sliced	450 g
1/2 cup	finely chopped onion	125 ml
12 oz	long-grain and wild rice mix	350 g
1/4 cup	chopped parsley	60 ml
	salt and pepper	
	soft butter	
	Orange Glaze (recipe follows)	
	Sauterne Gravy (recipe follows)	

Remove giblets from capons, wash them, set livers aside to use later and put remaining giblets and necks in large saucepan. Add water, carrot, celery, onion, slice, 1 1/2 tsp (7 ml) salt, peppercorns, parsley sprigs, marjoram and thyme. Bring to a boil, turn down heat, cover and simmer 2 hours. Add livers and simmer 6 to 8 minutes or until tender. Strain stock, discarding vegetables. Chop giblets finely.

Heat 1/4 cup (60 ml) butter in large saucepan. Add mushrooms and cook quickly until lightly browned, stirring. Lift out with a slotted spoon and set aside. Add chopped onion to drippings left in pan and cook gently 3 minutes, stirring. Add 4 cups (1 L) giblet stock and bring to a boil. Add rice mix and chopped parsley. Cover and cook according to directions on rice mix package.

Remove pan from heat when rice is cooked. Add mushrooms and chopped giblets and toss all together with a fork. Cool.

Heat oven to 325 °F (160 °C).

Sprinkle insides of capons with salt and pepper and stuff rice mixture into them lightly. Truss. Rub outside of capons with soft butter, set them on a rack in a shallow roasting pan, cover with a tent of foil (do not wrap — just lay the foil over them loosely) and roast about 3 hours or until done. Remove foil for last hour of cooking so capons will brown well. Baste often with drippings in pan.

Make Orange Glaze while capons are cooking. Brush them with the glaze when they test done and continue roasting 15 minutes more, brushing with glaze often. Put on hot platter and keep hot while preparing Sauterne Gravy.

Note: Use large roasting chickens or small turkeys in place of capons if desired.

— SERVES 8 TO 10 —

Orange Glaze

1/4 cup	thinly slivered orange rind	60 ml
1/2 cup	orange juice	125 ml
1 cup	corn syrup	250 ml
1/4 tsp	chopped ginger root	1 ml

Cut all white membrane from inside orange rind and discard. Sliver enough of the orange rind to make 1/4 cup (60 ml). Combine rind with remaining ingredients and use to brush on cooked capons as directed.

Orange Glazed Capon

Sauterne Gravy

1/4 cup	thinly slivered orange rind	60 ml
	boiling water	
3/4 cup	golden raisins	180 ml
1/3 cup	flour	80 ml
4 cups	liquid (stock remaining from cooking giblets plus water)	1 L
1/2 tsp	salt (approx.)	2 ml
1/4 tsp	pepper	1 ml
1/2 tsp	dried leaf thyme	2 ml
1 cup	sweet white table wine (Sauterne)	250 ml

Cut all white membrane from inside orange rind and discard. Sliver enough of orange rind to make the 1/4 cup (60 ml) called for.

Pour boiling water over raisins and orange rind and let stand, covered, 15 minutes. Drain.

Pour drippings out of roasting pans into a heat-proof container. Chill quickly by setting in ice water. Lift off fat and put 1/3 cup (80 ml) of the fat in a large saucepan. Add flour and cook until lightly browned, stirring. Stir in liquid gradually. Add any cooking juices and browned bits from roasting pan. Cook until boiling, slightly thickened and smooth. Stir in salt, pepper, thyme, raisins-orange mixture and wine. Heat and taste, adding more salt and pepper if necessary.

Chicken Pie

3/4 cup	coarsely grated carrots	180 ml
1/2 cup	thinly sliced celery	125 ml
1/2 cup	boiling water	125 ml
1/2 cup	frozen peas	125 ml
3 cups	cut-up cooked chicken	750 ml
3 tbsp	butter or chicken fat	45 ml
1 medium	onion, sliced	1 medium
3 tbsp	flour	45 ml
1 tsp	salt	5 ml
1/4 tsp	pepper	1 ml
1/4 tsp	dried leaf savory	1 ml
1 cup	light cream	250 ml

3/4 cup	chicken stock	180 ml
	pastry for 2 crust 9-inch (23-cm) pie	
1 tsp	celery seed	5 ml
1	egg yolk	1
1 tbsp	water	15 ml

Cook carrots and celery 3 minutes in the boiling water.

Add peas for the last minute of cooking. Drain, saving cooking liquid.

Combine chicken, carrots, celery and peas in a large bowl.

Melt butter or chicken fat in a medium saucepan. Add onion and cook gently 5 minutes. Sprinkle in flour, salt, pepper and savory and stir to blend. Remove from heat. Add cream, chicken stock and liquid left from cooking vegetables. Stir to blend. Return to heat and cook until boiling, thickened and smooth, stirring constantly. Pour over chicken-vegetable mixture and mix lightly with a fork. Cool.

Heat oven to 425 °F (220 °C). Have ready a 9-inch (23-cm) pie pan.

Prepare pastry from your favorite recipe or a mix, adding the 1 tsp (5 ml) celery seed to the dry ingredients. Line the pie pan with half the pastry. Spoon in the chicken filling. Top with remaining pastry, sealing top and bottom crusts together well and fluting edge. Beat egg yolk and 1 tbsp (15 ml) water together with a fork and brush over top of pastry (not on edge). Cut a large vent in the top of the pie to let the steam escape.

Bake at 425 °F (220 °C) 10 minutes. Reduce oven control to 350 °F (175 °C) and bake about 50 minutes longer or until crust is very well browned and filling is bubbling well. Serve hot.

——— SERVES 4 TO 6 ———

Chicken Pie

Special Chicken Pie

1	Stewed Chicken (recipe p. 153)	1
1 lb	sweetbreads	450 g
	juice of 1 lemon	
1/4 tsp	salt	1 ml
4	carrots, diced	4
1 medium	onion, sliced	1 medium
2 tbsp	chopped parsley	30 ml
1/4 tsp	dried leaf thyme	1 ml
small piece	bay leaf, crumbled	small piece
1/2 tsp	salt	2 ml
1/4 tsp	pepper	1 ml
1 1/2 cups	chicken stock	375 ml
1/2 lb	bacon, cut in thin strips crosswise	225 g
2 tbsp	chicken fat, butter or margarine	30 ml
1/2 lb	mushrooms, sliced	225 g
1/4 cup	chicken fat, butter or margarine	60 ml
1/4 cup	flour	60 ml
1 tsp	salt	5 ml
1/2 tsp	pepper	2 ml
1/4 tsp	dried leaf thyme	1 ml
1/2 tsp	nutmeg	2 ml
2 cups	chicken stock	500 ml
1/4 cup	brandy	60 ml
1/4 cup	Madeira	60 ml
1/4 cup	chopped parsley	60 ml
4 cups	cut-up cooked chicken (from stewed chicken)	1 L
	pastry for 2 crust 9-inch (23-cm) pie	
1	egg yolk	1
1 tbsp	water	15 ml

Soak sweetbreads in ice water 1 hour. Put in saucepan with lemon juice and 1/4 tsp (1 ml) salt. Cover with cold water and bring to a boil. Turn down heat and boil gently 5 minutes. Drain and drop sweetbreads into ice water immediately. Remove thin outer membrane and tubes from sweetbreads when they are cold. Slice crosswise.

Heat oven to 375 °F (190 °C).

Put diced carrots, onion, 2 tbsp (30 ml) parsley, 1/4 tsp (1 ml) thyme and bay leaf in a small baking dish. Add sliced sweetbreads. Sprinkle with 1/2 tsp (2 ml) salt and 1/4 tsp (1 ml) pepper. Pour 1 1/2 cups (375 ml) chicken stock over all. Cover pan tightly and put in oven for about 30 minutes or until sweetbreads are tender. Baste occasionally.

Fry bacon just until transparent. Lift out and drain on paper towelling.

Heat 2 tbsp (30 ml) chicken fat or butter in large saucepan. Add mushrooms and fry quickly 3 minutes, stirring. Lift out with slotted spoon and set aside. Add 1/4 cup (60 ml) chicken fat or butter to same pan and heat. Sprinkle in flour, 1 tsp (5 ml) salt, 1/2 tsp (2 ml) pepper, 1/4 tsp (1 ml) thyme and 1/2 tsp (2 ml) nutmeg. Stir to blend. Remove from heat. Add 2 cups (500 ml) chicken stock, brandy and Madeira. Return to heat and bring to a boil, stirring constantly. Turn down heat and simmer 5 minutes. Taste and add salt and pepper if necessary. Add sweetbreads and their cooking liquid, bacon bits and mushrooms. simmer 3 minutes. stir in parsley and chicken. Pour into 3-qt (4-L) casserole.

Roll pastry thicker than usual into a round a little larger than the top of the casserole. Lay it over the chicken mixture, crimping edges and sealing well to sides of casserole. Cut a large vent in the centre of the pastry.

Beat egg yolk and water together with a fork and brush over pastry (not on edge). Bake about 40 minute or until pastry is dark golden brown and filling is bubbling well.

SERVES 8 TO 10

Chicken Sea Pie

4 cups	*sifted all-purpose flour*	1 L
4 tsp	*baking powder*	20 ml
1 tsp	*salt*	5 ml
pinch	*pepper*	pinch
3/4 cup	*shortening*	180 ml
1 1/4 cups	*cold water (approx.)*	310 ml
1 3-lb	*chicken,* *cut in 12 pieces*	1 1.4-kg
1/2 cup	*thinly sliced green onion*	125 ml
2 tbsp	*chopped parsley*	30 ml
2 tbsp	*chopped celery leaves*	30 ml
1 tsp	*salt*	5 ml
1/4 tsp	*pepper*	1 ml
1/2 tsp	*dried leaf marjoram*	2 ml
1/4 tsp	*dried leaf savory*	1 ml
1/4 tsp	*dried leaf thyme*	1 ml
	boiling water	
1 cup	*hot milk*	250 ml

Heat oven to 450 °F (230 °C). Grease a round 8-cup (2-L) casserole with a tight lid (a glass casserole with a lid that fits down inside works perfectly — the tight lid is important).

Sift flour, baking powder, 1 tsp (5 ml) salt and pinch of pepper into bowl. Add shortening and cut in finely with pastry blender or 2 knives. Add just enough of the cold water so dough will hold together. I use about 1 cup plus 3 tbsp (250 ml plus 45 ml). Press dough into a ball and knead gently about 6 times to smooth up.

Roll a little less than 1/2 of the dough into a circle large enough to line bottom and sides of casserole — dough will be about 1/4 inch (0.5 cm) thick. Ease it into the casserole, anchoring it on the sides by pressing it to the edge.

Put half of the chicken pieces on the dough (you may bone the chicken pieces but I use them bones and all). Sprinkle with half the onion, parsley, celery leaves and seasonings.

Divide the remaining dough in 2 pieces. Roll out one half to just fit over the chicken. Cut 3 large slits in the circle of dough and lay it over the chicken. Top with remaining chicken pieces and seasonings.

Roll out remaining dough so it is just a little larger than the top of the casserole. Cut 3 large slits in the circle of dough and lay it over the chicken. Fold this top down outside the dough that lines the casserole and press the two pieces of dough together to seal well. Flute edge.

Pour boiling water over and into the pie so you can see it all around and up to the top of the pie inside. (This sounds

→

Chicken Wings Polynesian Style

wrong — but you'll see it isn't!) Put lid on casserole and bake 25 minutes. Turn heat down to 325 °F (160 °C) and continue baking with lid on for about 2 hours or until chicken is tender. (At this point I find the crust of the pie is dark golden brown and has risen enough that it has sealed the lid on the casserole.)

Remove lid and pour as much milk as possible into the slits in the pie (move chicken pieces with a fork so milk gets in between) and over top of pie. Cover and bake 15 minutes. Remove cover and bake 15 minutes more. (Now you have a crispy brown crust with chicken pieces in sauce inside.) Serve immediately.

—— SERVES 6 ——

1/3 cup	soya sauce	80 ml
1/3 cup	pineapple juice	80 ml
1 small clove	garlic, crushed	1 small clove
1/2 tsp	ginger	2 ml
8	chicken wings	8
1 cup	diced canned pineapple	250 ml
1 cup	chicken stock	250 ml
3 tbsp	cold water	45 ml
1 tbsp	cornstarch	15 ml
	hot cooked rice	

Combine soya sauce, pineapple juice, garlic and ginger in a dish that will just hold the chicken wings. Add chicken wings and marinate several hours, turning often.

Heat oven to 350 °F (175 °C). Grease a shallow baking dish about 12 x 7 x 2 inches (30.5 x 18 x 5 cm).

Lift chicken wings out of marinade and put in prepared baking dish. Add pineapple to marinade and heat to boiling. Pour over chicken. Bake 30 to 40 minutes or until chicken is very tender, basting often.

Put chicken wings on serving plate and keep hot. Heat chicken stock to boiling and pour it into baking pan, stirring to blend any browned bits in pan into chicken stock. Pour into a saucepan and heat to boiling. Combine cold water and cornstarch, stirring until smooth. Stir into boiling liquid gradually. Boil 1 minute. Pour over chicken wings. Serve with rice.

Note: If preferred, put sauce in 2 small dishes and serve as a dunking sauce with chicken wings.

—— SERVES 2 ——

Chicken Wings Polynesian Style

143

Chicken Rolls Véronique

4	whole chicken breasts, cut in half to make 8 sides	4
1/2 lb	ground veal	225 g
1/4 tsp	dried leaf tarragon	1 ml
1 tbsp	chopped green onion	15 ml
1 tbsp	chopped parsley	15 ml
1	egg	1
1 tbsp	dry white wine	15 ml
1/4 cup	flour	60 ml
1/2 tsp	salt	2 ml
1/4 tsp	pepper	1 ml
1/2 tsp	paprika	2 ml

1	egg	1
1 tbsp	milk	15 ml
1 cup	fine salted soda biscuit crumbs	250 ml
1/4 cup	butter or margarine	60 ml
2 tbsp	cooking oil	30 ml
1/2 cup	chopped green onions	125 ml
3/4 cup	chicken stock	180 ml
3/4 cup	dry white wine	180 ml
	salt and pepper	
1 lb	mushrooms, sliced	450 g
1/4 cup	butter or margarine	60 ml
3 cups	seedless green grapes	750 ml
1/4 cup	cold water	60 ml
1 tbsp	cornstarch	15 ml

Bone pieces of chicken by cutting close to the bones with a sharp point knife and loosening and pulling the flesh away carefully with the fingers so that it comes off in one piece. Remove skin from chicken pieces and lay them between 2 sheets of waxed paper with the side skin was removed from up. Pound the pieces of chicken with a rolling pin until they are thin and nearly double in size. Remove top paper and turn chicken over with the side skin was removed from down.

Combine veal, tarragon, 1 tbsp (15 ml) onion, parsley, 1 egg and 1 tbsp (15 ml) wine, blending well with a fork. Spread this mixture over the pieces of chicken and roll them up from one end, pinching to seal.

Combine flour, 1/2 tsp (2 ml) salt, 1/4 tsp (1 ml) pepper and paprika in a flat dish. Beat egg and milk together in another flat dish. Put soda biscuit crumbs in a third dish. Coat the chicken rolls first with the flour mixture, then the egg mixture and finally with the crumbs. Let stand a few minutes to allow the coating to dry.

→

Chicken Rolls Véronique

Heat oven to 375 °F (190 °C).

Heat 1/4 cup (60 ml) butter or margarine and oil in large heavy skillet. Add chicken rolls and fry until well browned all around. As they brown, lift out and put in a large shallow baking dish, about 13 x 9 x 2 inches (33 x 23 x 5 cm). Add 1/2 cup (125 ml) onions to fat left in pan (add a little more oil if needed) and cook gently 3 minutes. Add chicken stock and 3/4 cup (180 ml) wine and bring to a boil. Taste and add salt and pepper if needed (this will depend on seasoning in chicken stock). Pour over chicken rolls. Cover pan and bake about 45 minutes or until chicken is tender.

Fry mushrooms quickly in 1/4 cup (60 ml) butter or margarine for 3 minutes while chicken is cooking. Remove chicken from oven, uncover and add mushrooms and grapes. Return to oven and cook, uncovered, for about 10 minutes or until everything is hot.

Lift chicken, mushrooms and grapes out of cooking liquid onto a hot platter with a slotted spoon. Keep hot. Pour liquid in baking pan into a saucepan and bring to a boil. Stir water and cornstarch together until smooth and add to boiling liquid gradually, stirring constantly. Boil gently 1 minute, stirring. Pour over chicken and serve immediately.

——————— SERVES 8 ———————

Bone pieces of chicken. Remove skin from chicken pieces.

Lay them between 2 sheets of waxed paper with the side skin was removed from up. Pound the pieces of chicken with a rolling pin until they are thin and nearly double in size.

Spread veal mixture over the pieces of chicken.

Roll them up from one end, pinching to seal.

Corn Crisped Chicken

1 cup	coarsely crushed corn flakes	250 ml
1 tsp	salt	5 ml
2 tsp	curry powder	10 ml
1/4 tsp	ginger	1 ml
1 large	chicken breast (separated into 2 sides)	1 large
1/4 cup	evaporated milk	60 ml

Apple Chutney (recipe follows)

Heat oven to 350 °F (175 °C). Line a shallow baking pan just large enough to hold the two pieces of chicken with aluminum foil.

Combine corn flake crumbs, salt, curry powder and ginger in a flat dish.

Dip chicken pieces in evaporated milk then roll them in the corn flakes mixture to coat both sides. Put in foil-lined pan, skin side up and bake about 1 hour and 15 minutes or until chicken is very tender. Serve with Apple Chutney.

——— SERVES 2 ———

Apple Chutney

1 cup	apple slices	250 ml
2 tbsp	water	30 ml
1/4 cup	molasses	60 ml
2 tbsp	vinegar	30 ml
1/4 cup	raisins	60 ml
1 tsp	curry powder	5 ml
1/4 tsp	ginger	1 ml

Combine all ingredients in small saucepan. Cover and bring to a boil. Simmer 5 minutes or until apples are beginning to get tender. Remove cover and continue simmering until apples are very tender and mixture is thick. Serve hot or cold with chicken.

Easy Chicken Marengo

1 envelope	spaghetti sauce mix	1 envelope
1/2 tsp	seasoned salt	2 ml
1/2 cup	fine dry bread crumbs	125 ml
1	frying chicken, cut up	1
1/4 cup	cooking oil	60 ml
1/2 cup	dry white table wine	125 ml
1/2 cup	water	125 ml
3	tomatoes, peeled and chopped coarsely	3
2 cups	sliced fresh mushrooms	500 ml
1/2 tsp	salt	2 ml

hot buttered noodles

→

Blend spaghetti sauce mix and seasoned salt with bread crumbs. Roll chicken pieces in mixture to coat all sides.

Heat oil in large heavy skillet and add chicken pieces. Brown well on all sides. Add wine, water, tomatoes, mushrooms, salt and any leftover crumb mixture. Cover tightly and simmer 35 to 40 minutes or until chicken is tender. Serve with hot buttered noodles.

SERVES 4

Sesame Fried Chicken

	cooking oil	
1	egg	1
2 tbsp	milk	30 ml
1 tbsp	flour	15 ml
1/2 cup	sesame seeds	125 ml
1/2 cup	flour	125 ml
1 1/2 tsp	salt	7 ml
dash	pepper	dash
3-lb	chicken, cut up	1.4-kg

Put about 1/2 inch (1.25 cm) cooking oil in electric skillet. Set control for 350 °F (175 °C).

Beat egg, milk and 1 tbsp (15 ml) flour together with a fork in a flat dish. Combine sesame seeds, 1/2 cup (125 ml) flour, salt and pepper in another flat dish. Dip chicken pieces in egg mixture then roll them in flour mixture to coat all sides.

Drop chicken into hot oil, cover (leave vent in lid open) and cook about 15 minutes or until dark golden brown. Turn chicken pieces. Reduce temperature to 300 °F (150 °C) and continue cooking, uncovered, until golden on all sides and tender, about 15 minutes more. Serve immediately.

SERVES 4

Left: Easy Chicken Marengo
Right: Sesame Fried Chicken

Western Chicken

	cooking oil	
1/4 cup	flour	60 ml
1 tsp	salt	5 ml
1/4 tsp	pepper	1 ml
1/2 tsp	paprika	2 ml
3-lb	chicken, cut up	1.4-kg
3 tbsp	butter	45 ml
1 tbsp	cooking oil	15 ml
1 cup	regular long-grain rice	250 ml
1/2 cup	chopped onion	125 ml
1/4 cup	chopped green pepper	60 ml
	boiling water	
1 tsp	salt	5 ml
1/8 tsp	pepper	0.5 ml
12-oz can	whole kernel corn, drained	375-ml can

Heat 1/4 inch (0.5 cm) cooking oil in large heavy skillet.

Combine flour, 1 tsp (5 ml) salt, 1/4 tsp (1 ml) pepper and paprika in a clean paper or plastic bag. Shake chicken pieces in the bag a few at a time to coat with flour mixture. Put chicken pieces in hot oil and fry until well browned. Turn down heat, cover skillet tightly, and cook gently until chicken is tender, 30 to 40 minutes. Turn chicken occasionally and remove cover for last 10 minutes of cooking so that it becomes crisp.

Prepare rice while chicken is cooking. Heat butter and 1 tbsp (15 ml) oil in medium saucepan. Add rice, onion and green pepper and cook gently until rice is golden brown, stirring constantly. Add amount of boiling water called for on the rice package, 1 tsp (5 ml) salt and 1/8 tsp (0.5 ml) pepper. Cook rice according to package directions.

Add corn and toss together with a fork. Cover and heat gently until corn is heated through, about 5 minutes.

Put corn-rice mixture on platter. Top with chicken pieces.

SERVES 4

Chicken Spaghetti

3 tbsp	butter or margarine	45 ml
3-lb	chicken, cut up	1.4-kg
1 tsp	salt	5 ml
1/4 tsp	pepper	1 ml
1/2 cup	chopped celery leaves	125 ml
1 small	onion, chopped	1 small
1 cup	boiling water	250 ml
5 tbsp	butter or margarine	75 ml
4 cups	fresh mushrooms, sliced thick	1 L
3 tbsp	flour	45 ml
1 1/2 to 2 cups	light cream	375 to 500 ml
2/3 cup	grated Romano cheese	180 ml
1/4 cup	dry sherry	60 ml
1 lb	spaghetti, cooked	450 g

Heat 3 tbsp (45 ml) butter or margarine in heavy skillet. Add chicken pieces and brown lightly on all sides. Add salt, pepper, celery leaves, onion and water. Cover tightly and simmer until chicken is tender, about 35 minutes. Lift out chicken pieces and cool until they can be handled. Remove meat from bones and cut into bite-size pieces.

Strain chicken stock left in skillet. Discard vegetables.

Heat 5 tbsp (75 ml) butter or margarine in heavy saucepan. Add mushrooms and cook gently 3 minutes, stirring. Sprinkle in flour and stir to blend. Remove from heat.

Measure chicken stock and add enough light cream to make 3 cups (750 ml) liquid. Add to mushroom mixture all at once and stir to blend. Return to moderate heat and cook until boiling, thickened and smooth, stirring constantly. Add chicken pieces and cheese and heat well. Stir in sherry.

Serve over hot spaghetti.

SERVES 6

Western Chicken

Crusty Cold Chicken

12	chicken drumsticks	12
12	chicken thighs	12
1 cup	butter or margarine	250 ml
1 1/2 cups	fine dry bread crumbs	375 ml
1/2 tsp	dried leaf thyme	2 ml
1/2 tsp	dried leaf marjoram	2 ml
1/2 tsp	dried leaf rosemary	2 ml
2 tsp	paprika	10 ml
2 tsp	salt	10 ml
1/2 tsp	pepper	2 ml
3	eggs	3
3 tbsp	cold water	45 ml

Dipping Sauces (recipes follow)

Wash chicken pieces and dry well on paper towelling.

Heat oven to 375 °F (190 °C). Put 1/2 cup (125 ml) butter or margarine in each of 2 large shallow baking pans that will hold the chicken pieces in a single layer. Put the pans in the oven to melt the butter.

Combine bread crumbs, thyme, marjoram, rosemary, paprika, salt and pepper in a large flat dish. Beat eggs and water together with a fork in another flat dish.

Roll each chicken piece in the egg mixture then in the crumbs to coat well and put the pieces in the prepared pans, turning them over once in the butter. Try to place chicken pieces so that they are not quite touching each other.

Bake 1 hour or until tender and browned, turning chicken pieces after first 30 minutes. (If your oven won't hold both pans at once it won't hurt to let one pan stand while the other is baking.)

Cool and chill. Serve with any or all of the following dips.

———— SERVES 8 TO 12 ————

Leek Dip

1 cup	whipping cream	250 ml
1 1/2 cups	plain yogurt	375 ml
1 envelope	leek soup mix	1 envelope
1/4 lb	farmer's (Colby) cheese, grated	

Whip cream until soft peaks form. Stir in yogurt, dry soup mix and cheese. Chill.

Curried Cheese Dip

8-oz pkg	cream cheese (room temperature)	225-g pkg
1/4 cup	commercial mayonnaise	60 ml
6 oz	plain yogurt	165 g
1 tbsp	curry powder	15 ml
2 tsp	finely grated onion	10 ml
pinch	salt	pinch

Combine cheese, mayonnaise and yogurt and beat until smooth and blended. Stir in curry powder, onion and salt. Chill. Let warm up a little before using as dip.

Onion Dip

1 cup	whipping cream	250 ml
12 oz	plain yogurt	350 g
1 envelope	onion soup mix	1 envelope

Whip cream until soft peaks form. Stir in yogurt and dry soup mix. Chill.

Dill Dip

1 cup	commercial sour cream	250 ml
1/2 cup	commercial mayonnaise	125 ml
1 tsp	dried dill weed	10 ml
	or	
1 tbsp	snipped fresh dill	15 ml

Combine all ingredients. Chill.

Pineapple Dip
(to be served hot)

1 cup	pineapple jam	250 ml
1/4 cup	prepared mustard	60 ml
1/4 cup	prepared horseradish	60 ml
1/4 tsp	ginger	1 ml

Combine all ingredients in small saucepan and heat.

Crusty Cold Chicken and, from top to bottom, Dill Dip, Curried Cheese Dip and Pineapple Dip

Crispy Chili Chicken

Soya Butter Baked Chicken

3-lb	chicken, cut up	1.4-kg
1/3 cup	water	80 ml
3 tbsp	soya sauce	45 ml
1/2 tsp	salt	2 ml
1/8 tsp	pepper	0.5 ml
1 1/2 tbsp	lemon juice	22 ml
1 tsp	crushed dried chili peppers	5 ml
1/2 cup	butter or margarine	125 ml
	hot cooked rice	

Heat oven to 400 °F (205 °C). Have ready a baking dish about 12 x 7 x 2 inches (30.5 x 18 x 5 cm).

Put chicken in baking dish in a single layer. Combine all remaining ingredients, except rice, in a small saucepan, bring to a boil, turn down heat and boil gently 10 minutes. Pour over chicken.

Bake about 45 minutes or until chicken is very tender. Turn chicken pieces half way through baking and baste occasionally. Serve with rice.

———————— SERVES 4 ————————

Crispy Chili Chicken

1 1/2 cups	coarsely crushed potato chips	375 ml
1/2 tsp	salt	2 ml
2 tsp	chili powder	10 ml
3 1/2-lb	frying chicken, cut up	1.6-kg
1/3 cup	evaporated milk	80 ml
	Spicy Sauce (recipe follows)	

Heat oven to 350 °F (175 °C). Line a 13- x 9- x 2-inch (33- x 23- x 5-cm) baking pan with aluminum foil.

Combine potato chips, salt and chili powder in a flat dish.

Dip chicken pieces in evaporated milk then roll them in potato chip mixture to coat all sides. Put in prepared baking pan, skin side up. Bake about 1 1/2 hours or until chicken is very tender. Serve with Spicy Sauce.

—————— SERVES 4 ——————

Spicy Sauce

1 tbsp	cooking oil	15 ml
1 medium	onion, chopped	1 medium
1/2 medium	green pepper, chopped	1/2 medium
19-oz can	tomatoes	540-ml can
1 tsp	sugar	5 ml
3/4 tsp	chili powder	3 ml
3/4 tsp	salt	3 ml
dash	Tabasco	dash
1/3 cup	sliced stuffed olives	80 ml

Heat oil in saucepan. Add onion and green pepper and cook gently 3 minutes, stirring. Add remaining ingredients and simmer 30 minutes, uncovered, stirring occasionally.

Stewed Chicken

5-lb	stewing chicken, cut up	2.2-kg
	boiling water	
1 large	carrot, cut up	1 large
1 large stalk	celery (with leaves), cut up	1 large stalk
1 thick slice	onion	1 thick slice
4 sprigs	parsley	4 sprigs
6	peppercorns	6
6 whole	cloves	6 whole
1 small	bay leaf	1 small
2 tsp	salt	10 ml

Wash chicken and put in a large kettle. Add water to nearly cover. Add carrot, celery, onion, parsley, peppercorns, cloves, bay leaf and salt. Bring to a boil, turn down heat, cover and simmer until tender, 2 to 3 hours. Cool.

Lift out chicken and remove meat in large pieces, discarding bones. Strain stock, chill and lift off fat. Keep meat, stock and fat refrigerated until needed.

—————— MAKES ABOUT 4 CUPS (1 L) CHICKEN MEAT ——————
—————— AND 3 TO 4 CUPS (750 ML TO 1 L) STOCK ——————

Cornish Game Hens with Cranberry Gravy

8	*frozen Cornish game hens, thawed*	8
	salt and pepper	
	bay leaves	
	garlic cloves	
8	*whole cloves*	8
8 small thin slices	*onion*	*8 small thin slices*
4 slices	*lemon*	*4 slices*
8 small sprigs	*celery leaves*	*8 small sprigs*
8 sprigs	*parsley*	*8 sprigs*
4 slices	*bacon*	*4 slices*
2 large	*onions, quartered*	*2 large*
3 cups	*chicken stock*	*750 ml*
1/4 cup	*dry vermouth*	*60 ml*
3/4 cup	*water*	*180 ml*
1/3 cup	*white vinegar*	*80 ml*
6	*whole cloves*	*6*
1 stick	*cinnamon, broken up*	*1 stick*
14-oz can	*whole cranberry sauce*	*398-ml can*
1/4 cup	*cold water*	*60 ml*
2 tbsp	*cornstarch*	*30 ml*

Heat oven to 450 °F (230 °C). Have ready a large shallow roasting pan big enough to hold the 8 birds with a little space between.

Wash Cornish hens and dry well inside and out with paper towelling. Sprinkle inside of each with salt and pepper. Add a small piece of bay leaf, a sliver of garlic, a clove, a slice of onion, half a slice of lemon, a sprig of celery leaves and a sprig of parsley to the inside of each bird. Tie legs and wings close to bodies and set birds in lightly oiled roasting pan. Lay a half strip of bacon over the breast of each bird.

Add onion quarters, giblets, chicken stock and vermouth to the pan.

Roast 15 minutes, at 450 °F (230 °C). Turn heat to 350 °F (175 °C) and continue roasting until the birds are tender, about 45 minutes. Baste occasionally and remove bacon for last 15 minutes cooking.

Heat 3/4 cup (180 ml) water, vinegar, 6 cloves and cinnamon in a saucepan until boiling while birds are cooking. Turn down heat and simmer 10 minutes. Strain and return liquid to saucepan. Add cranberry sauce and heat and stir until blended. Set aside for gravy.

→

Put cooked birds on large hot platter and set in warm oven. Strain cooking stock into a large measuring cup and add water, if necessary, to make 3 cups (750 ml) liquid. Put this liquid into a saucepan and bring to a boil. Combine 1/4 cup (60 ml) cold water and cornstarch in small jar with a tight lid and shake together until well blended. Stir into boiling liquid gradually and cook until thick and clear, stirring. Taste and add salt and pepper, if desired. Stir in spiced cranberry mixture and heat well. Serve as gravy.

———— 8 PORTIONS ————

Rice and Chicken Livers

1/4 cup	butter or margarine	60 ml
1 medium	onion, chopped	1 medium
1 lb	chicken livers, cut in halves	450 g
1/2 cup	chopped fresh mushrooms	125 ml
1/2 cup	chopped sweet red pepper (see note)	125 ml
1 1/2 tsp	salt	7 ml
1/4 tsp	pepper	1 ml
1 cup	long-grain regular rice	250 ml
1/4 tsp	dried leaf basil	1 ml
4 medium	tomatoes, peeled and chopped	4 medium
2 cups	hot chicken stock	500 ml
1/3 cup	grated Parmesan cheese	80 ml

Heat oven to 350 °F (175 °C). Butter a 2 1/2-qt (3-L) casserole.

Heat butter in heavy skillet. Add onion and cook gently 3 minutes.

Add chicken livers and cook gently 1 minute, stirring. Add mushrooms and red pepper and cook 1 minute, stirring. Stir in salt, pepper and rice. Cook gently until rice begins to turn a golden color, stirring constantly. This will take about 3 minutes.

Remove from heat. Add basil and tomatoes. Spoon into prepared casserole. Pour chicken stock over. Cover and bake 45 minutes or until rice is tender and most of liquid is absorbed. (If you find there is still quite a lot of liquid on rice continue baking, uncovered, until most of liquid disappears.) Remove from oven and turn on broiler.

Sprinkle rice mixture with cheese and slip low under broiler to brown lightly. Serve immediately.

———— SERVES 6 ————

Left: Cornish Game Hens with Cranberry Gravy
Right: Rice and Chicken Livers

Turkey Pies

8 lb	turkey meat, cut up	3.6 kg
	water	
2 large	carrots, cut coarsely	2 large
2 large stalks	celery (with leaves), cut coarsely	2 large stalks
1 small	onion	1 small
6	cloves	6
6 large sprigs	parsley	6 large sprigs
12	peppercorns	12
1	bay leaf	1
3 tsp	salt (or to taste)	15 ml
1/4 cup	turkey fat, butter or vegetable oil	60 ml
1 lb	mushrooms, sliced	450 g
2 cups	turkey stock	500 ml
12 medium	carrots, sliced thin	12 medium
1 medium	bunch celery, sliced thin on diagonal	1 medium
3 tsp	salt	15 ml
1/2 tsp	pepper	2 ml
2 tsp	dried leaf thyme	10 ml
1 tsp	dried leaf marjoram	5 ml
1 tsp	dried leaf chervil	5 ml
1 cup	chopped parsley	250 ml
1 lb	cooked ham, cut in strips (canned ham is fine)	450 g
1 cup	butter or margarine	250 ml
1 cup	chopped onion	250 ml
1 cup	flour	250 ml
6 cups	liquid (vegetable cooking liquid plus turkey stock)	1.5 L
2 tsp	salt	10 ml
1/4 tsp	pepper	1 ml
1/4 tsp	nutmeg	1 ml
1 tsp	lemon juice	5 ml
2 cups	light cream	500 ml
	Sage Pastry (recipe follows)	
1	egg yolk	1
1 tbsp	cold water	15 ml

Put turkey in large kettle and cover with cold water. Add coarsely cut carrots, celery, onion stuck with the cloves, parsley, peppercorns, bay leaf and salt. Bring to a boil, turn down heat, cover and simmer until turkey is just tender, 2 to 3 hours. Lift out pieces of turkey and cool. Strain, cool and chill turkey stock. Lift fat off top of stock and set aside to use later. Take turkey meat off bones and cut into bite-size pieces. Refrigerate stock, fat and meat until you are ready to make the pie (all of this step can be done the day ahead). You should have about 10 cups (2.5 L) turkey meat and 14 cups (3.5 L) stock.

Have ready two 3-qt (4-L) casseroles when you start to make the pies.

Heat 1/4 cup (60 ml) turkey fat, butter or vegetable oil in large heavy skillet. Add mushrooms and cook gently 5 minutes, stirring. Remove from heat.

Heat 2 cups (500 ml) turkey stock to boiling in large sauce-pan. Add sliced carrots and celery. Bring back to a boil, turn down heat, cover and cook until vegetables are tender-crisp, about 10 minutes. Drain, saving cooking liquid.

Combine 3 tsp (15 ml) salt, pepper, thyme, marjoram, chervil and parsley in a small dish.

Put layers of turkey, mushrooms, vegetables and ham strips in each of the casseroles, sprinkling each vegetable layer with a little of the salt-herb mixture and continuing the layers until all ingredients are used.

Heat the 1 cup (250 ml) butter (or margarine) in a large saucepan. Add chopped onion and cook and stir 3 minutes or until onion is limp. Sprinkle in flour. Let bubble. Remove from heat. Add the 6 cups (1.5 L) liquid. (Save any left-over stock for soup for another day). Stir to blend. Add 2 tsp (10 ml) salt, pepper and nutmeg. Return to heat and cook until boiling, thickened and smooth, stirring. Stir in lemon juice and cream.

Pour half of this gravy over the layers in each casserole. Cool to lukewarm.

Heat oven to 400 °F (205 °C) if you are going to bake the pies immediately (see note).

Prepare Sage Pastry and top pies with it, sealing pastry well to the edges of the casseroles. Cut a large vent in the top of each pie. Beat egg yolk and 1 tbsp (15 ml) water together lightly with a fork and brush some of this mixture over pastry (not on edge). Bake about 1 hour or until turkey mixture is bubbling well and pastry is dark golden brown. Serve very hot.

Note: If you want to make the pies a day ahead of time, refrigerate them after the pastry topping is added. Remove from refrigerator about an hour before baking time to let them warm up a little. Then cut the vent in the top, and brush with egg yolk mixture and bake as directed.

———— 2 LARGE PIES ENOUGH TO SERVE 12 ————

Turkey Pie

Sage Pastry

2 cups	sifted all-purpose flour	500 ml
1 tsp	salt	5 ml
2 tsp	sage	10 ml
3/4 cup	shortening	180 ml
1/4 cup	ice water	60 ml

Measure flour into a bowl. Mix in salt and sage with a fork. Add shortening and cut in coarsely with a pastry blender or two knives. Sprinkle in water, a little at a time, mixing lightly with a fork just until all flour is dampened. Gather dough into a ball and press together firmly. Divide into 2 equal parts and use to top pies as directed in recipe.

Roast Turkey with Oyster Stuffing

1 pt	*fresh oysters*	625 ml
	flour	
1	*egg*	1
1 tbsp	*milk*	15 ml
3/4 cup	*fine soda biscuit crumbs (approx.)*	180 ml
1 tbsp	*butter*	15 ml
1 tbsp	*cooking oil*	15 ml
1 cup	*butter or margarine*	250 ml
1/2 cup	*chopped onion*	125 ml
1 1/2 cups	*chopped celery (with leaves)*	375 ml
1 cup	*chopped green pepper*	250 ml
1 cup	*sliced mushrooms*	250 ml
6 cups	*soft bread crumbs*	1.5 L
1 tbsp	*salt*	15 ml
1/2 tsp	*pepper*	2 ml
1/4 cup	*chopped parsley*	60 ml
1/2 tsp	*sage*	2 ml
1/4 tsp	*dried leaf rosemary*	1 ml
1/4 tsp	*dried leaf marjoram*	1 ml
1 tbsp	*lemon juice*	15 ml
2 tbsp	*oyster liquid*	30 ml
1 12-lb	*turkey*	1 5.4-kg
	melted butter	

Drain oysters and dry them on paper towelling. Measure out and set aside 2 tbsp (30 ml) of the oyster liquid. Dip oysters in flour, then in egg beaten with 1 tbsp (15 ml) milk and finally in soda biscuit crumbs to coat well.

Heat 1 tbsp (15 ml) butter and 1 tbsp (15 ml) oil in large heavy skillet and drop in the oysters. Fry about 1 minute or just until lightly browned, turning and lifting out with an egg turner. Set them aside.

Heat 1 cup (250 ml) butter in same skillet. Add onion, celery and green pepper. Cook gently 3 minutes, stirring. Add mushrooms and continue cooking and stirring 2 minutes more. Add half of bread crumbs and cook and stir until bread is lightly browned.

Put remaining bread in a large bowl. Add salt, pepper, parsley, sage, rosemary and marjoram. Add hot bread-vegetable mixture, lemon juice and the 2 tbsp (30 ml) oyster liquid you set aside. Toss all together lightly.

Stuff neck end of turkey lightly with some of bread mixture. Skewer opening closed. Put a handful of bread mixture into breast of turkey then add a few of the oysters. Add another handful of bread mixture and more oysters, continuing until turkey is loosely stuffed. Skewer opening closed and tie wings and legs of bird close to body.

Heat oven to 325 °F (160 °C).

Set turkey on rack in roasting pan and brush all over with melted butter. Cover with a loose tent of aluminum foil. Roast about 5 hours or until drumstick moves easily. Uncover for last hour so turkey browns well. Baste occasionally.

——————— SERVES 6 ———————

Turkey Divan

Turkey Divan

1/3 cup	*butter or margarine*	80 ml
1/3 cup	*all-purpose flour*	80 ml
3/4 tsp	*salt*	3 ml
1/4 tsp	*pepper*	1 ml
3 cups	*milk*	750 ml
1/4 tsp	*dry mustard*	1 ml
1/4 tsp	Worcestershire sauce	1 ml
1 cup	*grated old cheddar cheese*	250 ml
20-oz pkg	*frozen broccoli*	560-g pkg
1 tsp	*salt*	5 ml
1/4 tsp	*pepper*	1 ml
6 large slices	*leftover turkey breast*	6 large slices
2	*egg yolks, beaten*	2
6 thick slices	*tomato*	6 thick slices

Heat oven to 375 °F (190 °C). Butter a 13- x 9- x 2-inch (33- x 23- x 5-cm) glass baking dish.

Melt butter or margarine in saucepan. Sprinkle in flour, 3/4 tsp (3 ml) salt and 1/4 tsp (1 ml) pepper and let bubble. Remove from heat and add milk all at once. Add mustard and Worcestershire sauce and stir to blend. Return to moderate heat and cook until thick and smooth, stirring. Remove from heat. Stir in about 3/4 cup (180 ml) of the cheese.

Cook broccoli according to package directions using the minimum time suggested. Drain and lay pieces in prepared baking dish. Sprinkle with 1 tsp (5 ml) salt and 1/4 tsp (1 ml) pepper. Lay turkey slices on top of broccoli in a single layer.

Beat egg yolks into cheese sauce and pour sauce over turkey. Top with tomato slices and sprinkle them with the remaining 1/4 cup (60 ml) cheese. Bake 10 to 15 minutes or until bubbling well. Turn on broiler to lightly brown top. Watch carefully so that it doesn't burn. Serve immediately.

SERVES 6

Goose with Onion-Sage Stuffing

3 lb	onions	1.4 kg
1/2 cup	butter or margarine	125 ml
1/2 cup	chopped celery, with leaves	125 ml
6 cups	soft bread crumbs	1.5 L
1 tbsp	salt	15 ml
1/2 tsp	pepper	2 ml
1 tbsp	sage	15 ml
1 tsp	dried leaf savory	5 ml
1/2 tsp	dried leaf marjoram	2 ml
1/4 tsp	nutmeg	1 ml
1 10- to 12-lb	goose	1 4.5- to 5.4-kg
1 tbsp	lemon juice	15 ml
	salt and pepper	
2	chicken bouillon cubes	2
2 cups	boiling water	500 ml

Giblet Gravy (recipe follows)

Peel onions (cut large ones into quarters) and put them in a large saucepan. Add boiling water to cover and simmer, covered, about 15 minutes or until just tender. Drain. Chop rather coarsely.

Heat butter (or margarine) in large heavy skillet. Add celery and cook gently 3 minutes, stirring. Add half of bread crumbs and cook gently, until crumbs are lightly browned, stirring.

Put remaining crumbs in large bowl. Add salt, pepper, sage, savory, marjoram and nutmeg. Toss lightly. Add onions and celery-crumb mixture and toss again lightly. Cool.

Heat oven to 400 °F (205 °C). Rub goose inside and out with lemon juice. Sprinkle inside generously with salt and pepper. Stuff neck cavity with some of stuffing and fasten neck skin to body with a skewer. Stuff body cavity with rest of stuffing, skewer opening closed and lace closed with string. Tie legs and wings close to body. Prick skin all over bird to let fat escape.

Put bird, breast side down, on rack in large roasting pan. Add bouillon cubes to 2 cups (500 ml) boiling water and stir until dissolved. Pour over goose.

Roast 1 hour, uncovered. Pour off and discard all drippings. Turn goose over and pour 2 cups (500 ml) boiling water over it. Continue roasting for another hour. Pour off drippings in pan again. Prick goose again all over and continue roasting about 1 1/2 hours more or until tender. Put goose on hot platter and keep warm while making gravy.

Note: Goose has a high proportion of fat and bone to meat, so allow at least 1 lb (450 g) per person.

SERVES 10 TO 12

Giblet Gravy

	goose giblets (except liver)	
	boiling water	
2 large sprigs	celery leaves	2 large sprigs
2 large sprigs	parsley	2 large sprigs
1 large	carrot, cut up coarsely	1 large
4	peppercorns	4
1/2 tsp	salt	2 ml
	goose drippings	
1/4 cup	all-purpose flour	60 ml

Put goose giblets in a saucepan while goose is cooking. Cover them with boiling water and add celery leaves, parsley, carrot, peppercorns and salt. Bring to a boil, turn down heat, cover and simmer about 2 hours. Lift out giblets and strain liquid, discarding vegetables. Chop giblets finely.

Pour all but 1/4 cup (60 ml) drippings out of roasting pan. Put pan on stove and heat drippings. Stir in flour and let bubble and brown slightly. Gradually stir in liquid left from cooking giblets, stirring until smooth after each addition. Stir in enough boiling water to make the gravy a good consistency. Taste and add salt and pepper if necessary. Stir in chopped giblets and heat well.

Duckling à l'Orange

2	ducklings, 4 to 5 lb (1.8 to 2.2 kg) each	2
1/3 cup	butter	80 ml
1 large	carrot, chopped coarsely	1 large
1 medium	onion, chopped coarsely	1 medium
2 large sprigs	parsley	2 large sprigs
2 large sprigs	celery leaves	2 large sprigs
small piece	bay leaf	small piece
1 tsp	dried leaf savory	5 ml
	salt and pepper	
2 cups	white wine	500 ml
2 cups	Brown Stock (recipe follows)	500 ml
2	oranges	2
2 tbsp	cold water	30 ml
1 tsp	cornstarch	5 ml
2	oranges	2
	cranberry or red currant jelly	
	parsley or watercress	

Dry ducklings well inside and out with paper towelling.

Heat butter in small saucepan until it foams up. Skim off and discard foam. Pour clear yellow oil into large heavy skillet and heat. (Discard sediment left in small saucepan.) Brown ducklings well on all sides in this clarified butter.

Heat oven to 325 °F (160 °C). Put carrot, onion, 2 sprigs parsley, celery leaves, bay leaf and savory in an extra-large Dutch oven or pot with a tight lid (if you don't have one large enough, use a large baking dish and use heavy-duty aluminum foil as a cover). Sprinkle ducklings well inside and out with salt and pepper and lay them on top of vegetables in pan. Add wine and brown stock. Cover tightly and roast in oven about 2 hours or until birds are just tender. Uncover and roast 15 minutes more to crisp skin.

Squeeze 2 of the oranges while the ducklings are cooking. Strain the juice and set it aside to add to the sauce. Cut the peel of these 2 oranges into pieces and lay the pieces flat on the table, white side up. Cut away all the white membrane with a sharp pointed knife and discard. Cut the orange part of the peel into short, thin slivers. Put them in a small saucepan, cover with boiling water, cover and simmer until tender, about 10 minutes. Drain and set aside for sauce.

Lift ducklings out of pan, put them on a hot platter and keep warm.

Strain drippings in roasting pan, discard vegetables and chill drippings quickly by setting in ice water. Lift off fat and discard. Put remaining liquid in a saucepan and boil hard, uncovered, until reduced to about 1/4 of the amount.

Stir water and cornstarch together and stir this mixture into the boiling liquid gradually. Turn down heat. Add orange juice and orange rind and simmer 5 minutes.

Cut remaining 2 oranges into thick slices and centre each slice with a dab of cranberry or red currant jelly. Use these orange slices to garnish platter and add a few large sprigs parsley or watercress. Spoon a little of orange sauce over each serving of duckling.

SERVES 6 TO 8

Brown Stock

1 1/2 lb	shin of beef, cut up	675 g
1 1/2 lb	veal knuckle, cut up	675 g
2 tbsp	cooking oil	30 ml
2	carrots, coarsely cut	2
2	onions sliced	2
6	peppercorns	6
4	cloves	4
1 tbsp	salt	15 ml
16 cups	boiling water	4 L
2 sprigs	celery leaves	2 sprigs
2 large sprigs	parsley	2 large sprigs
1 small	bay leaf	1 small

Duckling à l'Orange

Heat oven to 375 °F (190 °C). Spread pieces of shin of beef and veal knuckle out on shallow roasting pan and drizzle oil over them. Put in oven and brown well (this will take about 30 minutes). Turn the pieces several times. Sprinkle carrots and onions over all and let them brown a little, about 10 minutes.

Turn all the meat, bones and vegetables into a large kettle. Add all remaining ingredients. Bring to a boil, skim, then turn heat down to low, cover and simmer about 3 hours or until all meat is falling off bones.

Cool, lift off fat and strain liquid. Store liquid in jars in refrigerator or freeze — be sure to leave about 2 inches (5 cm) headroom in jars if you are freezing.

Pheasants with Wild Rice

2	pheasants, about 2 1/2 lb (1.1 kg) each	2
4	green onions, sliced thin	4
2 large bunches	celery leaves	2 large bunches
2 large sprigs	parsley	2 large sprigs
6 tbsp	clarified butter (see note)	90 ml
	salt and pepper	
2 cups	dry red table wine	500 ml
1/2 lb	fresh mushrooms	225 g
1 tbsp	butter	15 ml
1 tbsp	flour	15 ml
12	small white onions	12
1 cup	wild rice	250 ml
1 tsp	salt	5 ml
1/4 cup	butter, melted	60 ml
1/4 cup	chopped parsley	60 ml

Thaw pheasants if they are frozen and wash. Dry thoroughly with paper towels. Put green onions, celery leaves and parsley inside birds.

Heat clarified butter in large heavy skillet. Cook birds gently in butter, turning often, until golden brown all over (this will take about 30 minutes).

Put them in buttered casserole just large enough to hold them side by side. Sprinkle with salt and pepper.

Heat oven to 375 °F (190 °C).

Pour wine into skillet. Add stems from mushrooms. Cook hard until liquid is reduced in half (scrape up browned bits from bottom of skillet during cooking). Turn down heat.

Cream 1 tbsp (15 ml) butter and flour together and stir into hot liquid bit by bit. Cook until slightly thickened, stirring. Add salt and pepper to taste and strain over birds.

Peel onions, cover with boiling water and simmer 5 minutes or until just beginning to get tender. Drain and add to casserole. Cover tightly. Cook until very tender, about 1 hour.

Cook rice while pheasants are cooking. Wash rice well under cold running water. Put in saucepan and cover with boiling water. Add 1 tsp (5 ml) salt. Cover and simmer over low heat until rice grains have split open and are tender, about 40 minutes. Check after 30 minutes, adding more water if necessary. Fluff with a fork when tender and cook uncovered, 5 minutes.

Chop mushroom caps. Heat 1/4 cup (60 ml) butter in large heavy skillet and add mushrooms. Cook and stir 2 minutes. Remove from heat, stir in parsley and add to rice. Toss together with a fork. Serve with pheasants.

Note: To make clarified butter, heat in small saucepan until it foams up. Skim off foam. Pour off clear oil, which is clarified butter. Discard sediment in bottom of the pan.

——————— SERVES 4 ———————

Fish and

Shellfish

*F*ish and *Shellfish*

Streams, rivers, lakes and oceans have yielded a vast and varied harvest of fish and shellfish for man to enjoy since first he walked this earth. And enjoy them we should.

I often hear people say, "I don't like fish". Yet many a fish scorner has been converted to a fish lover through the subtleties of good fish cookery. Remember, all fish comes to us tender and only the cook can spoil good fresh or properly frozen or stored fish and shellfish. Overcooked, these tender water dwellers become dry tough and tasteless. On the other hand fish that is treated with the reverence it deserves will reward the cook and please the diners with delicate, flavorful morsels to savour.

Fish is some of the most healthy fare available, at any cost. It is rich in minerals as well as A, B and D vitamins. Legends have been written of the longevity of those whose exclusive protein intake is from the sea's harvest. And why not, are there not countless varieties of fish and shellfish, and even more ways to prepare them for an infinite supply of delicious meals?

For a taste treat that your company will never forget try Baked Haddock and Grapefruit or go the distance with the Paella. The classical taste of fresh sole is unmistakable and the methods to cook it included here will enhance your reputation as a cook while delighting the taste buds of your family or friends. All the recipes that follow are long time favorites and they wont disappoint.

Haddock en Casserole

2 lb	haddock fillets	900 g
2 sprigs	celery leaves	2 sprigs
2 sprigs	parsley	2 sprigs
1/4 tsp	dried leaf thyme	1 ml
1 small	bay leaf	1 small
1 tbsp	lemon juice	15 ml
2	peppercorns	2
1 tsp	salt	5 ml
	boiling water	
3 tbsp	butter	45 ml
1 medium	onion, sliced paper-thin	1 medium
2 cups	sliced mushrooms	500 ml
1/4 cup	slivered pimento	60 ml
1/4 cup	butter	60 ml
1/4 cup	flour	60 ml
1 cup	fish cooking water	250 ml
1/2 tsp	salt	2 ml
1/4 tsp	pepper	1 ml
1/4 tsp	dried leaf tarragon	1 ml
pinch	dried leaf marjoram	pinch
pinch	dried leaf chervil	pinch
1 cup	light cream	250 ml
2	egg yolks	2
1 cup	1/4-inch (0.5-cm) bread cubes	250 ml
2 tbsp	melted butter	30 ml

Heat oven to 325 °F (160 °C). Butter a baking dish about 12 x 7 x 2 inches (3.5 x 18 x 5 cm).

Cut fish into serving size pieces. Lay in large skillet. Add celery leaves, parsley, thyme, bay leaf, lemon juice, peppercorns and 1 tsp (5 ml) salt. Add boiling water to just cover. Bring to a boil, turn down heat, cover and simmer about 5 minutes or just until fish flakes easily with a fork. Lift fish out of water. Strain cooking water and measure out 1 cup (250 ml) to use in sauce.

Melt 3 tbsp (45 ml) butter in same skillet and add onion. Cook gently 3 minutes, stirring. Add mushrooms and cook and stir 2 minutes more. Remove from heat and stir in pimento.

Melt 1/4 cup (60 ml) butter in saucepan. Sprinkle in flour and stir to blend. Remove from heat and add the 1 cup (250 ml) fish cooking water all at once. Add 1/2 tsp (2 ml) salt, 1/4 tsp (1 ml) pepper, tarragon, marjoram and chervil. Stir to blend and return to moderate heat. Cook until boiling, thickened and smooth, stirring constantly. Beat cream and egg yolks together with a fork and stir into hot mixture. Heat but do not boil.

Put a little of the sauce in the prepared baking dish. Lay fish pieces in sauce and sprinkle onion-mushroom mixture over. Top with remaining sauce.

Add bread cubes to 2 tbsp (30 ml) melted butter and toss to coat bread with butter. Sprinkle over casserole.

Bake 30 minutes or until bubbling and lightly browned on top.

SERVES 4 TO 6

Baked Haddock and Grapefruit

Baked Haddock and Grapefruit

1 1/2 lbs	haddock fillets	675 g
1 tsp	salt	5 ml
1/8 tsp	pepper	0.5 ml
2 tbsp	grapefruit juice	30 ml
3/4 cup	1/2-inch (1.25-cm) soft bread cubes	180 ml
3 tbsp	butter, melted	45 ml
1/4 tsp	dried leaf thyme	1 ml
1	grapefruit, sectioned	1
	melted butter	

Heat oven to 400 °F (205 °C). Butter a shallow baking pan, about 12 x 7 x 2 inches (30.5 x 18 x 5 cm).

Cut fish into serving-size pieces. Sprinkle both sides with the salt and pepper and lay in prepared pan in a single layer. Sprinkle with grapefruit juice.

Mix bread cubes, butter and thyme and sprinkle over fish. Bake 15 minutes. Lay sections of grapefruit on top of fish. Brush them lightly with butter and continue baking 10 minutes more or until fish flakes easily with a fork. Serve immediately.

SERVES 4

171

Oven Fried Fish

2 lb	frozen fish fillets (sole or haddock)	900 g
1/2 cup	buttermilk	125 ml
2 tsp	salt	10 ml
1/8 tsp	pepper	0.5 ml
1/2 tsp	dried leaf thyme	2 ml
1 cup	fine dry bread crumbs	250 ml
2 tbsp	finely chopped parsley	30 ml
2 tbsp	cooking oil	30 ml

Hot Tartare Sauce
(recipe follows)

Thaw fish enough to separate fillets.

Heat oven to 500 °F (260 °C). Oil a 13- x 9- x 2-inch (33- x 23- x 5-cm) glass baking dish.

Dip fish in a combination of buttermilk, salt, pepper and thyme then in a mixture of crumbs and parsley to coat both sides. Lay the fillets in prepared baking dish in a single layer if possible. Drizzle with cooking oil.

Bake 15 to 20 minutes or until fish is golden and flakes easily with a fork. Do not turn. Serve immediately with Hot Tartare Sauce.

——————— SERVES 6 ———————

Hot Tartare Sauce

1 tbsp	butter	15 ml
1 tbsp	flour	15 ml
1/2 cup	milk	125 ml
1/4 tsp	salt	1 ml
dash	pepper	dash
1/4 cup	commercial mayonnaise	60 ml
1/2 tsp	grated onion	2 ml
6 small	stuffed olives, sliced finely	6 small
1 tbsp	finely chopped sweet pickle	15 ml
1 tbsp	finely chopped parsley	15 ml

Melt butter in small saucepan. Sprinkle in flour and stir to blend. Remove from heat and stir in milk all at once. Add salt and pepper. Return to moderate heat and cook until boiling, thickened and smooth, stirring.

Add all remaining ingredients and heat but do not boil. Serve hot.

Oven Fried Fish

Fish à la King

1 lb	*frozen haddock fillets*	450 g
2 tbsp	*butter or margarine*	30 ml
2 tbsp	*flour*	30 ml
1/2 tsp	*salt*	2 ml
1/8 tsp	*cayenne*	0.5 ml
1 cup	*milk*	250 ml
1 tbsp	*chopped pimento*	15 ml
1 cup	*cooked peas*	250 ml
	hot cooked rice or baked potatoes	

Cut block of fish into 3 pieces. Boil water 1 inch (2.5 cm) deep in a large skillet. Add pieces of fish and simmer about 10 minutes or until fish flakes easily with a fork. Lift fish out of water with an egg turner and flake into a bowl.

Heat butter or margarine in medium saucepan. Sprinkle in flour, salt and cayenne. Stir to blend. Remove from heat and add milk all at once. Return to moderate heat and cook and stir until thickened and smooth. Add pimento, peas and flaked fish and heat gently about 4 minutes, stirring occasionally.

Serve over cooked rice or split baked potatoes.

——————— SERVES 4 ———————

Fish in Beer Batter

2 lb	*fresh or frozen fish fillets (haddock or cod)*	900 g
	oil for deep frying	
	lemon juice	
1 cup	*sifted all-purpose flour*	250 ml
1 tsp	*salt*	5 ml
1 tbsp	*paprika*	15 ml
12-oz bottle	*beer*	341-ml bottle
	flour	

If using frozen fish, thaw fish until fillets can be separated easily.

Heat oil to 400 °F (205 °C) in deep saucepan or electric deep fryer. Fill pan about 1/3 full of oil. Cut fish into serving-size pieces. Sprinkle lightly with lemon juice.

Sift 1 cup (250 ml) flour, salt and paprika into mixing bowl. Add beer gradually, beating until batter is smooth.

Put a little flour in a flat dish and dip the fish fillets in it to coat both sides. Then draw each piece of fish through the beer mixture to coat well with batter.

Fry in hot oil about 4 minutes, turning once. Batter should be dark golden brown and crisp and fish should be cooked through. Drain on paper towelling. Serve very hot.

——————— SERVES 4 TO 6 ———————

Sole and Asparagus

1 lb	*frozen sole fillets*	450 g
10-oz pkg	*frozen asparagus*	280-g pkg
2 tbsp	*cooking oil*	30 ml
1/2 tsp	*salt*	2 ml
1 tbsp	*oil*	15 ml
1/2 tsp	*salt*	2 ml
	black pepper	
1/2 cup	*cold water*	125 ml
1 tsp	*cornstarch*	5 ml

Thaw sole just until it can be separated. Cut into serving-size pieces if necessary.

Cut frozen asparagus on the diagonal into pieces about 1 inch (2.5 cm) long.

Heat 2 tbsp (30 ml) oil in heavy skillet. Add asparagus and sprinkle with 1/2 tsp (2 ml) salt. Cook over high heat, stirring constantly or shaking the pan, until asparagus is thawed, hot and just barely cooked. Lift out of pan with a slotted spoon and put on small platter. Keep hot in a low oven.

Add remaining 1 tbsp (15 ml) oil to same pan and add fish pieces. Fry quickly 2 minutes. Turn carefully, sprinkle with remaining 1/2 tsp (2 ml) salt and lightly with pepper and continue frying until fish flakes easily with a fork, about 2 minutes. Add to platter.

Combine water and cornstarch while fish is frying and stir mixture into any drippings in pan gradually as soon as fish has been removed. Cook until slightly thickened and clear, stirring. Pour over fish and serve immediately.

SERVES 3

Sole Amandine

1/2 cup	*flour*	125 ml
1 tsp	*salt*	5 ml
1/4 tsp	*pepper*	1 ml
1 tsp	*paprika*	5 ml
2 lb	*sole fillets*	900 g
3 tbsp	*butter*	45 ml
3 tbsp	*slivered almonds*	45 ml
3 tbsp	*lemon juice*	45 ml
1 tsp	*grated lemon rind*	5 ml
3 tbsp	*chopped chives*	45 ml
1/3 cup	*salad oil*	80 ml

Combine flour, salt, pepper and paprika in a flat dish. Cut fish in serving-size pieces (if using frozen fish let it thaw enough so you can separate fillets) and dip into flour mixture to coat both sides.

Heat butter in small skillet. Add almonds and cook gently until almonds are golden, stirring. Stir in lemon juice, lemon rind and chives.

Heat oil in large heavy skillet and fry fish quickly on both sides until golden. Lift out onto hot platter and pour almond mixture over. Serve immediately.

SERVES 6

Sole and Avocado

Sole and Avocado

1 lb	fresh or frozen fillets of sole	450 g
	salt and pepper	
1 tbsp	lime juice	15 ml
1 large	avocado	1 large
1/4 cup	flour	60 ml
1/4 cup	butter	60 ml
1/4 cup	light cream	60 ml
1 1/2 tsp	lime juice	7 ml
1/4 cup	toasted flaked coconut	60 ml

If you are using frozen fish, thaw fish enough so it can be separated into pieces. Put in a single layer in a shallow dish. Sprinkle pieces of fish lightly with salt and pepper and drizzle 1 tbsp (15 ml) lime juice over all. Let stand 10 minutes.

Cut avocado in half and remove stone. Peel avocado and cut into 1/2-inch (1.25-cm) cubes.

Put the flour in a shallow dish.

Heat 2 tbsp (30 ml) of the butter in a large skillet. Dip the fish pieces into the flour and drop them into the hot butter. Brown on first side. Add another 1 tbsp (15 ml) butter, turn fish pieces and brown on second side. Do not overcook.

Lift fish pieces out onto hot platter. Add remaining 1 tbsp (15 ml) butter, cream and cubes of avocado to the skillet and heat gently 1 minute, stirring. Pour over fish. Sprinkle with 1 1/2 tsp (7 ml) lime juice and coconut. Serve immediately.

—————— SERVES 2 TO 3 ——————

Fish Rolls with Lemon Sauce

2 lb	sole fillets	900 g
3 cups	water	750 ml
2 thin slices	onion	2 thin slices
1 medium	carrot, sliced	1 medium
1 small	bay leaf	1 small
1 sprig	celery leaves	1 sprig
2 sprigs	parsley	2 sprigs
2 whole	allspice	2 whole
6	peppercorns	6
2 tsp	salt	10 ml
2 tbsp	butter	30 ml
2 tbsp	flour	30 ml
1 cup	fish cooking water	250 ml
1 tbsp	lemon juice	15 ml
dash	pepper	dash
1	egg yolk	1
1/4 cup	heavy cream	60 ml
2 tbsp	chopped parsley	30 ml

Split fish fillets down their natural divisions to make 2 narrow strips from each fillet. Roll these strips up and fasten with a toothpick.

Heat water, onion, carrot, bay leaf, celery leaves, parsley sprigs, allspice, peppercorns and salt together in a deep skillet. Cover and boil 10 minutes. Put fish rolls in skillet, cover again and simmer about 10 minutes or until centres of little rolls of fish are tender. Lift fish out of cooking water, remove toothpicks, and put on hot platter. Keep warm.

Strain fish cooking water and measure out 1 cup (250 ml) for sauce.

→

Sole with Shrimp Sauce

Melt butter in saucepan. Sprinkle in flour and stir to blend. Remove from heat and add the 1 cup (250 ml) fish stock, lemon juice and pepper. Stir to blend.

Return to moderate heat and cook until boiling, thickened and smooth, stirring constantly. Beat egg yolk and cream together with a fork and stir a little of the hot sauce into this mixture. Stir back into sauce and heat but do not boil. Stir in 2 tbsp (30 ml) parsley. Pour over fish and serve immediately.

———————— SERVES 4 TO 6 ————————

2 lb	*frozen fillets of sole*	900 g
3 tbsp	*butter*	45 ml
2 small	*onions, chopped finely*	2 small
1/2 lb	*mushrooms, chopped finely*	225 g
2 tbsp	*flour*	30 ml
1 1/2 tsp	*salt*	7 ml
1/4 tsp	*pepper*	1 ml
1 cup	*light cream*	250 ml
2/3 cup	*dry white table wine*	160 ml
1/4 cup	*water*	60 ml
2 tbsp	*finely chopped parsley*	30 ml
4-oz can	*small shrimp, drained and rinsed with cold water*	115-g can
1/2 cup	*grated Gruyère cheese*	125 ml

Thaw fish just until fillets can be separated.

Heat oven to 400 °F (205 °C). Butter a large baking dish about 13 x 9 x 2 inches (33 x 23 x 5 cm).

Lay fish fillets out in baking dish in a single layer if possible.

Heat butter in large skillet. Add onions and mushrooms and cook and stir until onions are limp. Sprinkle in flour, salt and pepper and stir to blend. Remove from heat. Stir in cream, wine and water. Return to moderate heat and cook until boiling, thickened and smooth, stirring constantly. Remove from heat and stir in parsley and shrimp. Pour over fish fillets. Sprinkle with cheese.

Bake about 25 minutes or until fish flakes easily with a fork.

———————— SERVES 6 ————————

Left: Fish Rolls with Lemon Sauce
Right: Sole with Shrimp Sauce

177

Ocean Perch Thermidor

2 lb	*frozen ocean perch fillets*	900 g
1/4 cup	melted butter	60 ml
2 tbsp	lemon juice	30 ml
1 tsp	finely chopped onion	5 ml
dash	Tabasco	dash
2 tbsp	butter	30 ml
2 tbsp	flour	30 ml
1/4 tsp	dry mustard	1 ml
1/4 tsp	paprika	1 ml
1/2 tsp	salt	2 ml
3 tbsp	dry white wine	45 ml
1 cup	milk	250 ml
1/4 tsp	dried leaf chervil	1 ml
pinch	dried leaf tarragon	pinch
2	egg yolks	2
1/2 cup	heavy cream	125 ml
	paprika	

Thaw fish enough to separate. Skin fish if desired. While the fillets are partly frozen the skin will pull off easily.

Heat oven to 375 °F (190 °C). Butter 6 individual baking dishes about 12 oz (375 ml) in size. Cut fish into 1-inch (2.5-cm) squares and divide evenly among the baking dishes. Combine melted butter, lemon juice, onion and Tabasco. Pour over fish pieces. Bake 25 minutes or until fish flakes easily with a fork.

Heat 2 tbsp (30 ml) butter in saucepan while fish is cooking. Sprinkle in flour, mustard, 1/4 tsp (1 ml) paprika and salt and stir to blend. Remove from heat and add wine, milk, chervil and tarragon. Stir to blend. Return to heat and cook until boiling, thickened and smooth, stirring constantly.

Beat egg yolks and cream together with a fork. Stir some of the hot mixture into the egg yolk mixture gradually, then stir into the remaining hot sauce. Cook gently 2 minutes, stirring.

Remove fish from oven when it is baked and turn on broiler.

Pour sauce over cooked fish. Sprinkle with paprika. Put under the broiler at least 5 inches (12.5 cm) from heat source until sauce bubbles and browns lightly. Serve immediately.

———————— SERVES 6 ————————

Barbecued Perch

1 lb	*frozen ocean perch fillets*	450 g
1/4 cup	*melted butter or margarine*	60 ml
1 tbsp	*lemon juice*	15 ml
2 tbsp	*ketchup*	30 ml
1 tsp	*Worcestershire sauce*	5 ml
1/8 tsp	*dry mustard*	0.5 ml
1/2 tsp	*salt*	2 ml
dash	*pepper*	dash
1 tbsp	*finely chopped onion*	15 ml
2 tbsp	*chopped parsley*	30 ml

Thaw fish just enough to separate pieces.

Heat broiler. Grease a shallow baking pan large enough to hold the pieces in a single layer. Lay fish pieces on pan, skin side down.

Combine all remaining ingredients and spoon mixture over fish. Broil about 3 inches (7.5 cm) from the heat (do not turn) until fish flakes easily with a fork, about 10 minutes. Serve immediately.

SERVES 3

Barbecued Perch

Halibut in Tomato Sauce

2	halibut steaks, about 12 oz (350 g) each	2
1/2 tsp	salt	2 ml
1/8 tsp	pepper	0.5 ml
1 tsp	lemon juice	5 ml
3 tbsp	olive oil	45 ml
2 large	tomatoes, peeled and chopped	2 large
1 medium	onion, chopped	1 medium
1 clove	garlic, crushed	1 clove
1/2 tsp	salt	2 ml
1 tsp	sugar	5 ml
1/4 cup	chopped parsley	60 ml
3 tbsp	tomato paste	45 ml
1/4 cup	sherry	60 ml
1/2 cup	water	125 ml
1/4 tsp	dried mint	1 ml
4 slices	lemon	4 slices
1 tbsp	butter	15 ml
	hot cooked rice	

Heat oven to 375 °F (190 °C). Grease a shallow baking dish just large enough to hold the halibut steaks in a single layer. Put the steaks in the dish and sprinkle with 1/2 tsp (2 ml) salt, pepper and lemon juice.

Heat olive oil in medium saucepan. Add tomatoes, onion and garlic and cook gently, stirring, until soft, about 5 minutes. Add 1/2 tsp (2 ml) salt, sugar, parsley, tomato paste, sherry, water and mint and simmer uncovered, 10 minutes.

Pour tomato mixture over fish. Lay lemon slices on fish. Dot with butter. Cover baking dish tightly with aluminum foil. Bake about 30 minutes or until fish flakes easily with a fork. Serve with rice.

SERVES 4

Cod à la Portuguese

2 lb	frozen cod fillets	900 g
	corn oil	
2 cups	peeled, seeded and finely chopped tomatoes	500 ml
1/2 cup	finely chopped onion	125 ml
1/4 cup	finely chopped green pepper	60 ml
1 tsp	salt	5 ml
1/8 tsp	black pepper	0.5 ml
1/2 tsp	dried leaf basil	2 ml
1/4 tsp	dried leaf thyme	1 ml
1/4 tsp	dried leaf tarragon	1 ml
1/4 cup	corn oil	60 ml

Thaw fish just until fillets can be separated.

Heat oven to 500 °F (260 °C). Lightly grease large baking dish with corn oil.

Combine tomatoes, onion, green pepper, salt, pepper, herbs and 1/4 cup (60 ml) corn oil in bowl.

Lay fish fillets in baking dish in a single layer if possible. Spread with tomato mixture. Bake 10 to 15 minutes or until fish flakes easily with a fork. Serve immediately.

SERVES 6

Halibut in Tomato Sauce

Salmon with Cucumber Stuffing

1/4 cup	*butter*	60 ml
1/2 cup	*finely chopped onion*	125 ml
1/2 cup	*finely chopped celery*	125 ml
3 cups	*soft bread crumbs*	750 ml
1 1/2 cups	*peeled, seeded and finely chopped cucumber*	375 ml
1 tsp	*salt*	5 ml
1/4 tsp	*pepper*	1 ml
1/2 tsp	*dill weed or seed*	2 ml
4-lb piece	*salmon*	1.8-kg piece
	salt and pepper	
1 tbsp	*cooking oil*	15 ml

Heat oven to 450 °F (230 °C). Butter a shallow baking dish large enough to hold the piece of salmon.

Heat butter in large skillet. Add onion and celery and cook gently until onion is limp but not brown, stirring. Add half of bread crumbs and continue cooking until crumbs brown very lightly, stirring. Add the remaining bread crumbs along with cucumber, 1 tsp (5 ml) salt, 1/4 tsp (1 ml) pepper and dill weed or seed.

Sprinkle inside of fish lightly with salt and pepper. Add stuffing and skewer opening closed. Lace tightly with string. Measure thickness of fish and stuffing. Put fish in prepared baking dish and drizzle with the oil. Put in oven and cook, allowing 10 minutes per inch of stuffed thickness. (Fish is done when it flakes easily with a fork — be sure to check at backbone.) Serve immediately.

SERVES 8

Salmon with Cucumber Stuffing

Sprinkle inside of fish lightly with salt and pepper. Add stuffing.

Skewer opening closed.

Lace tightly with string.

Salmon with Asparagus

2 lb	fresh asparagus	900 g
1/4 cup	butter, melted	60 ml
1/2 tsp	dried leaf basil	2 ml
1 tbsp	lemon juice	15 ml
4 3/4-inch	salmon steaks	4 1.75-cm
1 tbsp	butter	15 ml
1/2 cup	sliced mushrooms	125 ml
10-oz can	cream of mushroom soup	284-ml can
1/2 cup	milk	125 ml

Wash asparagus and break off tough ends. Put spears in a single layer in a large skillet and add 1/4 inch (0.5 cm) boiling water. Cover and cook until tender, 8 to 10 minutes. Drain and keep warm.

Combine 1/4 cup (60 ml) butter, basil and lemon juice in a small dish. Lay salmon steaks on greased broiler pan and brush with lemon-butter mixture. Put under hot broiler and broil until fish flakes easily with a fork, about 5 minutes a side.

Heat 1 tbsp (15 ml) butter in small saucepan while asparagus and fish are cooking. Add mushrooms, and cook gently 3 minutes, stirring. Add soup and milk and heat.

Put asparagus and salmon on serving plates and spoon mushroom mixture over the asparagus.

SERVES 4

Broiled Salmon Steaks

1/3 cup	salad oil	80 ml
1 1/2 tsp	grated lemon rind	7 ml
1/3 cup	lemon juice	80 ml
1 small clove	garlic, crushed	1 small clove
1 tsp	sugar	5 ml
1/4 tsp	pepper	1 ml
1 tsp	salt	5 ml
1/2 tsp	dried leaf oregano	2 ml
4 1-inch	salmon steaks	4 2.5-cm
1/3 cup	sliced stuffed olives (optional)	80 ml

→

Salmon Steaks with Crab Sauce

Combine oil, lemon rind, lemon juice, garlic, sugar, pepper, salt and oregano.

Grease rack of broiler pan very well. Lay salmon steaks on it and brush well with oil mixture. Put about 4 inches (7.5 cm) from the heat and broil about 5 minutes. Turn salmon steaks carefully, brush with oil mixture again and continue broiling 2 to 3 minutes or until salmon flakes easily with a fork.

Add sliced olives to remaining oil mixture if desired and heat just to boiling point. Serve over salmon.

———— SERVES 4 ————

2 cups	water	500 ml
2 thin slices	lemon	2 thin slices
1/4 tsp	salt	1 ml
1/2 tsp	dill seed	2 ml
small piece	bay leaf	small piece
6 3/4-inch	salmon steaks	6 1.75-cm
1/4 cup	cold water	60 ml
1 tbsp	cornstarch	15 ml
1/4 cup	commercial sour cream	60 ml
2 tbsp	butter	30 ml
dash	nutmeg	dash
1/4 cup	chopped parsley	60 ml
6-oz can	crab meat, drained and flaked	165-g can

Put water, lemon slices, salt, dill seed and bay leaf in large skillet. Bring to a boil. Add salmon steaks, cover and simmer about 5 minutes or until salmon flakes easily with a fork (check around backbone particularly). Lift salmon out of water carefully and put on hot platter. Keep hot in a warm oven.

Strain water salmon was cooked in and measure out 1 cup (250 ml). Put this liquid in a saucepan and bring to a boil. Combine cold water and cornstarch and stir until smooth. Stir this mixture into boiling fish liquid gradually. Boil until thick and clear. Remove from heat. Stir in sour cream, butter, nutmeg, parsley and crab meat. Heat but do not boil.

Serve the salmon topped with sauce.

———— SERVES 6 ————

Left: Broiled Salmon Steak
Right: Salmon Steaks with Crab Sauce and vegetable side-dish

Salmon Loaf with Egg Sauce

2 8-oz cans	pink salmon	2 227-g cans
2	eggs	2
1 cup	liquid (salmon liquid plus milk)	250 ml
1 tsp	salt	5 ml
1/4 tsp	sage	1 ml
1 cup	drained canned mixed peas and carrots	250 ml
2 cups	fine noodles, cooked	500 ml

Egg Sauce (recipe follows)

Heat oven to 350 °F (175 °C). Grease a 9- x 5- x 3-inch (23- x 12.5- x 7.5-cm) loaf pan.

Drain salmon, saving liquid. Pour liquid into measuring cup and add enough milk to make the 1 cup (250 ml) liquid called for. Flake salmon.

Beat eggs lightly. Stir in liquid, salt and sage. Add flaked salmon, mixed peas and carrots and noodles and blend lightly.

Pour mixture into prepared pan. Bake about 1 hour or until loaf is set. Turn out of pan onto hot serving platter. Cut in thick slices and top with egg sauce to serve.

Note: Use left over vegetables in place of canned if desired.

Egg Sauce

6 tbsp	butter or margarine	90 ml
6 tbsp	flour	90 ml
3/4 tsp	salt	3 ml
1/8 tsp	pepper	0.5 ml
1 1/2 cups	milk	375 ml
2	hard-cooked eggs, diced	2

Melt butter in saucepan. Sprinkle in flour, salt and pepper. Let bubble. Remove from heat and add milk all at once. Stir to blend and return to moderate heat. Cook until thick and smooth, stirring constantly. Add hard-cooked eggs and heat well.

SERVES 6

Salmon and Potato Casserole

4 cups	thinly sliced potatoes	1 L
8-oz can	salmon	225-g can
3 tbsp	butter	45 ml
1/4 cup	flour	60 ml
1 tsp	salt	5 ml
1/8 tsp	pepper	0.5 ml
2 cups	liquid (salmon liquid plus milk)	500 ml
2 tbsp	prepared mustard	30 ml
1 cup	thin slices onion	250 ml

Heat oven to 350 °F (175 °C). Butter 6-cup (1.5-L) casserole.

Cook sliced potatoes in boiling salted water 10 minutes. Drain immediately.

Drain salmon, saving liquid. Break salmon into bite-size pieces. Put liquid in cup and add enough milk to make the 2 cups (500 ml) liquid called for.

Heat butter in medium saucepan. Add flour, salt and pepper and stir to blend. Remove from heat and add the 2 cups (500 ml) liquid all at once. Stir to blend. Stir in mustard. Return to moderate heat and cook until boiling, thickened and smooth, stirring constantly. Turn heat to low and continue cooking and stirring 2 minutes longer.

Put a layer of 1/4 of the potatoes in the prepared casserole. Top with 1/3 of the salmon, 1/3 of the onions and about 1/4 of the sauce. Repeat these layers twice more and end with a final layer of potatoes and sauce.

Bake 45 minutes or until potatoes are tender and sauce is bubbling well.

———————————— SERVES 4 ————————————

Salmon and Potato Casserole

Tuna-Bean Macaroni

2 cups	macaroni	500 ml
2 1/2 cups	French-style green beans	685 ml
2 tbsp	French dressing	30 ml
7-oz can	tuna, drained	190-g can
10-oz can	mushroom pieces	284-ml can
1/4 cup	butter	60 ml
1/3 cup	finely chopped onion	80 ml
3 tbsp	flour	45 ml
1 1/2 tsp	salt	7 ml
1/4 tsp	pepper	1 ml
2 cups	liquid (mushroom liquid plus milk)	500 ml
1 cup	grated old cheddar cheese	250 ml

Heat oven to 375 °F (190 °C). Butter a 12- x 7- x 2-inch (30.5- x 18- x 5-cm) glass baking dish.

Cook macaroni in plenty of boiling salted water until just tender, about 7 minutes.

Cook beans in a small amount of water just until tender-crisp. Drain. Spread in prepared baking dish. Drizzle French dressing over. Break up tuna and spread pieces evenly over beans.

Drain mushrooms into a measuring cup. Set liquid aside. Heat butter in medium saucepan. Add mushroom pieces and onion and cook gently 3 minutes. Sprinkle in flour, salt and pepper and stir to blend. Remove from heat. Add enough milk to the mushroom liquid to make the 2 cups (500 ml) liquid called for. Add this liquid, all at once, to butter-flour mixture and stir to blend. Return to moderate heat and cook until boiling, thickened and smooth, stirring constantly. Stir 1/2 cup (125 ml) of the cheese and the cooked macaroni into this sauce and pour it all over the tuna layer in the baking dish. Sprinkle with the remaining 1/2 cup (125 ml) cheese.

Bake 20 minutes or until very hot.

SERVES 6

Tuna-Bean Macaroni

Cheese-Coated Smelts

1 lb	frozen smelts	450 g
1/4 cup	butter or margarine, melted	60 ml
1 clove	garlic, crushed	1 clove
1/4 cup	fine dry bread crumbs	60 ml
1/4 cup	grated Parmesan cheese	60 ml
1 tbsp	finely chopped parsley	15 ml
1/4 tsp	salt	1 ml

Thaw smelts and clean and bone if necessary (see following note). Wash and pat dry with paper towels.

Heat oven to 450 °F (230 °C). Grease a shallow baking pan about 12 x 7 x 2 inches (30.5 x 18 x 5 cm).

Combine melted butter or margarine and garlic in a flat dish. Combine bread crumbs, cheese, parsley and salt in another flat dish. Dip each fish in garlic butter then in bread crumb mixture to coat both sides. Put in prepared pan, skin side down. Bake about 8 minutes or until browned and fish flakes easily with a fork.

Note: Cleaning and boning smelts is easy. With kitchen shears cut off heads just below the gills. Trim off fins and tails. Slit fish open with shears and clean. Spread fish flat, skin side down, and loosen backbones at head end by slipping the tip of a small knife under them. Work fingers under the backbones and lift carefully to pull all bones away without tearing the fish. Cook them spread flat.

SERVES 3

189

Lobster Thermidor

4 small	cooked lobsters	4 small
1 tbsp	butter	15 ml
1 1/2 tsp	finely minced onion	7 ml
2 tbsp	flour	30 ml
1 1/2 cups	milk, scalded	375 ml
1/4 tsp	salt	1 ml
dash	white pepper	dash
sprig	parsley	sprig
pinch	nutmeg	pinch
1/3 cup	heavy cream	80 ml
2 tsp	lemon juice	10 ml
1 tbsp	dry sherry	15 ml
1 tsp	dry mustard	5 ml
pinch	cayenne	pinch
dash	Worcestershire sauce	dash
	salt and pepper	
1/4 cup	grated Parmesan cheese	60 ml
	paprika	
1/4 cup	soft butter	60 ml

Split lobsters in halves lengthwise. Remove claws. Lift meat out of bodies and claws and cut in large pieces. Keep body shells whole.

Melt butter in saucepan. Add onion and cook gently 3 minutes. Sprinkle in flour and cook and stir until golden. Remove from heat and stir in hot milk. Stir in 1/4 tsp (1 ml) salt, white pepper, parsley and nutmeg. Return to moderate heat and cook until mixture comes to a boil, stirring constantly. Turn heat to low and continue cooking 20 minutes, stirring often. Strain and return to saucepan.

Stir in heavy cream, lemon juice, sherry, mustard, cayenne and Worcestershire sauce. Taste and season with salt and pepper. Add lobster meat and heat.

Set lobster shells in shallow pan. Pile lobster mixture into them. Sprinkle evenly with Parmesan cheese, dust with paprika and dot with butter.

Slip under hot broiler and broil until golden brown. Serve immediately.

Note: This same recipe can be used with 2 large or 3 medium size lobsters.

SERVES 4

Lobster Thermidor

Seafood-Avocado Cocktail

6-oz can	lobster, broken up coarsely	165-ml can
4 1/2-oz can	small shrimp (cocktail size)	130-ml can
5-oz can	crab, flaked	140-ml can
3 3/4-oz can	tuna, broken up coarsely	110-ml can
2 tsp	capers	10 ml
2 tsp	chopped chives	10 ml
2 tsp	chopped parsley	10 ml
1/2 cup	commercial sour cream	125 ml
1/3 cup	mayonnaise	80 ml
1/4 tsp	dry mustard	1 ml
2 tsp	caper juice	10 ml

1/4 tsp	salt	1 ml
dash	pepper	dash
2 large	ripe avocados (or 4 small)	2 large
	lettuce	

Combine lobster, shrimp, crab, tuna, capers, chives and parsley in a bowl and toss together lightly with a fork. Blend sour cream, mayonnaise, mustard, caper juice, salt and pepper and add to seafood. Toss again lightly with a fork. Cover and chill well.

Serve over wedges of avocado set on lettuce or, if you have small avocados, fill a half for each serving.

SERVES 8

Stuffed Lobster Tails

12	frozen lobster tails	12
1 small slice	onion	1 small slice
1 small	carrot, cut up	1 small
1 stalk	celery (with leaves), cut up	1 stalk
2 sprigs	parsley	2 sprigs
small piece	bay leaf	small piece
2 tsp	salt	10 ml
4	peppercorns	4
3/4 cup	butter	180 ml
6 tbsp	flour	90 ml
1 1/2 tsp	salt	7 ml
1 1/2 tsp	paprika	7 ml
1/4 tsp	dried leaf tarragon	1 ml
dash	cayenne	dash
3 cups	light cream	750 ml
3 tbsp	lemon juice	45 ml
1/2 cup	grated Parmesan cheese	125 ml
1/2 cup	fine dry bread crumbs	125 ml
2 tbsp	melted butter	30 ml

Put frozen lobster tails in large kettle. Add onion slice, carrot, celery, parsley, bay leaf, 2 tsp (10 ml) salt and peppercorns. Add enough boiling water to completely cover the tails. Bring to a boil, turn down heat, cover and boil until tender. (Time varies with size of lobster tails. General rule is to cook them 1 minute per oz (30 g) plus 2 minutes when frozen, or 1 minute per oz (30 g) plus 1 minute if thawed first.) Drain and rinse quickly under cold running water.

Clip away the undershells with kitchen shears and pull the meat free from the shells with the fingers (do not discard shells — you will need them later). Chill lobster meat.

Dice lobster meat.

Heat 3/4 cup (180 ml) butter in large heavy skillet. Add pieces of lobster and cook gently 3 minutes, stirring. Sprinkle in flour, 1 1/2 tsp (7 ml) salt, paprika, tarragon and cayenne and stir to blend. Remove from heat and add cream all at once. Stir to blend well then return to moderate heat. Cook until boiling, thickened and smooth, stirring constantly. Stir in lemon juice. Remove from heat immediately.

Put shells in a shallow baking pan that will just hold them in a single layer (if you fit them in rather snugly they will support each other and won't tip over when you are filling them). Spoon the lobster mixture into the shells piling it up as high as possible. Cover pan with transparent wrap and refrigerate until shortly before serving time.

Heat oven to 350 °F (175 °C) soon enough to allow 30 minutes for heating lobster.

Combine cheese, bread crumbs and melted butter. Sprinkle mixture generously over tops of lobster tails. Heat about 30 minutes or until mixture in shells is bubbling and crumb mixture is brown. Serve immediately.

Note: If you want to complete the cooking when the tails are filled rather than refrigerating them, heat oven to 450 °F (230 °C). Sprinkle the hot filling with the crumb mixture and heat about 12 minutes or until crumb mixture is golden.

——————— SERVES 6 ———————

Seafood-Avocado Cocktail

Broiled Shrimp

2 lb	large raw shrimp	900 g
1/2 cup	olive oil	125 ml
1/2 tsp	salt	2 ml
1/4 tsp	pepper	1 ml
2 tbsp	finely chopped parsley	30 ml
pinch	dried leaf tarragon	pinch
1/4 cup	butter	60 ml
3 tbsp	lemon juice	45 ml
	hot cooked rice	

Shell and clean shrimp. Mix oil, salt, pepper, parsley and tarragon thoroughly in a small bowl. Dip shrimp in mixture to coat well. Lay on shallow metal baking pan.

Heat broiler. Slip shrimp under hot broiler and broil about 3 minutes a side or until cooked. Put shrimp on hot platter.

Heat butter and lemon juice together while shrimp are cooking. Add the oil mixture left in pan shrimp were cooked in. Heat well and pour over shrimp. Serve with rice.

SERVES 4 TO 6

Curried Shrimp and Egg Cocktail

3 tbsp	mayonnaise	45 ml
1/4 cup	natural yogurt	60 ml
2 tsp	curry powder	10 ml
1/4 cup	commercial chutney, chopped if necessary	60 ml
2 tsp	lemon juice	10 ml
1 tbsp	raisins	15 ml
1 lb	small frozen cooked shrimp, thawed	450 g
3	hard-cooked eggs, chopped	3
	iceberg lettuce	

Combine mayonnaise, yogurt, curry powder, chutney and lemon juice, stirring to blend well. Add remaining ingredients except lettuce. Blend and chill.

Shred enough lettuce to line the bottoms of 8 sherbet glasses or seafood cocktail glasses. Put the lettuce in the glasses at serving time and spoon in shrimp mixture. Serve immediately.

SERVES 8

Above: Broiled Shrimp
Below: Curried Shrimp and Egg Cocktail

Scallop Cocktail

1 lb	scallops	450 g
2/3 cup	dry white table wine	160 ml
1/3 cup	water	80 ml
2 sprigs	parsley	2 sprigs
1 small	onion, halved	1 small
1 tbsp	lemon juice	15 ml
1 tbsp	tarragon vinegar	15 ml
2	hard-cooked eggs	2
2 tbsp	Dijon mustard	30 ml
1/4 tsp	salt	1 ml
dash	white pepper	dash
1/4 tsp	dried leaf tarragon	1 ml
1/2 cup	olive oil	125 ml
	juice of 1/2 lemon	
1 1/2 tsp	chopped capers	7 ml
1 1/2 tsp	chopped parsley	7 ml
	lettuce	

Rinse scallops well under cold water.

Heat wine, water, parsley and onion to boiling. Add scallops and simmer 5 minutes. Drain. Cut any large scallops in half. Cool. Sprinkle with 1 tbsp lemon juice and tarragon vinegar. Cover and chill well, stirring occasionally.

Cut hard-cooked eggs in halves. Lift out yolks and press through a fine sieve. Add mustard, salt, pepper and tarragon. Add oil and lemon juice drop by drop, blending well. Stir in finely-chopped egg whites, capers and parsley.

Put scallops in sherbet glasses lined with lettuce. Spoon sauce over.

SERVES 4

Crab in Shrimp Sauce

1/4 lb	fresh raw shrimp	115 g
1 cup	boiling water	250 ml
small bunch	celery leaves	small bunch
2 sprigs	parsley	2 sprigs
3	peppercorns	3
2 tbsp	butter	30 ml
1 tbsp	finely chopped onion	15 ml
2 tbsp	flour	30 ml
3/4 cup	light cream	180 ml
3/4 cup	shrimp cooking liquid	180 ml
1 tsp	salt	5 ml
1/4 tsp	pepper	1 ml
pinch	tarragon	pinch
1 tsp	lemon juice	5 ml
1 1/2 cups	cooked crab	375 ml
1 tbsp	chopped parsley	15 ml
1 tbsp	butter	15 ml
	hot cooked rice	
	chopped parsley	

Put washed shrimp in small saucepan. Add boiling water, celery leaves, parsley sprigs and peppercorns. Bring to a boil, turn down heat, cover and simmer 5 minutes. Remove from heat and cool shrimp in liquid. Drain, saving liquid. Shell, clean and chop shrimp finely. Strain shrimp liquid and measure out the 3/4 cup (180 ml) needed for next step.

Melt 2 tbsp (30 ml) butter in saucepan. Add onion and cook gently 3 minutes, stirring. Sprinkle in flour and blend well. Remove from heat and add cream and shrimp cooking liquid all at once. Return to moderate heat and cook until boiling, thickened and smooth, stirring constantly. Turn heat to low and stir in salt, pepper, tarragon and lemon juice. Simmer 5 minutes, stirring often. Stir in chopped shrimp, crab, 1 tbsp (15 ml) parsley and 1 tbsp (15 ml) butter. Heat well.

Serve over hot rice, sprinkled with more chopped parsley.

SERVES 3 TO 4

Scallop Cocktail

Paella

3	whole chicken breasts	3
1/2 cup	olive oil	125 ml
2 cloves	garlic, slivered	2 cloves
1 large	green pepper, slivered	1 large
1/3 cup	finely chopped onion	80 ml
2 tsp	paprika	10 ml
1/2 tsp	pepper	2 ml
2 cups	regular long-grain rice	500 ml
12-oz pkg	frozen peas	350-g pkg
2 large	tomatoes, peeled and chopped coarsely	2 large
4 cups	chicken stock	1 L
1/4 tsp	saffron	1 ml
1 lb	raw shrimp, shelled and cleaned	450 g
16	clams (in the shell)	16
	chopped parsley	
	lemon wedges	

Have butcher cut each chicken breast in half, and each half, through the bone, into 4 pieces (24 small pieces).

Heat 1/4 cup (60 ml) of the olive oil in each of two 10-inch (25-cm) heavy iron skillets (see note below). Add half of chicken pieces to each and brown well. Add half of garlic, green pepper, onion, paprika and pepper to each pan. Stir to blend and cook gently 3 minutes. Remove from heat.

Add half of rice, peas and tomatoes to each pan. Bring chicken stock to a boil. Add saffron and stir until dissolved. Add half of stock to each pan. Cook 10 minutes over moderately high heat, uncovered. Do not stir.

Add shrimp, pushing down well into liquid. Lower heat, cover tightly and simmer 10 to 15 minutes more or until chicken and rice are tender.

Heat oven to 350 °F (175 °C).

Uncover skillets. Stir mixture lightly with a fork, put in oven and cook another 15 minutes or until almost all liquid is absorbed.

Scrub clam shells very well with a brush. Put in steamer or sieve over boiling water and cover tightly. Steam until shells open, about 10 minutes.

Sprinkle cooked paella with chopped parsley and top with steamed clams and lemon wedges.

Note: If you happen to have a paella pan use only the one pan for the whole recipe.

If fresh shrimp and clams are not available use 18 oz (510 g) of canned shrimp (drained and rinsed) and a 5-oz (140-g) can clams (drained). Add them for the last 15 minutes of cooking, pushing them well down into the rice mixture.

———————— SERVES 8 ————————

Paella

Broiled Scampi

1 1/2 lb	*fresh or thawed frozen scampi*	675 g
2 cloves	*garlic, crushed*	2 cloves
2 tsp	*salt*	10 ml
3/4 cup	*olive oil*	180 ml
1/4 cup	*finely chopped parsley*	60 ml
1/8 tsp	*dried leaf tarragon*	0.5 ml
2 tbsp	*lemon juice*	30 ml
	freshly ground black pepper	
3/4 cup	*butter, melted*	180 ml
1/2 cup	*fine dry bread crumbs*	125 ml

Wash scampi and cut away undershells with kitchen shears.

Heat broiler.

Add garlic, salt, oil, parsley, tarragon, lemon juice and a grating of pepper to melted butter. Dip each scampi into this mixture and then into bread crumbs. Put in a single layer on shallow baking pan, shell side down.

Broil low under the broiler 5 minutes, spooning a little of the remaining sauce over during broiling. Pour remaining sauce mixture into small individual dishes for dipping scampi meat. Serve immediately.

———————— SERVES 4 ————————

199

Curried Scallops

1 lb	frozen scallops, thawed	450 g
1/4 cup	fine dry bread crumbs	60 ml
1/4 tsp	salt	1 ml
3 tbsp	butter	45 ml
1 tsp	curry powder	5 ml
2 tsp	lemon juice	10 ml
4 thin slices	fresh lemon	4 thin slices

Heat oven to 450 °F (230 °C). Butter 4 large scallop shells or shallow individual baking dishes.

Rinse scallops under cold water and dry well on paper towelling. Combine bread crumbs and salt in a flat dish and roll each scallop in the mixture to coat with crumbs on all sides. Divide scallops evenly among the scallop shells or baking dishes, putting them in a single layer.

Melt butter in a small saucepan. Add curry powder and cook gently 2 minutes, stirring. Stir in lemon juice. Drizzle this mixture over the scallops. Lay a lemon slice on top of each serving. Bake 15 minutes or until scallops are tender. Serve immediately.

———— SERVES 4 AS AN APPETIZER ————

Scallops Sauté

1 1/2 lb	scallops	675 g
1/2 cup	chili sauce	125 ml
1/2 cup	ketchup	125 ml
1 tbsp	prepared horseradish	15 ml
1 tsp	Worcestershire sauce	5 ml
1 tbsp	lemon juice	15 ml
2 tsp	prepared mustard	10 ml
pinch	tarragon	pinch
2 tbsp	butter	30 ml
1 tbsp	cooking oil	15 ml
1 clove	garlic, peeled and cut in half	1 clove
	chopped parsley	

Wash scallops and dry well on paper towelling.

Mix chili sauce, ketchup, horseradish, Worcestershire sauce, lemon juice, mustard and pinch tarragon.

Heat butter, oil and garlic in large heavy skillet. Add scallops and cook quickly, stirring, until lightly browned and tender, about 5 minutes. Discard garlic. Pour chili sauce mixture over all and heat just to boiling point. Sprinkle generously with parsley. Good served with noodles.

———— SERVES 4 TO 6 ————

Above: Scallops Sauté
Below: Curried Scallops

Quick Coquilles St.Jacques

1 lb	scallops	450 g
2/3 cup	dry white table wine	160 ml
1/3 cup	water	80 ml
2 sprigs	parsley	2 sprigs
1 small	onion, cut in half	1 small
3 tbsp	butter	45 ml
1 cup	sliced fresh mushrooms	250 ml
1 tbsp	flour	15 ml
1/2 tsp	salt	2 ml
1/8 tsp	pepper	0.5 ml
2 tbsp	lemon juice	30 ml
10-oz can	cream of shrimp soup	284-ml can
1	egg yolk	1
1/3 cup	heavy cream	80 ml
1/4 cup	butter	60 ml
1 cup	1/4 -inch (0.5-cm) bread cubes	250 ml
1/2 cup	grated Parmesan cheese	125 ml
	paprika	

Rinse scallops. Heat wine, water, parsley and onion to boiling in saucepan. Add scallops and simmer 5 minutes. Drain, saving cooking water but discard parsley and onion. Cut scallops in halves if large.

Heat 3 tbsp (45 ml) butter in saucepan and add mushrooms. Cook gently 3 minutes. Sprinkle in flour, 1/2 tsp (2 ml) salt, 1/8 tsp (0.5 ml) pepper and let bubble. Remove from heat and add lemon juice and 1/2 cup (125 ml) of scallop cooking water all at once. Return to heat and cook gently, stirring until boiling and smooth.

Add undiluted shrimp soup and blend well.

Beat egg yolk and cream together with a fork. Stir into soup mixture. Add scallops and heat.

Melt 1/4 cup (60 ml) butter in skillet. Add bread cubes and heat, stirring until bread is golden brown. Remove from heat and mix in cheese lightly.

Pile scallop mixture into 6 scallop shells or individual serving dishes. Sprinkle with bread cubes-cheese mixture and then with paprika.

Put low under broiler (middle of the oven) and broil about 5 minutes or until heated through and browned (watch carefully so tops don't burn). Serve immediately.

——————— SERVES 6 ———————

202

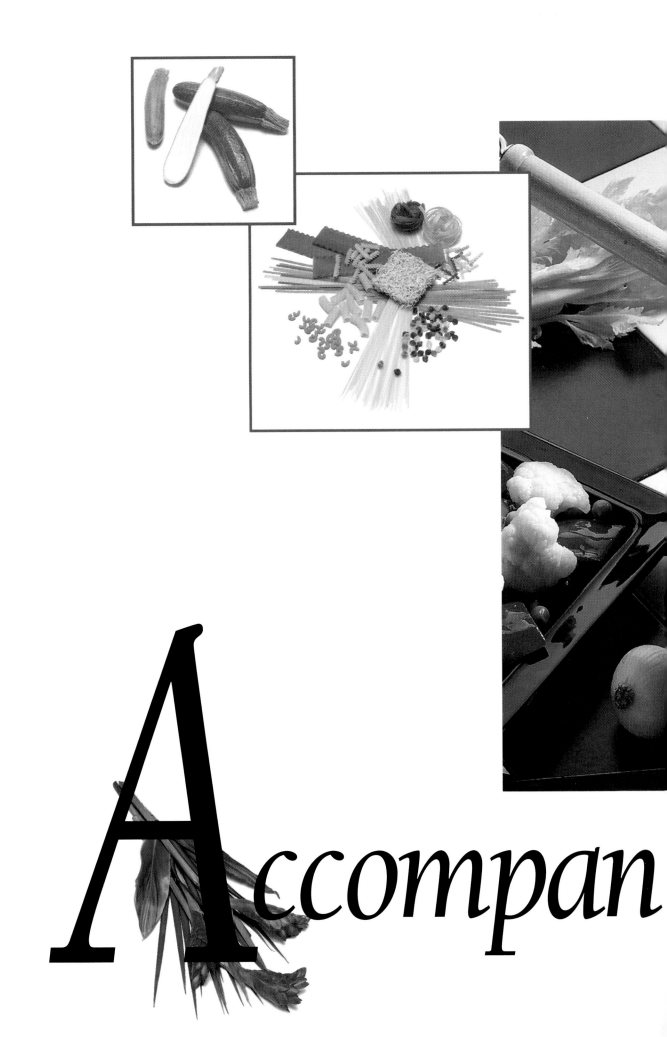

Accompan

nents

Accompaniments

Vegetables, Eggs, Pasta and Rice

In France, vegetables are often served as a separate course so they get the appreciation they deserve. That is because in France even the most humble vegetable is treated with respect and imagination. Like the French, we should highlight our beautiful vegetables. Today many are turning to vegetables as main dishes to reduce their intake of fats. Some have become semi-vegetarian by serving nutritious  vegetable casseroles using cheese or eggs for added protein. In this section I have included several vegetable recipes that can be served as main dishes, even complete meals.

Of course, vegetables must be cooked perfectly to retain their natural color, food value and texture. A good rule of thumb is if vegetables gain more vivid color in the cooking, you are on the right track, if they lose their vibrancy, they have been overcooked. Cook vegetables until tender crisp — no longer. And remember only a pinch of herbs, a touch of onion or a smidgen of brown sugar is enough to raise a vegetable out of the humdrum to the heights of elegance.

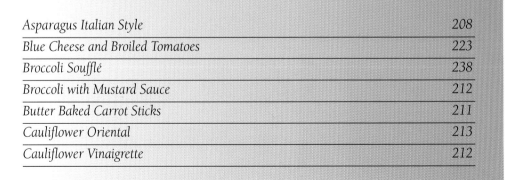

Less simple but simply delicious are the rice, pasta and egg dishes that complete this section. In many recipes they are combined with vegetables to a delightful effect.

Rice Stuffed Avocados

(vegetable or main dish)

2 tbsp	butter	30 ml
1/2 cup	regular rice	125 ml
1/4 cup	finely chopped onion	60 ml
1/4 cup	finely chopped celery	60 ml
1 cup	boiling chicken stock (see note)	250 ml
1/2 tsp	salt	2 ml
1	egg, beaten	1
1 cup	grated old cheddar cheese	250 ml
1/4 tsp	Worcestershire	1 ml
1/2 cup	chopped parsley	125 ml
3 medium	avocados	3 medium
1/2 cup	fine dry bread crumbs	125 ml
2 tbsp	melted butter	30 ml

Heat 2 tbsp (30 ml) butter in medium saucepan. Add rice and cook until rice is golden, stirring. Add onion and celery and continue cooking gently 3 minutes, stirring. Add chicken stock and salt, cover and simmer 20 minutes or until rice is tender (if rice is still very moist cook with cover off for a few minutes). Remove from heat. Stir egg, cheese and Worcestershire sauce together with a fork and mix into rice along with parsley.

Heat oven to 350 °F (175 °C).

Cut avocados in half, remove stones and put avocado halves in a shallow baking pan. Add 1/4 inch (0.5 cm) hot water to pan. Spoon rice mixture into hollows in avocados. Combine bread crumbs and melted butter and sprinkle over rice mixture. Bake 20 minutes or until crumbs are browned and avocados are hot. Good served with chicken.

Note: Replace chicken stock with 1 chicken bouillon cube dissolved in 1 cup (250 ml) water if desired.

———————— SERVES 6 ————————

Asparagus Italian Style

8 oz	fine noodles	225 g
1 small clove	garlic, peeled	1 small clove
1 lb	fresh asparagus	450 g
3 tbsp	cooking oil	45 ml
5-oz can	sliced mushrooms, drained	142-ml can
1/2 tsp	salt	2 ml
1/4 cup	grated Romano cheese	60 ml

Fill a large saucepan with boiling salted water. Add noodles. Stick a toothpick in the clove of garlic and add (the toothpick will help you find the garlic when you want to discard it). Cook the noodles as directed on the package or for about 5 minutes. Drain. Discard clove of garlic and rinse noodles under cold water.

Wash asparagus and snap off tough ends. Cut stalks into 1/2-inch (1.25-cm) slices on the diagonal. Leave tips whole.

Heat oil in large heavy skillet. Add asparagus, cover and cook over medium heat, shaking the pan often, 5 to 8 minutes or until asparagus is tender-crisp. Add noodles and mushrooms. Toss together with a fork over moderate heat until everything is hot. Sprinkle with salt and cheese. Serve immediately. Good with fried chicken.

———————— SERVES 4 ————————

Above: Rice Stuffed Avocado
Below: Asparagus Italian Style

*Green Beans with Almonds
and Butter Baked Carrot Sticks*

Green Beans with Almonds

1/4 cup	butter or margarine	60 ml
1/2 cup	slivered blanched almonds	125 ml
1/2 tsp	salt	2 ml
2 tsp	lemon juice	10 ml
1 1/2 lb	frozen French-style green beans	675 g

Heat butter or margarine in heavy saucepan or skillet. Add almonds and cook slowly until golden, stirring often. Remove from heat and stir in salt and lemon juice.

Cook beans as directed on package. Drain. Pour almond mixture over beans. Serve immediately.

SERVES 6

Zesty Carrot Strips

1 lb	carrots (about 6 medium)	450 g
1/2 cup	water	125 ml
1 cube	chicken bouillon	1 cube
1/4 cup	butter	60 ml
3 medium	onions, sliced	3 medium
1 tbsp	flour	15 ml
1/2 tsp	salt	2 ml
dash	pepper	dash
pinch	sugar	pinch
1/4 tsp	dried leaf thyme	1 ml
3/4 cup	water	180 ml

Peel carrots and cut into thin strips 2 inches (5 cm) long.

Heat 1/2 cup (125 ml) water to boiling in medium saucepan and add bouillon cube. Stir until cube is dissolved. Add carrots and cook 10 minutes, covered. Do not drain.

Heat butter in skillet while carrots are cooking. Add onions and cook 5 minutes, covered, shaking the pan so onions don't stick. Remove cover and stir in flour, salt, pepper, sugar and thyme. Remove from heat and add 3/4 cup (180 ml) water all at once. Return to moderate heat and cook until boiling, thickened and smooth, stirring constantly. Add carrots and their cooking liquid and simmer, uncovered, until carrots are tender, about 5 minutes.

——————— SERVES 4 TO 6 ———————

Butter Baked Carrot Sticks

1 lb	carrots	450 g
2 tsp	sugar	10 ml
1 tsp	salt	5 ml
1/8 tsp	pepper	0.5 ml
2 tsp	snipped fresh dill	10 ml
1/4 cup	butter or margarine	60 ml

Heat oven to 400 °F (205 °C). Butter a shallow baking dish about 10 x 6 x 2 inches (25 x 15 x 5 cm).

Scrape or peel carrots and cut into sticks about 2 inches long (3.75 cm). Put in baking dish. Sprinkle with sugar, salt, pepper and dill. Dot with butter or margarine. Cover (use foil if pan has no cover).

Bake about 30 minutes or until carrots are tender.

——————— SERVES 4 ———————

Cauliflower Vinaigrette

1 medium	cauliflower	1 medium
2	green peppers, cut in strips lengthwise	2
2	tomatoes, peeled and cut in one-sixths	2
1/4 cup	wine vinegar	60 ml
3/4 cup	olive oil	80 ml
1 tsp	salt	5 ml
1/8 tsp	pepper	0.5 ml
1 tsp	paprika	5 ml
2 tbsp	chopped stuffed olives	30 ml
1 tbsp	sweet pickle relish	15 ml
2	green onions, chopped	2
	lettuce	

Break cauliflower into small florets. Cook, covered, in a small amount of boiling water 3 minutes. Add strips of green pepper and continue cooking just until vegetables are tender-crisp, about 5 minutes more. Drain.

Put hot vegetables in a shallow glass dish. Add tomatoes.

Combine vinegar, oil, salt, pepper, paprika, olives, relish and onions in a small jar with a tight lid and shake until well blended. Pour over vegetables. Cool, stirring gently 2 or 3 times. Cover with transparent wrap and chill until serving time.

Lift out of oil mixture with a slotted spoon at serving time and serve on lettuce as a salad.

—————— SERVES 4 ——————

Broccoli with Mustard Sauce

1/4 cup	butter	60 ml
1 tbsp	finely chopped onion	15 ml
1/4 cup	flour	60 ml
3/4 cup	milk	80 ml
3/4 cup	chicken stock	80 ml
1 1/2 tbsp	lemon juice	22 ml
1 tbsp	Dijon mustard	15 ml
1 tsp	sugar	5 ml
1/2 tsp	salt	2 ml
3 lb	broccoli	1.4 kg

Melt butter in medium saucepan. Add onion and cook gently 3 minutes, stirring. Add flour and stir to blend. Remove from heat and add milk and chicken stock all at once. Stir to blend. Return to moderate heat and cook until boiling, thickened and smooth, stirring constantly. Stir in lemon juice, mustard, sugar and salt. Keep hot. (If you are making the sauce ahead of time set it over hot water.)

Cook broccoli in a little boiling salted water until just tender. Serve immediately with mustard sauce spooned over.

—————— SERVES 8 ——————

Left: Cauliflower Oriental
Right: Broccoli with Mustard Sauce

Cauliflower Oriental

1 medium	cauliflower	1 medium
2 tbsp	butter	30 ml
1 medium	onion, finely chopped	1 medium
1/2 cup	chopped celery	125 ml
1 cube	chicken bouillon	1 cube
1 cup	hot water	250 ml
1/4 cup	cold water	60 ml
1 tbsp	cornstarch	15 ml
1 tbsp	soya sauce	15 ml
2 tbsp	finely chopped parsley	30 ml

Wash cauliflower and break into florets. Drop into boiling salted water and cook until just tender, about 10 minutes.

Heat butter in saucepan while cauliflower is cooking. Add onion and celery and cook gently 5 minutes, stirring. Add bouillon cube and hot water and bring to a boil. Combine cold water, cornstarch and soya sauce, stirring until smooth and stir into boiling liquid gradually. Boil 1 minute. Stir in parsley.

Put cauliflower in serving dish, pour sauce over and serve.

SERVES 4

Turnip Casserole

(vegetable or main dish)

2 tbsp	butter	30 ml
1 1/2 cups	chopped green pepper	375 ml
1 1/2 tbsp	finely chopped onion	22 ml
1 tbsp	flour	15 ml
1 tsp	salt	5 ml
1/4 tsp	pepper	1 ml
1/2 cup	chili sauce	125 ml
1/4 cup	water	60 ml
4 cups	3/4-inch (2-cm) cubes turnip, cooked	1 L
1/2 cup	grated Gruyère cheese	125 ml

Heat oven to 350 °F (175 °C). Butter a 8-cup (2-L) casserole.

Heat 2 tbsp (30 ml) butter in medium saucepan. Add green pepper and onion and cook gently until onion is very lightly browned, stirring. Sprinkle in flour, salt and pepper and stir to blend. Remove from heat and add chili sauce and water. Stir to blend. Return to moderate heat and cook until thickened, stirring constantly. Stir in cooked turnip. Pour into prepared casserole. Sprinkle with cheese.

Bake about 20 minutes or until cheese is melted and mixture is very hot.

———— SERVES 6 ————

Fried Onion Rings in Batter

2 medium	Spanish onions	2 medium
1 cup	milk	250 ml
1/2 tsp	salt	2 ml
	fat for deep frying	
1 cup	sifted all-purpose flour	250 ml
1/2 tsp	salt	2 ml
1/2 tsp	paprika	2 ml
1/2 tsp	dried leaf marjoram	2 ml
2/3 cup	water	160 ml
2 tbsp	olive oil	30 ml
1	egg white	1

→

Creamed Onions

Peel onions and cut into thick slices. Separate the slices into rings.

Combine milk and 1/2 tsp (2 ml) salt in a glass baking pan. Add onion rings and let stand at least 30 minutes, turning rings over in milk often.

Heat fat for deep frying.

Sift flour, 1/2 tsp (2 ml) salt and paprika into a bowl. Add marjoram. Add water and beat until smooth. Beat in oil. Beat egg white until stiff but not dry and fold into batter.

Dip onion rings in batter a few at a time, shaking each one to remove excess batter. Fry a few at a time in hot fat until nicely browned, about 2 minutes. Drain on paper towelling and sprinkle with salt. Serve hot.

———————— SERVES 4 ————————

2 lb	small onions (26 to 32 depending on size)	900 g
2 tbsp	butter or margarine	30 ml
2 tbsp	flour	30 ml
1/2 tsp	salt	2 ml
dash	pepper	dash
1/4 tsp	dried leaf savory	1 ml
dash	paprika	dash
1 1/2 cups	milk	375 ml
1/2 cup	coarsely chopped salted peanuts	125 ml
1/3 cup	fine dry bread crumbs	80 ml
2 tbsp	melted butter or margarine	30 ml

Cook peeled onions in boiling, lightly salted water until just tender, about 10 minutes. Drain, saving 1/2 cup (125 ml) of the cooking liquid.

Heat oven to 375 °F (190 °C). Butter a 8-cup (2-L) casserole.

Melt 2 tbsp (30 ml) butter or margarine in saucepan. Sprinkle in flour, salt, pepper, savory and paprika and stir to blend. Remove from heat and add milk and the 1/2 cup (125 ml) onion cooking water. Stir to blend. Return to moderate heat and cook and stir until boiling, thickened and smooth. Stir in peanuts.

Put onions in prepared casserole. Pour sauce over and stir lightly with a fork.

Combine crumbs and melted butter or margarine and sprinkle over onion mixture. Bake about 20 minutes or until bubbling well.

———————— SERVES 6 ————————

Left: Turnip Casserole
Right: Creamed Onions

Crispy Celery Casserole

(vegetable or main dish)

3 cups	sliced celery, cut 1/4 inch (0.5 cm) thick	750 ml
1/2 cup	boiling water	125 ml
1/4 tsp	salt	1 ml
1/4 cup	butter or margarine	60 ml
5-oz can	water chestnuts, sliced	142-ml can
10-oz can	cream of chicken soup	284-ml can
1/4 tsp	salt	1 ml
dash	pepper	dash
5 oz can	Chinese noodles	142 ml can

Heat oven to 400 °F (205 °C). Butter a 1 1/2-qt (2-L) casserole.

Cook celery in boiling water, with 1/4 tsp (1 ml) salt added, just until tender-crisp, about 10 minutes. Remove from heat. Do not drain. Add butter or margarine, water chestnuts, soup, 1/4 tsp (1 ml) salt and pepper to celery. Mix lightly to blend.

Put a layer of 1/3 of the Chinese noodles in the prepared casserole. Top with half of celery mixture. Repeat these layers and end with a layer of noodles. Bake 10 minutes, covered. Uncover and continue baking 5 minutes more or until bubbling.

———— SERVES 4 ————

Scalloped Parsnips

1 1/2 lb	parsnips	675 g
3 tbsp	butter	45 ml
1/4 cup	chopped onion	60 ml
3 tbsp	flour	45 ml
1/2 tsp	salt	2 ml
dash	pepper	dash
1 tsp	sugar	5 ml
1/4 tsp	dried leaf basil	1 ml
1 1/2 cups	tomato juice	375 ml
1/4 cup	fine dry bread crumbs	60 ml
1 tbsp	melted butter	15 ml

Peel parsnips and cut into 1/2-inch (1.25-cm) cubes. Cook in boiling salted water until tender. Drain.

Heat oven to 400 °F (205 °C). Butter a 1 1/2-qt (2-L) casserole.

Melt 3 tbsp (45 ml) butter in medium saucepan. Add onion and cook gently 3 minutes, stirring. Sprinkle in flour, salt, pepper, sugar and basil and stir to blend. Remove from heat and add tomato juice all at once. Stir to blend and return to heat. Cook until boiling, thickened and smooth, stirring constantly.

Put parsnips in prepared baking dish. Pour tomato mixture over and mix lightly with a fork. Combine bread crumbs and 1 tbsp (15 ml) melted butter and sprinkle over top. Bake about 15 minutes or until bubbling well.

———— SERVES 6 ————

Creamed Peas

Creamed Peas

2 tbsp	butter	30 ml
2 tbsp	chopped green onion	30 ml
1 tbsp	flour	15 ml
1 tsp	sugar	5 ml
pinch	dried leaf thyme	pinch
pinch	nutmeg	pinch
1/2 tsp	salt	2 ml
dash	pepper	dash
3/4 cup	milk	180 ml
24-oz pkg	frozen peas	675-g pkg

Melt butter in a small saucepan. Add onion and cook gently 5 minutes, stirring. Sprinkle in flour, sugar, thyme, nutmeg, salt and pepper. Stir to blend and remove from heat. Add milk all at once. Stir to blend and return to moderate heat. Cook until boiling, thickened and smooth, stirring constantly. Turn heat to low and continue cooking 10 minutes, stirring occasionally.

Cook peas in a little boiling salted water just until tender-crisp. Drain. Stir in hot sauce. Serve immediately. If you must hold the peas for a little while, keep them hot by putting them over hot water in a double boiler.

SERVES 8

Swiss Style Potato Cake

Cheesy Potatoes

(for the barbecue)

4 slices	bacon	4 slices
3 large	baking potatoes	3 large
1 large	onion, sliced	1 large
1 cup	1/2-inch (1.25-cm) cubes processed cheese	250 ml
3/4 tsp	salt	3 ml
1/4 tsp	pepper	1 ml
1/2 tsp	dried leaf chervil	2 ml
2 tbsp	butter or margarine	30 ml
1 tbsp	bacon fat	15 ml

Fry bacon until crisp. Drain on paper towelling and crumble. Peel and slice potatoes onto a large piece of doubled heavy-duty aluminum foil. Add onion separated into rings. Add bacon bits, cheese, salt, pepper and chervil and toss all together lightly. Dot with butter or margarine and drizzle bacon fat over all. Wrap foil loosely around the potatoes, making double folds to seal well. Cook about 4 inches (10 cm) from hot coals for 1 hour or until tender, turning the package often.

Note: Bake in oven at 400 °F (205 °C) for about the same time, if desired.

SERVES 4

Swiss Style Potato Cake

(main dish)

9 medium	potatoes	9 medium
1 1/2 tsp	salt	7 ml
4 slices	bacon, diced	4 slices
1/4 cup	chopped onion	60 ml
1/4 cup	chopped green pepper (optional)	60 ml
1/3 cup	cooking oil (approx.)	80 ml
1/4 cup	butter (approx.)	60 ml

Scrub potatoes (do not peel) and put them in a large saucepan. Add enough boiling water to cover completely. Bring to a boil and boil hard for 10 minutes or until the point of a knife can be stuck into them about 1 inch before it hits a firm centre. Drain immediately and cool until they can be handled. Peel potatoes and put them in a bowl. Cover with transparent wrap and chill 1 hour.

Grate potatoes just before cooking time. Use the fine grater and grate them into shreds that are as long as possible. Add salt and toss gently with a fork.

Fry bacon bits in a small skillet until transparent. Add onion and green pepper and continue frying until vegetables are limp, stirring. Remove from heat.

Heat 3 tbsp (45 ml) of the oil and 2 tbsp (30 ml) of the butter in a 10-inch (25-cm) heavy iron skillet. Add half of the potatoes. Press down firmly with the back of an egg turner. Spread the bacon mixture over this layer of potatoes to within 1 inch (2.5 cm) of the edge. Add remaining potatoes and spread them evenly. Pack them down firmly around the edges and press with the back of the egg turner as before.

Cook over moderately high heat until very well browned on the underside, 8 to 10 minutes. Lay a large flat plate or cookie sheet over the skillet. Invert the plate or cookie sheet and the skillet, holding them firmly together.

Return skillet to heat and add more oil and butter (I find I have to use the same amount as the first time — 3 tbsp (45 ml) oil and 2 tbsp (30 ml) butter. Heat well. Slide the potato cake carefully off the plate or cookie sheet back into the pan, browned side up. Press down firmly again. Continue cooking until well browned and crisp around the edges, about 8 minutes.

Invert on a large hot serving plate, cut into wedges and serve immediately.

SERVES 6 TO 8

Curried Squash

2 medium	acorn or butternut squash	2 medium
	salt and pepper	
2 tbsp	butter	30 ml
1/2 tsp	curry powder	2 ml
1 1/2 tsp	flour	7 ml
1 cup	light cream	250 ml

Heat oven to 375 °F (190 °C). Butter a 12- x 7- x 2-inch (30.5- x 18- x 5-cm) baking dish.

Cut squash into slices lengthwise. Remove seeds and peel. Drop pieces into lightly salted boiling water and cook until almost tender, 5 to 10 minutes. Drain and put pieces in a single layer in prepared baking dish. Sprinkle lightly with salt and pepper.

Heat butter in saucepan. Add curry powder and cook gently 2 minutes, stirring. Sprinkle in flour and stir to blend. Remove from heat and add cream all at once. Add 1/4 tsp (1 ml) salt and dash pepper and stir to blend. Return to moderate heat and cook until boiling, thickened and smooth, stirring constantly. Pour over squash pieces.

Heat in oven 10 to 15 minutes or just until bubbling.

SERVES 4

Glazed Squash

(for the barbecue)

1	acorn squash	1
1/4 cup	butter or margarine	60 ml
1/4 cup	brown sugar, packed	60 ml
1/4 tsp	nutmeg	1 ml
1/2 tsp	salt	2 ml
1/8 tsp	pepper	0.5 ml

Cut squash lengthwise into strips about 1/2 inch (1.25 cm) thick. Peel each strip. Put the squash pieces on a large piece of doubled heavy-duty aluminum foil. Melt butter or margarine and stir in remaining ingredients. Pour over squash and wrap the foil loosely around the vegetable, making double folds to seal well. Cook about 4 inches (10 cm) from hot coals for 45 minutes or until tender, turning the package halfway through cooking.

Note: Bake in oven at 400 °F (205 °C) for about 1 hour, if desired.

SERVES 2

Left: Glazed Squash
Right: Curried Squash

Stewed Tomatoes with Yogurt

4 large	tomatoes, peeled	4 large
2 tbsp	butter	30 ml
1 tsp	mustard seeds	5 ml
2 tbsp	finely chopped green onions	30 ml
3 tbsp	finely chopped green pepper	45 ml
1/2 tsp	salt	2 ml
1/8 tsp	pepper	0.5 ml
1/3 cup	plain yogurt	80 ml

Cut tomatoes into quarters and scrape out seeds. Chop pulp into fairly small pieces.

Heat butter in medium-size skillet. Add mustard seeds and heat and stir until butter browns lightly and seeds begin to pop. Add tomato pieces, onions and green pepper. Simmer 10 minutes, uncovered. Add salt and pepper. Stir in yogourt. Serve immediately.

———————— SERVES 4 ————————

Blue Cheese Broiled Tomatoes

4 large	tomatoes	4 large
1 tsp	sugar	5 ml
1/2 tsp	dried leaf basil	2 ml
1/4 tsp	salt	1 ml
dash	pepper	dash
1 cup	soft bread crumbs	250 ml
2 tbsp	melted butter	30 ml
1/4 cup	crumbled blue cheese	60 ml

Cut stem ends off tomatoes and cut each tomato into 2 thick slices. Put on broiler rack.

Combine sugar, basil, salt and pepper and sprinkle little of mixture on each tomato slice. Slip under hot broiler and broil 2 minutes.

Add bread crumbs to melted butter and toss lightly with a fork. Add blue cheese and toss again lightly. Spoon on tomato slices and slip under broiler until crumbs are nicely browned, about 1 minute. Serve immediately.

———————— SERVES 4 ————————

Above: Stewed Tomatoes with Yogurt
Below: Blue Cheese Broiled Tomatoes

Stuffed Zucchini

(vegetable or main dish)

6 small	zucchini	6 small
1 cup	small soft bread cubes	250 ml
1/2 cup	finely chopped cooked spinach	125 ml
1 tbsp	finely chopped onion	15 ml
2	eggs, lightly beaten	2
2 tbsp	cooking oil	30 ml
1/2 tsp	salt	2 ml
1/4 tsp	pepper	1 ml
1/4 tsp	paprika	1 ml
1/4 tsp	dried leaf thyme	1 ml
dash	garlic salt	dash

Heat oven to 350 °F (175 °C). Butter a shallow baking dish, about 12 x 7 1/2 x 2 inches (30.5 x 19 x 5 cm).

Wash zucchini and cut off ends. Drop (whole) into boiling, salted water and boil 5 minutes. Drain and cool until they can be handled.

Cut zucchini in half lengthwise and scrape out pulp, leaving a "wall" about 1/4 inch (0.5 cm) thick to hold filling. Chop pulp finely and combine with all remaining ingredients. Pile back into zucchini shells. Put in prepared baking dish and bake about 30 minutes or until zucchini is tender.

SERVES 6

Best Mustard Pickles

4 cups	tiny silver onions	1 L
24 small	cucumbers, 3 to 4 inches (7.5 to 10 cm) long	24 small
1 medium	cauliflower	1 medium
1	sweet red pepper	1
8 cups	cold water	2 L
1 cup	pickling salt	250 ml
pinch	alum	pinch
2 1/2 cups	sugar	625 ml
1/2 cup	flour	125 ml
1/2 cup	dry mustard	125 ml
2 tbsp	turmeric	30 ml
2 tbsp	celery seed	30 ml
5 cups	cider vinegar	1.25 L

Peel onions. Wash cucumbers well and cut into slices about 1/4 inch (0.5 cm) thick. Separate cauliflower into bite-size pieces. Cut red pepper into short strips.

Measure cold water into a large bowl. Add the salt and alum and stir until salt is dissolved. Add vegetables. Let stand overnight. Drain very well.

Combine sugar, flour, mustard, turmeric and celery seed in a large kettle. Stir until very well blended. Blend in vinegar gradually, stirring until smooth. Set over moderate heat and cook until boiling, thickened and smooth, stirring constantly. Add vegetables and heat over moderate heat 15 minutes, stirring occasionally.

Ladle into hot sterilized jars. Seal.

MAKES ABOUT 8 CUPS (2 L)

Zucchini and Onions

(for the barbecue)

3 medium	zucchini	3 medium
2 medium	onions, sliced very thin	2 medium
1 envelope	Italian salad dressing mix	1 envelope
2 tbsp	wine vinegar	30 ml
1/4 cup	salad oil	60 ml
2 tbsp	grated Parmesan cheese	30 ml

Slice zucchini 1/4 inch (0.5 cm) thick onto a large piece of doubled heavy-duty aluminum foil. Add onions. Turn up edges of foil slightly.

Combine salad dressing mix, vinegar and oil and pour over vegetables. Sprinkle with cheese.

Wrap loosely, sealing the foil with double folds. Cook about 4 inches (10 cm) from hot coals for 25 minutes or until tender, turning package halfway through cooking.

Note: Bake in oven at 400 °F (205 °C) for about 40 minutes, if preferred.

SERVES 3

Stuffed Zucchini

Soybean-Vegetable Casserole

(main dish)

1 cup	dried soybeans	250 ml
4 cups	cold water	1 L
1 tsp	salt	5 ml
12-oz can	whole kernel corn	341-ml can
19-oz can	tomatoes	540-ml can
2 tbsp	flour	30 ml
1 tsp	sugar	5 ml
1 tsp	garlic salt	5 ml
1/4 tsp	dried leaf basil	1 ml
1/8 tsp	pepper	0.5 ml
1 cup	1/4-inch (0.5-cm) bread cubes	250 ml
2 tbsp	melted butter	30 ml
1/2 cup	grated old cheddar cheese	125 ml

Wash beans. Soak overnight in cold water to cover (see note).

Put beans, soaking water and salt into large saucepan. Bring to a boil, turn down heat, cover and simmer until tender, 2 to 3 hours. Add water if necessary during cooking. Drain.

Heat oven to 375 °F (190 °C). Butter a 1 1/2-qt (2-L) casserole.

Combine beans and corn and put in prepared casserole. Put 2 tbsp (30 ml) of the liquid from the tomatoes in a small dish. Put remaining tomatoes in medium saucepan. Heat to boiling.

Add flour, sugar, garlic salt, basil and pepper to the 2 tbsp (30 ml) tomato liquid and stir until smooth. Stir into boiling tomatoes. Bring back to a boil, stirring constantly. Pour over beans and corn. Stir lightly to blend.

Add bread cubes to melted butter and stir lightly with a fork to coat bread cubes with butter. Add cheese and toss with fork to blend. Sprinkle mixture over top of casserole.

Bake about 30 minutes or until bread cubes are browned and sauce is bubbling.

Note: To soak beans quickly, boil 2 minutes, remove from heat and let stand 1 hour.

SERVES 4 TO 6

Red, White and Green Vegetable Mélange

(vegetable or main dish)

1 large	sweet red pepper	1 large
1 tbsp	olive oil	15 ml
2 cups	small cauliflower florets	500 ml
10-oz pkg	frozen peas	280-g pkg
1/2 cup	water	125 ml
1/2 tsp	salt	2 ml
1/4 tsp	pepper	1 ml
1/4 tsp	ground cumin seed	1 ml

Cut red pepper into 1-inch (2.5-cm) squares.

Heat oil in large heavy skillet. Add red pepper, cauliflower, peas (unthawed), water, salt, pepper and cumin. Cover tightly and cook over high heat, shaking the pan often, until cauliflower is just tender, about 8 minutes.

——— SERVES 4 TO 6 ———

Stir Fried Vegetables

(vegetable or main dish)

4 large stalks	celery	4 large stalks
2 medium	onion	2 medium
1/2 large	green pepper	1/2 large
2 tbsp	water	30 ml
1 tsp	cornstarch	5 ml
2 tbsp	peanut oil	30 ml
1/2 tsp	salt	2 ml
2 tsp	soya sauce	10 ml
1/4 cup	water	60 ml

Cut celery in 1/4-inch (0.5-cm) slices on diagonal. Cut onions in half lengthwise and lay on board, cut side down. Slice paper thin lengthwise. Cut pepper into thin strips lengthwise. Mix 2 tbsp (30 ml) water and cornstarch, blending until smooth.

Heat oil in large heavy skillet or wok until very hot. Sprinkle in salt. Add celery and cook over high heat 30 seconds, stirring constantly. Add onions and cook and stir 30 seconds. Add green pepper and cook and stir another 30 seconds. Add soya sauce and 1/4 cup (60 ml) water. Cover, turn heat to medium and simmer 2 minutes. Move vegetables to one side of pan and stir enough of the cornstarch mixture into boiling liquid to make a sauce thick enough to cling to the vegetables. Stir all together and serve immediately.

Note: This is a good basic way of cooking any vegetable or combination of vegetables. Double recipe if main dish.

——— SERVES 2 TO 3 ———

Left: Stir Fried Vegetables
Right: Red, White and Green Vegetable Mélange

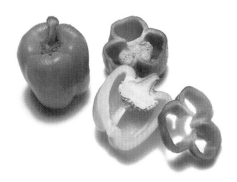

Rice and Peppers

(vegetable or main dish)

1/4 cup	cooking oil	60 ml
1 cup	regular long-grain rice	250 ml
2 large	green peppers, seeded and cut in 1-inch (2.5-cm) squares	2 large
1 medium	onion, chopped	1 medium
19-oz can	tomato juice	540-ml can
1/2 cup	ketchup	125 ml
1 tsp	salt	5 ml
1/4 tsp	pepper	1 ml

Heat oven to 350 °F (175 °C). Grease a 1 1/2-qt (2-L) casserole.

Heat oil in medium saucepan. Add rice. Cook over moderate heat until rice is golden, stirring. Add pepper pieces and onion and cook gently 1 minute. Stir in all remaining ingredients. Heat to boiling. Pour into prepared casserole. Cover and bake about 45 minutes or until liquid is absorbed and rice is tender. Especially good served with chicken, fish or veal.

—————— SERVES 6 ——————

Herbed Rice

1/4 cup	butter	60 ml
1/2 cup	chopped onion	125 ml
1 1/2 cups	regular long-grain rice	375 ml
1 1/4 cups	chicken stock	300 ml
2 1/2 cups	water	625 ml
1/8 tsp	dried leaf thyme	0.5 ml
1/8 tsp	dried leaf marjoram	0.5 ml
2 tsp	salt	10 ml
1/8 tsp	pepper	0.5 ml
1/2 cup	slivered toasted almonds	125 ml

Heat butter in a large saucepan. Add onion and cook gently 3 minutes, stirring. Add rice and continue cooking and stirring until rice is golden brown.

Heat chicken stock and water to boiling. Add to rice mixture along with thyme, marjoram, salt and pepper. Bring to a boil, turn heat to low, cover tightly and simmer 20 minutes or until rice is tender and liquid is absorbed. Add almonds and toss lightly with a fork.

—————— SERVES 8 ——————

From left to right:
Rice and Peppers, Herbed Rice, Savory Rice

Savory Rice

1 cup	regular long-grain rice	250 ml
1 cup	thinly sliced mushrooms	250 ml
1/4 cup	water	60 ml
1 tsp	lemon juice	5 ml
1 tbsp	butter	15 ml
2 cups	boiling water	500 ml
1 1/2 oz	envelope onion soup mix	45 g

Heat oven to 400 °F (205 °C). Spread rice on a large shallow baking pan and put in oven. Heat, stirring once or twice, until rice is dark golden brown, about 5 minutes. Remove from oven. Reduce oven temperature to 350 °F (175 °C).

Heat mushrooms, 1/4 cup (60 ml) water and lemon juice to simmering in a small saucepan. Simmer, uncovered, 3 minutes, shaking the pan often. Drain.

Combine rice, mushrooms, butter, boiling water and onion soup mix in 1 1/2-qt (2-L) casserole. Stir together with a fork. Cover tightly and bake 30 minutes. Stir lightly with a fork and continue baking, uncovered, until liquid is absorbed but rice is still moist, about 15 minutes. Good with broiled meat patties, steak or fish.

SERVES 4

Rice and Cheese Balls

(main dish)

1 1/2 cups	regular long-grain rice (before cooking)	375 ml
1/8 tsp	nutmeg	0.5 ml
1/4 tsp	black pepper	1 ml
3 tbsp	grated Parmesan cheese	45 ml
2	eggs	2
1/4 lb	Mozzarella cheese, cut in 1/4-inch (0.5-cm) cubes	115 g
1 tbsp	grated Parmesan cheese	15 ml
pinch	salt	pinch
1 tbsp	finely chopped parsley	15 ml
	oil for deep frying	
1/3 cup	all-purpose flour (approx.)	80 ml
1/2 cup	fine dry bread crumbs (approx.)	125 ml

Cook rice as directed on package. Stir in nutmeg, 1/4 tsp (1 ml) pepper and 3 tbsp (45 ml) Parmesan cheese lightly with a fork. Cover with transparent wrap and chill well.

Beat the eggs with a fork in a shallow dish (a pie pan is fine).

Combine Mozzarella cheese cubes, 1 tbsp (15 ml) Parmesan cheese, pinch salt, 1 tbsp (15 ml) of the beaten eggs (the rest will be used later) and parsley shortly before you plan to make the rice balls. Heat oil in deep fryer to 400 °F (205 °C).

Dip hands into cold water, shake to remove excess and put a heaping tablespoon of the cold rice in the palm of the hand. Add a heaping teaspoon of the Mozzarella cheese mixture to the centre of the rice and cover with another heaping tablespoon of rice. Shape into a ball about 2 inches (5 cm) in diameter. Continue in the same way until all rice and cheese are used. Set each ball on waxed paper as it is shaped and dampen hands with cold water before starting each one.

Put the flour in a shallow dish and the bread crumbs in another. Roll each ball first in flour to coat lightly, then in beaten egg and finally in bread crumbs.

Fry, a few at a time, in the hot oil until golden, about 5 minutes. Keep hot in a low oven until all are fried. Good for lunch with salads or with meat dishes.

———————— SERVES 6 ————————

*Rice and Cheese Balls
and Vegetable Rice*

Vegetable Rice

2 tbsp	olive oil	30 ml
4 strips	bacon, chopped	4 strips
1/3 cup	chopped onion	80 ml
4	tomatoes, peeled and chopped	4
1 1/2 cups	regular long-grain rice	375 ml
2 1/2 cups	beef stock	625 ml
	or 1 can beef consommé plus 1 can water	
1 tsp	salt	5 ml
1/8 tsp	pepper	0.5 ml
1 cup	finely chopped cauliflower	250 ml
1 cup	cut up fresh green beans	250 ml
1 cup	frozen peas	250 ml

Heat oven to 350 °F (175 °C).

Heat oil and bacon in large heavy saucepan or Dutch oven which can be put in the oven. Add onion and cook gently 5 minutes, stirring. Stir in tomatoes and rice.

Add beef stock or consommé-water mixture, salt and pepper. Bring to a boil. Add cauliflower and beans. Cover tightly and simmer 15 minutes. Stir lightly with a fork, add peas, cover and simmer 5 minutes more.

Put pan in oven, uncovered, for about 10 minutes or until liquid is absorbed but mixture is still moist. Stir lightly with a fork and serve immediately.

SERVES 6 TO 8

Spaghetti with Eggplant Sauce

(main dish)

1/2 cup	olive oil	125 ml
1/2 cup	finely chopped onion	125 ml
2	cloves garlic, crushed	2
3 cups	1/2-inch (1.25-cm) cubes eggplant (1 medium)	750 ml
1 cup	slivered green pepper (1 small)	250 ml
3 cups	peeled, chopped tomatoes (4 large)	750 ml
1/2 tsp	dried leaf basil	2 ml
1/2 tsp	salt	2 ml
1/4 tsp	pepper	1 ml
1/2 cup	slivered ripe olives	125 ml
6	anchovies, chopped very fine	6
1 tbsp	capers, chopped	15 ml
1 lb	spaghetti, cooked and drained	450 g
2 tbsp	melted butter	30 ml
1/4 cup	grated Parmesan cheese	60 ml
2 tbsp	chopped parsley	30 ml

grated Parmesan cheese

Heat oil in heavy saucepan. Add onion and garlic and cook gently 10 minutes, stirring. Add eggplant and green pepper and continue cooking and stirring 5 minutes.

Add tomatoes, basil, salt and pepper. Cover and simmer 30 minutes, stirring several times. Add olives, anchovies and capers and continue cooking gently 5 minutes. Taste and add more salt if necessary.

Toss hot spaghetti with butter, 1/4 cup (60 ml) Parmesan cheese and parsley and put on deep platter. Pour eggplant mixture over. Pass more Parmesan cheese.

———————— SERVES 4 TO 6 ————————

Macaroni and Vegetables

(main dish)

2 cups	elbow macaroni (before cooking)	500 ml
2 tbsp	butter	30 ml
1 medium	green pepper, coarsely chopped	1 medium
1 cup	thinly sliced celery	250 ml
2 tbsp	finely chopped onion	30 ml
1/2 lb	wieners, sliced thin	225 g
2 small	zucchini, cut coarsely	2 small
12-oz can	whole kernel corn	350-g can
2	tomatoes, cut in wedges	2
1 tsp	salt	5 ml
1/4 tsp	pepper	1 ml
2 cups	grated processed cheese	500 ml

Cook macaroni in plenty of boiling salted water until tender, about 7 minutes. Drain. Keep hot.

Melt butter in large skillet. Add green pepper, celery, onion and wieners and cook gently until vegetables are tender-crisp and wieners are lightly browned. Add zucchini pieces, corn and tomato wedges. Sprinkle in salt and pepper. Cook over medium heat until zucchini is just tender and everything is hot, stirring occasionally. Sprinkle in cheese and stir over low heat until melted.

Put macaroni on hot serving plate and spoon vegetable mixture over. Serve immediately.

———————— SERVES 4 TO 6 ————————

Creamy Garlic Noodles

Creamy Garlic Noodles

(main dish)

1/4 cup	soft butter or margarine	60 ml
8-oz pkg	cream cheese (room temperature)	225-g pkg
1/4 cup	chopped parsley	60 ml
1 tsp	dried leaf basil	5 ml
1/4 tsp	salt	1 ml
1/2 tsp	pepper	2 ml
8-oz pkg	fine noodles	225-g pkg
1 clove	garlic, crushed	1 clove
1/2 cup	butter or margarine	125 ml
1/2 cup	grated Parmesan cheese	125 ml
2/3 cup	boiling water	160 ml
1/2 cup	grated Parmesan cheese	125 ml

Beat 1/2 cup (125 ml) butter or margarine and cream cheese together until well blended with a rotary beater. Stir in parsley, basil, salt and pepper. Set aside.

Cook noodles in plenty of boiling, salted water until just tender, about 5 minutes. Drain. Return to cooking pan.

Cook garlic gently in the 1/2 cup (125 ml) butter or margarine for about 2 minutes while noodles are cooking. Add to cooked noodles and toss together with 2 forks over low heat until very hot. Remove from heat. Add 1/2 cup (125 ml) Parmesan cheese and toss again. Turn out on hot serving plate. Keep hot.

Add boiling water to cream cheese mixture and blend well. Pour over hot noodles. Sprinkle with 1/2 cup (125 ml) grated Parmesan cheese. Serve immediately. Good with veal.

SERVES 6

Herbed Noodles and Sauce

(main dish)

2 tbsp	olive oil	30 ml
1 cup	chopped onion	250 ml
2 cloves	garlic, minced	2 cloves
5 cups	coarsely chopped peeled tomatoes	1.25 L
1/2 cup	dry red wine	125 ml
1/4 cup	chopped parsley	60 ml
1 tsp	salt	5 ml
1/4 tsp	pepper	1 ml
1 tsp	paprika	5 ml
1 tsp	sugar	5 ml
1 tsp	dried leaf oregano	5 ml
1/2 tsp	dried leaf basil	2 ml
3 drops	Tabasco	3 drops
1/4 cup	butter	60 ml
1 cup	soft bread cubes	250 ml
1 tsp	dried leaf basil	5 ml
1 tsp	dried leaf chervil	5 ml
1 tbsp	chopped parsley	15 ml
1 cup	light cream	250 ml
1 cup	slivered ripe olives	250 ml
16-oz pkg	medium noodles	450-g pkg

Heat oil in large saucepan. Add onion and garlic and cook gently 3 minutes. Add tomatoes, wine, 1/4 cup (60 ml) parsley, salt, pepper, paprika, sugar, oregano, 1/2 tsp (2 ml) basil and Tabasco. Bring to a boil, turn down heat and simmer 40 minutes, uncovered.

Melt butter in saucepan when sauce is nearly ready. Add bread cubes and cook until golden, stirring. Add 1 tsp (5 ml) basil, chervil, 1 tbsp (15 ml) parsley and cream. Heat to simmering. Add olives. Let stand on lowest heat.

Cook noodles in plenty of boiling salted water until just tender. Drain. Mix butter-cream mixture through noodles, tossing lightly with a fork. Pile in centre of large deep serving platter. Pour tomato sauce around noodles. Serve immediately.

SERVES 6

Puffy California Omelet

(main dish)

6	egg yolks	6
4-oz pkg	cream cheese (room temperature)	115-g pkg
1/4 cup	milk	60 ml
3/4 tsp	salt	3 ml
1/8 tsp	pepper	0.5 ml
2 tbsp	butter	30 ml
1 tbsp	thinly sliced green onion	15 ml
6	egg whites	6
	California Sauce (recipe follows)	

Heat oven to 350 °F (175 °C).

Beat egg yolks until thick and lemon-colored, about 5 minutes at high speed on the mixer. Add cream cheese and continue beating until blended. Stir in milk, salt and pepper.

Heat butter in large heavy skillet — a 10-inch (25-cm) black iron skillet is fine. Add onion and cook gently 2 minutes.

Beat egg whites until stiff but not dry. Fold into egg yolk mixture and turn whole mixture into skillet. Cook slowly until firm and lightly browned on bottom, about 10 minutes. Put in oven and bake 10 to 15 minutes or until set and browned on top. Cut into wedges and serve with California Sauce.

———— SERVES 4 TO 6 ————

California Sauce

7 1/2-oz can	tomato sauce	215-ml can
1/4 tsp	chili powder	1 ml
1/2 cup	slivered ripe olives	125 ml

Combine tomato sauce and chili powder in small saucepan. Simmer 5 minutes. Stir in olives. Serve over wedges of Puffy California omelet as directed in recipe.

Puffy California Omelet

237

Broccoli Soufflé

(main dish)

10-oz pkg	frozen chopped broccoli	280-g pkg
6	eggs	6
1/4 tsp	cream of tartar	1 ml
1/3 cup	butter or margarine	80 ml
1/3 cup	flour	80 ml
1 1/4 cups	milk	300 ml
1/2 tsp	salt	2 ml
1/4 tsp	pepper	1 ml
1/4 tsp	garlic salt	1 ml
1/2 tsp	dried leaf marjoram	2 ml
1/2 cup	grated old cheddar cheese	125 ml
2 tbsp	grated old cheddar cheese	30 ml

Cook broccoli according to package directions using the minimum time suggested. Drain thoroughly.

Heat oven to 350 °F (175 °C). Fasten a doubled strip of aluminum foil tightly around an 8-cup (2-L) soufflé dish letting the foil extend about 3 inches (7.5 cm) above the top of the dish. Butter foil lightly. Do not butter soufflé dish.

Separate eggs, putting whites in one large bowl and yolks in another. Add cream of tartar to whites and beat until stiff peaks form. Set aside.

Melt butter or margarine in medium saucepan. Stir in flour and let bubble a little. Remove from heat. Add milk all at once and stir to blend. Return to heat and cook until very thick and smooth, stirring constantly. Remove from heat and stir in salt, pepper, garlic salt and marjoram.

Beat egg yolks well. Beat in hot mixture gradually. Add broccoli and 1/2 cup (125 ml) cheese and beat until blended.

Fold egg whites into broccoli mixture working as quickly as possible and folding just until the two mixtures are combined.

Turn mixture into prepared soufflé dish. Sprinkle with 2 tbsp (30 ml) cheese. Bake about 5 minutes or until soufflé is set. Serve immediately.

SERVES 6

Cottage Cheese Soufflé-Omelet

Cottage Cheese Soufflé-Omelet

(main dish)

4	egg yolks	4
1/2 tsp	salt	2 ml
1/8 tsp	pepper	0.5 ml
1/4 tsp	paprika	1 ml
1/4 tsp	dried leaf chervil	1 ml
1/4 cup	milk	60 ml
3/4 cup	cream-style cottage cheese	180 ml
3 tbsp	chopped pimento	45 ml
1 tbsp	chopped parsley	15 ml
4	egg whites	4
1 tbsp	butter	15 ml

Heat oven to 350 °F (175 °C).

Beat egg yolks until thick and lemon-colored, 5 minutes at high speed on the mixer. Stir in seasonings, milk, cheese, pimento and parsley.

Beat egg whites until stiff but not dry. Fold into egg yolk mixture.

Melt butter in heavy 10-inch (25-cm) skillet that can go in the oven (cast iron is fine). Pour in egg mixture. Cook slowly until firm and lightly browned on bottom, about 10 minutes.

Put in oven and bake 10 to 15 minutes or until browned on top. Crease across the centre, fold in half and turn out on platter or cut in wedges to serve. Serve immediately.

SERVES 4

Egg-Rice Luncheon Casserole

(main dish)

2 cups	cooked rice	500 ml
1 cup	grated old cheddar cheese	250 ml
3/4 cup	chopped parsley	180 ml
3/4 cup	slivered ripe olives	180 ml
2	hard-cooked eggs, chopped	2
1/4 cup	melted butter or margarine	60 ml
1/2 tsp	salt	2 ml
1/4 tsp	pepper	1 ml
2	eggs	2
1/4 cup	grated old cheddar cheese	60 ml

Heat oven to 350 °F (175 °C). Butter a 1-qt (1.25- L) casserole.

Combine rice, 1 cup (250 ml) cheese, parsley, olives, hard-cooked eggs, butter, salt and pepper, mixing lightly with a fork. Separate eggs and beat yolks lightly with a fork. Blend into rice mixture. Beat whites until stiff and fold into mixture. Turn into prepared casserole and sprinkle with 1/4 cup (60 ml) cheese.

Bake about 40 minutes or until lightly browned, puffed and set.

——————— SERVES 4 ———————

Eggs and Onions

(main dish)

2 large	Spanish onions	2 large
	boiling water	
2 tbsp	butter	30 ml
2 tbsp	olive oil	30 ml
1/4 cup	butter	60 ml
1/4 cup	flour	60 ml
1 cup	milk	250 ml
1/2 tsp	salt	2 ml
1/4 tsp	pepper	1 ml
2 tsp	dry mustard	10 ml
dash	cayenne	dash
1/2 cup	grated Swiss Emmentaler cheese	125 ml
1/4 cup	light cream	60 ml
6	hard-cooked eggs	6
3 tbsp	parsley	45 ml

Heat oven to 400 °F (205 °C). Butter a shallow baking dish, about 10 x 6 x 2 inches (25 x 15 x 5 cm).

Cut onions in half, then put cut sides down on board and slice paper-thin. Put cut onions in a bowl, cover with boiling water and let stand 5 minutes. Drain well.

Heat 2 tbsp (30 ml) butter and oil in large heavy skillet. Add onions and cook gently about 15 minutes, stirring. Onions should be limp but not brown.

Heat 1/4 cup (60 ml) butter in saucepan. Sprinkle in flour and stir to blend. Remove from heat and add milk all at once. Add salt, pepper, mustard and cayenne and stir to blend. Return to moderate heat and cook until boiling, thickened and smooth, stirring constantly. Stir in cheese and cream.

Cut eggs in halves and lift out yolks. Put yolks into a coarse sieve and slice whites thinly.

Put 1/3 of the onions in the prepared baking dish. Sprinkle with 1/3 of the egg whites then press about 1/3 of the egg yolks through the sieve over the egg whites. Sprinkle with 1 tbsp (15 ml) of the parsley. Repeat these layers twice more. Pour cheese sauce over all.

Bake about 15 minutes or until bubbling well and lightly browned.

———————————— SERVES 4 ————————————

Egg-Rice Luncheon Casserole

Sausage Quiche

(main dish)

pastry for 1 crust 9-inch (23-cm) pie		
10-oz pkg	frozen asparagus	280-g pkg
1/2 lb	sausages, cut in rounds 1/4 inch (0.5 cm) thick	225 g
1 large	onion, thinly sliced	1 large
1 cup	1/4-inch (0.5-cm) cubes old cheddar cheese	250 ml
4	eggs	4
1 1/2 cups	light cream	375 ml
1/4 tsp	dried leaf savory	1 ml
1/2 tsp	salt	2 ml
1/4 tsp	pepper	1 ml

Heat oven to 450 °F (230 °C). Have ready a 9-inch (23-cm) pie pan.

Line pie pan with pastry building up a high fluted edge to hold the filling. Cover the edge with a narrow strip of aluminum foil. Put in oven for 5 minutes (do not prick bottom of pastry — just press it down if it puffs up a little). Remove from oven and cool.

Cook asparagus just until tender-crisp. Drain very well. Dry on paper towel. Cut into 1/2-inch (1.25-cm) pieces.

Cook slices of sausage in a heavy skillet until cooked through and lightly browned. Lift out with slotted spoon and put pieces in prepared pastry shell. Pour all but 1 tbsp (15 ml) of the fat from the skillet and add the onion. Cook gently until limp, stirring. Spoon over sausage pieces. Add cheese cubes and asparagus pieces.

Beat eggs and cream together with a fork. Stir in seasonings. Pour over meat and vegetables in pie shell. Bake 15 minutes at 450 °F (230 °C). Turn heat down to 350 °F (175 °C) and continue baking another 30 minute or until a knife inserted 1 inch (2.5 cm) from the edge of the filling comes out clean. Serve hot.

SERVES 6

Salads

Salads

Good nutrition suggests uninteresting food to some people. But it shouldn't. Good nutrition is something to enjoy, not tolerate. What more splendid way is there to make it enjoyable than with salads? As for color, what is more pleasing to the eye than a salad displaying vibrant yellows, oranges, greens and reds. Tempting, satisfying, crackling-crisp and good for us too, no wonder salads are favorites with everyone.

The variety of salads you can make is infinite. From the simple to the elaborate, from first course to dessert and from those designed to whet the appetite to those that are a whole meal, there is a salad for every occasion. Salads can be composed of many types of greens, raw vegetables, fruits, and of course protein foods such as eggs, cheese, and nuts. And they can be combined with meat, fish and poultry to tempt the most jaded palate.

Salads should not be just a summer alternative to stove cooking. They will refresh and invigorate as well in January as in August. So don't be satisfied with a chunk of lettuce and a spoonful of bottled dressing when there are so many choice ingredients available all the year round.

Dutch Salad

4 cups	diced cooked potatoes	1 L
20-oz pkg	frozen peas, cooked	560-g pkg
1 lb	wieners	450 g
1 tbsp	butter	15 ml
1 small	onion, chopped	1 small
2 tbsp	brown sugar	30 ml
2 tbsp	cider vinegar	30 ml
2 tbsp	water	30 ml
1 tsp	salt	5 ml
1/4 tsp	pepper	1 ml
2 tbsp	chopped parsley	30 ml
	lettuce	

Combine potatoes and peas in a bowl (they should be warm).

Cut wieners into slices 1/4 inch (0.5 cm) thick.

Heat butter in skillet, add wieners and onion and cook gently about 3 minutes or until wieners are warmed through, stirring. Stir in sugar, vinegar, water, salt, pepper and parsley. Bring to boiling. Pour over potato mixture and toss lightly to blend.

Line bowl with lettuce and spoon in mixture. Serve immediately while still warm.

————————— SERVES 6 —————————

Swiss Peasant Cheese Salad

2 cups	1/4-inch (0.5-cm) cubes Swiss Emmentaler cheese	500 ml
3 cups	sliced boiled new potatoes	750 ml
1 1/2 cups	1-inch (2.5-cm) pieces cooked green beans	375 ml
1/2 cup	chopped Spanish onion	125 ml
2 tbsp	vinegar	30 ml
1 tbsp	prepared mustard	15 ml
3 tbsp	salad oil	45 ml
2 tbsp	mayonnaise	30 ml
1/2 tsp	salt	2 ml
dash	pepper	dash
	lettuce	

Combine cheese, potatoes, beans and onion in a large bowl and toss them together lightly. Blend remaining ingredients except lettuce and pour over cheese-potato mixture. Toss lightly to blend well. Chill several hours before serving. Serve on lettuce with crusty bread or pumpernickel as a complete lunch or supper.

————————— SERVES 4 —————————

Creamy Potato Salad

3 lb	potatoes	1.4 kg
2 tbsp	vinegar	30 ml
1/2 cup	thinly sliced celery	125 ml
1/2 cup	chopped sweet pickles	125 ml
1/2 cup	thinly sliced green onions	125 ml
1/4 cup	thinly sliced radishes	60 ml
2 tbsp	finely chopped parsley	30 ml
1 1/2 tsp	salt	7 ml
1/8 tsp	pepper	0.5 ml
2	egg yolks	2
2 tbsp	flour	30 ml
1 tsp	sugar	5 ml
1 tsp	dry mustard	5 ml
1 tsp	salt	5 ml
1 clove	garlic, crushed	1 clove
6 tbsp	vinegar	90 ml
1 tbsp	melted butter	15 ml
3/4 cup	whipping cream (not whipped)	180 ml

Peel potatoes and cook until just tender. Drain. Cut into small cubes as soon as they are cool enough to handle. Add 2 tbsp (30 ml) vinegar to hot potatoes and toss together. Cool to lukewarm. Add celery, pickles, onions, radishes, parsley, 1 1/2 tsp (7 ml) salt and pepper. Toss lightly. Cover and chill until shortly before serving time.

Combine egg yolks, flour, sugar, mustard and 1 tsp (5 ml) salt in top of double boiler. Beat together with rotary beater until blended. Stir in garlic, 6 tbsp (90 ml) vinegar and butter. Set over simmering water and cook until thick, stirring constantly. Remove from heat. Stir in cream. Cool.

Add dressing to potato mixture about 30 minutes before serving time. Toss lightly to blend, cover and return to refrigerator to chill.

SERVES 6

Creamy Potato Salad

Raw Broccoli Salad

1 1/2 lb	broccoli	675 g
1 tsp	salt	5 ml
1/4 tsp	pepper	1 ml
1/3 cup	salad oil	80 ml
2 tbsp	lemon juice	30 ml
4 medium	tomatoes	4 medium
1/3 cup	commercial sour cream	80 ml
1 tsp	prepared mustard	5 ml
	lettuce cups	

Wash broccoli and drain well. Cut off all the florets at the point where the small stems join the main stalk (refrigerate the main stalks to cook separately as a vegetable or to add to soup). Chop the florets very finely. Put broccoli in a large bowl and sprinkle with salt and pepper. Combine salad oil and lemon juice and pour over. Cover and chill for at least 30 minutes, stirring occasionally.

Peel tomatoes and cut in small pieces, discarding seeds. Add to broccoli. Combine cream and mustard and pour over. Mix well. Spoon into lettuce cups on serving plates and serve immediately.

———————— SERVES 4 ————————

Tomato Salad

1/2 tsp	salt	2 ml
1 large clove	garlic, peeled and cut in half	1 large clove
1/4 cup	wine vinegar	60 ml
1/8 tsp	pepper	0.5 ml
1/3 cup	olive oil	80 ml
8 large	green onions, white part only	8 large
6 medium	tomatoes	6 medium

Measure salt into small bowl. Add garlic and mash with a fork until almost a paste. Add wine vinegar and stir with fork until salt is dissolved. Lift out or strain out garlic. Add pepper and beat in olive oil gradually with a fork until mixture blends completely.

Slice green onions paper thin. Add to oil mixture.

Peel and cut tomatoes into 6 wedges each. Put in chilled bowl. Pour oil mixture over and toss lightly. Cover and chill for a few minutes before serving.

———————— SERVES 4 TO 6 ————————

Above: Tomato Salad
Below: Raw Broccoli Salad

Health Salad

10-oz pkg	spinach, torn up	280-g pkg
1 head	Boston lettuce, torn up	1 head
1 large bunch	watercress, stems removed	1 large bunch
1/2 cup	tiny sprigs parsley	125 ml
2 large stalks	celery, cut very thin on the diagonal	2 large stalks
1 clove	garlic, crushed	1 clove
1/2 tsp	salt	2 ml
1/2 tsp	grated lemon rind	2 ml
1/2 tsp	celery seed	2 ml
1/4 tsp	paprika	1 ml
1/4 tsp	pepper	1 ml
2 tbsp	tarragon vinegar	30 ml
1/2 cup	olive oil	125 ml
1 tbsp	heavy cream	15 ml
6 slices	bacon, fried very crisp, drained well and crumbled	6 slices

Wash greens and shake them dry in a towel. Put into large bowl with celery. Cover bowl and chill until they are very crisp.

Combine all remaining ingredients except bacon in a jar with a tight lid. Shake to blend well. Pour over vegetables and toss lightly. Sprinkle with bacon bits and serve immediately.

———————— SERVES 8 TO 10 ————————

Super Salad

10-oz pkg	plain yogurt	280-g pkg
1/2 cup	commercial mayonnaise	125 ml
2	green onions, sliced paper thin	2
1/4 cup	finely chopped parsley	60 ml
1/3 cup	finely crumbled blue cheese	80 ml
1/3 cup	slivered ripe olives	80 ml
1/4 tsp	salt	1 ml
dash	Tabasco	dash
8 to 10 cups	torn-up mixed salad greens	2 to 2.5 L
2 cups	slivered cooked chicken	500 ml
2	hard-cooked eggs, sliced	2
1/4 cup	slivered pimento	60 ml

Stir together yogourt, mayonnaise, onions, parsley, blue cheese, olives, salt and Tabasco.

Put greens in a large bowl and add yogurt mixture. Toss lightly. Transfer mixture to 6 or 8 individual salad bowls. Top each serving with some of chicken, egg slices and pimento. Serve immediately.

———————— SERVES 6 TO 8 ————————

Health Salad

Coleslaw Tartare

Coleslaw Tartare

1 small	coarsely grated or finely shredded cabbage	1 small
1 cup	paper-thin radish slices	250 ml
1 cup	commercial mayonnaise	250 ml
2 tsp	prepared mustard	10 ml
2 tsp	grated onion	10 ml
1/4 cup	finely chopped dill pickles	60 ml
2 tbsp	finely chopped parsley	30 ml

4 tsp	finely chopped pimento	20 ml
1/8 tsp	dried leaf tarragon	0.5 ml

Combine cabbage and radish slices in large bowl.

Combine all remaining ingredients, add to cabbage mixture and toss to blend well. Chill until serving time.

—————— SERVES 6 TO 8 ——————

Pepperoni Salad

6 cups	torn-up salad greens (use a mixture such as iceberg lettuce, leaf lettuce, Bibb or Boston lettuce and spinach)	1.5 L
1	cucumber (unpeeled if possible), cut in 2-inch (5-cm) strips	1
1/4 lb	Mozzarella cheese, cut in 1/4-inch (0.5-cm) cubes	115 g
1 small	zucchini, sliced paper thin	1 small
1 cup	cooked frozen baby lima beans	250 ml
1 cup	paper-thin sliced pepperoni	250 ml
1/4 cup	thinly sliced green onions	60 ml
	salt	
	fresh ground pepper	
1/4 cup	olive oil	60 ml
3 tbsp	tarragon wine vinegar	45 ml
2 tbsp	chopped parsley	30 ml
1 small clove	garlic, crushed	1 small clove
1/8 tsp	dry mustard	0.5 ml
1/8 tsp	dried leaf basil	0.5 ml
pinch	tarragon	pinch
1/2 tsp	salt	2 ml
1/8 tsp	pepper	0.5 ml
1/4 tsp	paprika	1 ml
12	cherry tomatoes, cut in half	12

Combine salad greens, cucumber strips, cheese, zucchini, lima beans, pepperoni and onions in large salad bowl. Sprinkle lightly with salt and pepper and toss together gently.

Combine all remaining ingredients except cherry tomatoes in a small jar with a tight lid. Shake to blend well. Pour just enough of this mixture over the salad to lightly coat all ingredients. Toss lightly. Add cherry tomatoes and toss again lightly. Serve immediately.

SERVES 6

Hot Macaroni Salad

1 lb	elbow macaroni, cooked and drained	450 g
4	wieners, thinly sliced	4
1 cup	chopped celery	250 ml
1/2 cup	small cubes green pepper	125 ml
2 tbsp	chopped pimento	30 ml
1 cup	diced bacon (about 8 slices)	250 ml
1/2 cup	finely chopped onion	125 ml
1/4 cup	flour	60 ml
3 tsp	salt	15 ml
1/4 tsp	pepper	1 ml
3/4 cup	white vinegar	180 ml
1/3 cup	sugar	80 ml
1 1/2 cups	water	375 ml

Combine macaroni, wieners, celery, green pepper and pimento in a large bowl. Fry bacon in a small skillet until crisp. Add onion and cook gently until onion is limp, stirring. Sprinkle in flour, salt and pepper and stir to blend. Remove from heat. Stir in vinegar, sugar and water. Return to moderate heat and cook until boiling and slightly thickened, stirring constantly. Pour over macaroni mixture while hot and toss lightly. Serve immediately.

SERVES 8

Fish Salad Mousse

3 lb	fresh or frozen haddock fillets	1.4 kg
2 cups	mayonnaise	500 ml
1/3 cup	lemon juice	80 ml
1 tbsp	grated onion	15 ml
2 tsp	salt	10 ml
1/2 tsp	pepper	2 ml
1 tsp	curry powder	5 ml
1 tsp	Worcestershire sauce	5 ml
1/8 tsp	Tabasco	0.5 ml
2 envelopes	unflavored gelatin	2 envelopes
1 cup	liquid (fish cooking liquid plus water if necessary)	250 ml
1/2 cup	chopped parsley	125 ml
	watercress	
	Marinated Shrimp (recipe follows)	

Wash the fresh fillets or thaw the frozen ones until they can be separated.

Put a large sheet of heavy-duty aluminum foil on a rack in a very large pan (I use my roaster). Lay the fish pieces on the foil and turn the foil up around the fish so it will hold the cooking liquid. Add about 1/2 inch (1.25 cm) boiling water to the pan (water will be under the fish so fish steams), cover tightly and simmer about 7 minutes or until fish flakes easily with a fork. Lift fish pieces out into a bowl and cool. Drain any liquid out of foil into a measuring cup. Cool.

Flake fish finely into large mixer bowl, discarding any bones and dark flesh or skin. You should have about 6 cups (1.5 L) flaked fish.

Combine mayonnaise, lemon juice, grated onion, salt, pepper, curry powder, Worcestershire sauce and Tabasco. Add fish and beat all together (medium speed on the mixer) until as smooth as possible.

Soak gelatin in 1 cup (250 ml) liquid 5 minutes in a small saucepan. Set over low heat and heat just until gelatin is dissolved. Pour into fish mixture in a thin stream, beating constantly. Stir in parsley.

Pour into 2-qt (2.5-L) mould with a tube in the centre. Chill several hours until very firm.

Unmould on a bed of watercress and fill centre with Marinated Shrimp. Garnish each serving with 2 or 3 shrimps.

_____ SERVES 8 _____

Marinated Shrimp

1 small	onion, sliced paper-thin and separated into rings	1 small
10 oz	large cleaned shrimp	270 g
1/2 cup	wine vinegar	125 ml
1/4 cup	salad oil	60 ml
dash	Worcestershire sauce	dash
dash	Tabasco	dash
1/2 tsp	paprika	2 ml
1/4 tsp	salt	1 ml
1/4 tsp	dry mustard	1 ml
pinch	garlic salt	pinch

Layer onion and shrimp in a jar with a tight lid.

Combine all remaining ingredients in a small jar with a tight lid and shake to blend well. Pour over shrimp and onion. Chill several hours, turning the jar upside down several times so all the shrimp have a chance to absorb some of the marinade. Lift shrimp out of marinade and drain before putting in centre of Fish Salad Mousse.

Crunchy Salmon Salad

Crunchy Salmon Salad

15 1/2-oz can	salmon	435-g can
1 small clove	garlic, crushed	1 small clove
3/4 tsp	salt	3 ml
1/2 cup	commercial mayonnaise	125 ml
1 tbsp	tarragon vinegar	15 ml
1/2 tsp	Worcestershire sauce	2 ml
5 cups	torn-up salad greens	1.25 L
1 cup	chopped celery leaves	250 ml
1/4 cup	thinly sliced radishes	60 ml
1/4 cup	thinly sliced stuffed olives	60 ml
2 cups	coarsely broken cheese flavored crackers	500 ml
	lettuce	
3	tomatoes, cut in wedges	3

Drain salmon and break into bite-size pieces. Cover and chill.

Combine garlic, salt, mayonnaise, vinegar, and Worcestershire sauce. Cover and chill.

Combine salmon, salad greens, celery leaves, sliced radishes, sliced olives and broken crackers in large salad bowl at serving time. Pour mayonnaise mixture over all and toss lightly. Spoon into lettuce cups and garnish with tomato wedges. Serve immediately.

SERVES 6

Shrimp in Avocado Halves

	boiling water	
1 small slice	onion	1 small slice
bunch	celery leaves	bunch
small piece	bay leaf	small piece
1 1/2 tsp	salt	7 ml
1/4 tsp	dried leaf thyme	1 ml
1/4 tsp	dried leaf chervil	1 ml
4	peppercorns	4
1 lb	raw shrimp	450 g
1 envelope	unflavored gelatin	1 envelope
1/4 cup	cold water	60 ml
1 1/2 cups	chicken stock	375 ml
1/4 tsp	dried leaf tarragon	1 ml
1/4 tsp	dried leaf chervil	1 ml
1 tbsp	wine vinegar	15 ml
2 tbsp	lemon juice	30 ml
1/2 tsp	salt	2 ml
pinch	pepper	pinch
	yellow food coloring (optional)	
3 large	ripe avocados	3 large
	watercress or parsley	

Put about 2 inches (5 cm) boiling water in saucepan. Add onion, celery leaves, bay leaf, 1 1/2 tsp (7 ml) salt, thyme, 1/4 tsp (1 ml) chervil and peppercorns and simmer 5 minutes. Drop in rinsed shrimp. Add more boiling water if necessary to cover shrimp. Bring to a boil. Turn down heat, cover and simmer just until shrimp are bright red, about 5 minutes. Remove from heat and drain. Cool shrimp, shell, clean and chill.

Add gelatin to cold water and let soak 5 minutes. Combine chicken stock, tarragon and 1/4 tsp (1 ml) chervil in saucepan and heat to boiling. Remove from heat and add gelatin mixture. Stir until gelatin is dissolved. Add vinegar, lemon juice, 1/2 tsp (2 ml) salt, pepper and a few drops of food coloring to tint the mixture a delicate yellow. Set in ice water and chill until beginning to set.

→

Crab Stuffed Tomatoes

Separate the unpeeled avocados into halves and set in a dish or pan, supporting them so they are level. Spoon a little of the slightly thickened gelatin mixture into the hollows of the avocados and over the cut edges (this will keep the cut part from darkening).

Arrange the chilled shrimp attractively in the hollows of the avocados. Spoon more gelatin mixture over shrimp. Chill until serving time.

Garnish each avocado half with a sprig of watercress or parsley at serving time. Set the salads on individual plates on a bed of watercress if it is available.

Note: Use 2 cans large shrimp rinsed under cold water and chilled instead of fresh shrimp, if desired.

SERVES 6

5 1/2-oz can	crab meat, flaked	155-g can
12-oz can	asparagus pieces, chopped	350-g can
2	hard-cooked eggs, chopped	2
1/2 cup	canned tiny peas or cooked fresh peas	125 ml
1 tbsp	cooking oil	15 ml
1/2 tsp	salt	2 ml
1/8 tsp	pepper	0.5 ml
1/4 tsp	dried leaf tarragon	1 ml
1/4 cup	mayonnaise	60 ml
1/2 tsp	lemon juice	2 ml
8 large	tomatoes	8 large
	salt	
	lettuce	
	parsley	

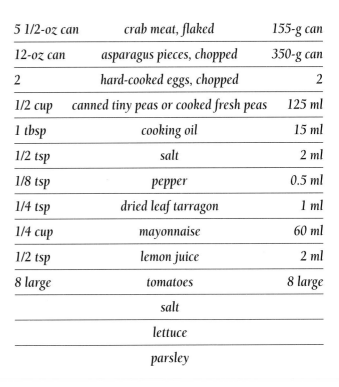

Combine crab, asparagus, eggs, peas, oil, 1/2 tsp (2 ml) salt, pepper, tarragon, mayonnaise and lemon juice, tossing lightly to blend. Chill.

Peel tomatoes, cut a thin slice from tops and hollow out leaving a good thick shell to hold filling. (Save tomato pulp to add to macaroni dishes, meat loaf, spaghetti sauce, etc.)

Sprinkle insides of tomatoes with salt and turn upside down on paper towelling to drain. Chill.

Fill tomato shells at serving time using 1/3 to 1/2 cup (80 to 125 ml) crab filling per tomato. Set on lettuce and garnish with parsley.

SERVES 8

Crab Stuffed Tomatoes

Chicken-Fruit Salad in Melon

2 cups	coarsely chopped cooked chicken	500 ml
5-oz can	water chestnuts, chopped	140-g can
2 cups	cubed peaches	500 ml
1/2 cup	thinly sliced celery	125 ml
1/2 cup	toasted slivered almonds	125 ml
2/3 cup	mayonnaise	160 ml
1/2 tsp	curry powder	2 ml
1/4 tsp	salt	1 ml
1 tsp	soya sauce	5 ml
6 large	melon wedges (cantaloup or honeydew)	6 large
	lettuce	

Combine chicken, water chestnuts, peaches, celery and almonds in a medium bowl.

Blend mayonnaise, curry powder, salt and soya sauce. Pour over chicken mixture and toss lightly to blend. Chill.

Spoon chicken mixture into melon wedges at serving time and set wedges on lettuce on serving plates.

———— SERVES 6 ————

Chicken and Lobster Salad

3	hard-cooked eggs	3
1 small	whole chicken breast, cooked (see note)	1 small
5-oz can	lobster (see note)	140-g can
1 cup	chopped celery	250 ml
1/4 cup	vinaigrette dressing	60 ml
1/2 cup	commercial mayonnaise	125 ml
2 tbsp	commercial chili sauce	30 ml
1 1/2 tsp	chopped chives	7 ml
1/4 tsp	salt	1 ml
1/4 cup	heavy cream, whipped	60 ml
2 cups	shredded lettuce	500 ml

Remove yolks from hard-cooked eggs and set aside. Chop whites.

Cut chicken meat into thin match-like strips about 1 1/2 inches (2.75 cm) long. Drain and chop lobster meat. Combine chicken, lobster, egg whites and celery in a bowl and pour the vinaigrette dressing over. Toss well with a fork, cover and chill about 1 hour, tossing occasionally.

Mash egg yolks with a fork. Blend with mayonnaise, chili sauce, chives and salt. Fold in whipped cream. Chill.

Line a salad bowl with shredded lettuce at serving time. Toss chicken-lobster mixture together with mayonnaise mixture and spoon into bowl. Serve immediately.

Note: The chicken breast can be poached or roasted wrapped in roasting paper or foil. You should have about 2 cups (500 ml) chicken meat when it is cut up. Crab may be substituted for lobster in this recipe.

———— SERVES 4 ————

Above: Chicken and Lobster Salad
Below: Chicken-Fruit Salad in Melon

Jellied Egg Salad

1 tbsp	unflavored gelatin	15 ml
3/4 cup	cold water	180 ml
1/2 cup	mayonnaise	125 ml
1 tbsp	prepared mustard	15 ml
1 cup	evaporated milk	250 ml
1 tsp	seasoned salt	5 ml
2 tbsp	lemon juice	30 ml
5	chopped hard-cooked eggs	5
1/2 cup	chopped celery	125 ml
1/2 cup	sliced stuffed olives	125 ml
	lettuce	

Add gelatin to cold water and let stand 5 minutes. Set in hot water and heat until gelatin dissolves. Stir into mayonnaise along with mustard, evaporated milk, seasoned salt and lemon juice. Set in ice water and chill until just beginning to set. Fold in eggs, celery and olives. Spoon into 1-qt (1.25-L) mould. Chill until set. Unmould on lettuce to serve.

——— SERVES 4 TO 6 ———

Vegetable-Egg Salad Mould

12	hard-cooked eggs	12
1/2 cup	chopped green pepper	125 ml
1/2 cup	chopped celery	125 ml
1/2 cup	chopped sweet pickles	125 ml
1/4 cup	chopped radishes	60 ml
1/4 cup	chopped pimento	60 ml
1/4 cup	thinly sliced green onions	60 ml
2 tbsp	chopped parsley	30 ml
8-oz pkg	cream cheese (room temperature)	225-g pkg
1/2 cup	commercial mayonnaise	125 ml
3 tbsp	chili sauce	45 ml
1/4 cup	cider vinegar	60 ml
1 1/2 tsp	salt	7 ml
1/4 tsp	pepper	1 ml
2 tbsp	unflavored gelatin	30 ml
1/2 cup	cold water	125 ml
	lettuce	

Chop eggs very finely. Combine with green pepper, celery, pickles, radishes, pimento, onions and parsley in a bowl.

Mash cheese with a fork and stir in mayonnaise, chili sauce, vinegar, salt and pepper, blending well.

Soak gelatin in cold water 5 minutes. Set in a pan of simmering water and heat until gelatin is dissolved. Stir gelatin into mayonnaise mixture, then stir into egg-vegetable mixture. Turn into a 9- x 5- x 3-inch (5- x 12.5- x 7.5-cm) loaf pan or 10-inch (25.5-cm) ring mould. Chill several hours or until very firm. Unmould and cut in thick slices or larges wedges and serve on lettuce.

——————— SERVES 6 ———————

Vegetable-Egg Salad Mould

Garden Mould with Salmon

(Be sure to do this when someone else is around)

1 cup	thinly sliced small carrots	250 ml
1 cup	peas (fresh or frozen)	250 ml
2 envelopes	unflavored gelatin	2 envelopes
1/2 cup	sugar	125 ml
1 tsp	salt	5 ml
1 1/2 cups	liquid (vegetable cooking water plus water)	375 ml
1 cup	cold water	250 ml
1/2 cup	white vinegar	125 ml
2 tbsp	lemon juice	30 ml
1 cup	finely cut cabbage	250 ml
2 tbsp	diced pimento	30 ml
	salad greens	
	chilled poached fresh salmon or canned red salmon	
	mayonnaise	
	capers	

Cook carrot slices about 2 minutes in a little boiling salted water (they should be tender-crisp). Drain, saving cooking water. Chill. Cook peas for as short a time as possible (if they are frozen, add a little boiling water, bring to a boil and drain immediately). Drain, saving cooking water. Chill.

Mix gelatin, sugar and salt in a small saucepan. Add enough cold water to vegetable cooking water to make 1 1/2 cups (375 ml) and add to the gelatin mixture. Let stand 5 minutes. Set over low heat and stir until gelatin is dissolved. Add cold water, vinegar and lemon juice. Chill by setting in ice water until beginning to thicken. Stir often during chilling.

Put cabbage and pimento in a medium bowl. Put carrots and peas in separate bowls. Add 1/3 of the gelatin mixture (a generous cup) to each vegetable. Blend well. Chill for a few minutes, watching carefully until the mixtures become quite thick but not set.

Rinse a 6-cup (1.5-L) ring mould with cold water. Have someone else standing by with two rubber scrapers or two large spoons. Spoon half of each vegetable mixture side by side into the mould. Your helper should hold the vegetable mixtures in place with the scrapers or spoons as you add each kind so they will run together as little as possible. Repeat, using the other half of the vegetable mixture. Chill until firm.

Unmould on salad greens on large serving plate. Fill centre with large pieces of chilled salmon. Add a little mayonnaise and a sprinkling of capers.

SERVES 6 TO 8

Garden Mould with Salmon

California Fruit Moulds

1 tbsp	unflavored gelatin	15 ml
1/2 cup	cold water	125 ml
1 medium	grapefruit	1 medium
1 cup	liquid	250 ml
1/4 cup	sugar	60 ml
1/4 cup	lemon juice	60 ml
pinch	salt	pinch
2/3 cup	chopped dates	160 ml
1 cup	cantaloup balls	250 ml
1 tbsp	chopped maraschino cherries	15 ml
2 tbsp	finely chopped preserved ginger (optional)	30 ml
	salad greens	
	mayonnaise	

Add gelatin to cold water and let stand 5 minutes. Peel and section grapefruit, holding it over a bowl to catch any juice. Drain grapefruit sections well and pour juice into a measuring cup. Add water to make 1 cup (250 ml) liquid. Heat this liquid to boiling in a small saucepan and add gelatin, stirring until gelatin is dissolved. Add sugar and stir until dissolved. Stir in lemon juice and salt.

Chill by setting in ice water until beginning to thicken. Cut grapefruit sections into bite-size pieces and fold into gelatin mixture along with dates, cantaloup, cherries and ginger. Spoon into 6-oz (180-ml) custard cups or other moulds and chill until firm.

Unmould onto salad greens at serving time and pass the mayonnaise.

SERVES 6

Orange-Avocado Salad

1/3 cup	olive oil	80 ml
1/4 cup	wine vinegar	60 ml
1 tsp	sugar	5 ml
1/2 tsp	salt	2 ml
1/4 tsp	dried leaf thyme	1 ml
1/4 tsp	dried leaf basil	1 ml
1/4 tsp	chili powder	1 ml
8 to 10 cups	torn-up mixed salad greens	2 to 2.5 L
2 large	oranges	2 large
1 large	ripe avocado	1 large
4	green onions, sliced paper thin	4

Combine oil, vinegar, sugar, salt, thyme, basil and chili powder in a small jar with a tight lid. Shake to blend well and set aside until needed.

Tear up salad greens shortly before serving time and put them in a large shallow bowl. Peel oranges, cut them into slices then cut each slice in half. Peel avocado and cut into slices lengthwise.

Toss about half of the oil and vinegar dressing with the salad greens. Top the greens with a ring of overlapping slices of orange and avocado. Sprinkle with onions. Bring to table along with remaining dressing in a small container. Drizzle remaining dressing over the salad and toss lightly. Serve immediately.

SERVES 8

Above: California Fruit Moulds
Below: Orange-Avocado Salad

Meat Ball Salad

1 lb	ground beef	450 g
1/4 cup	finely chopped green onions	60 ml
1 tbsp	finely chopped parsley	15 ml
1 tsp	salt	5 ml
1/8 tsp	pepper	0.5 ml
1	egg, beaten	1
1/4 tsp	chili powder	1 ml
1/4 tsp	dried leaf marjoram	1 ml
1 tbsp	fine dry bread crumbs	15 ml
2 tbsp	cooking oil	30 ml
	Herb-Garlic Dressing (recipe follows)	
2 14-oz cans	artichoke bottoms, drained, and cut in halves	2 398-ml cans
3 cups	cooked small carrots (slice if you use large)	750 ml
	lettuce leaves	
2 cups	torn up lettuce	500 ml

Combine beef, green onions, parsley, salt, pepper, egg, chili powder, marjoram and bread crumbs, blending well with a fork. Make into tiny meat balls — no larger than 1 inch (2.5 cm) in diameter.

Heat oil in large heavy skillet. Add meat balls and cook, turning often to brown all sides and cook through. Drain and cool on paper towelling when they are all cooked, then put them in a single layer in a shallow dish. Pour about half of the Herb-Garlic Dressing over the meat balls. Cover tightly and chill several hours, turning the meat balls at least once so they will absorb the flavor of the dressing.

Put the artichoke bottoms and carrots in a single layer in another shallow dish and pour the remaining Herb-garlic dressing over them. Cover tightly and chill well.

Line a large salad bowl with lettuce leaves at serving time. Toss artichoke bottoms and carrots and their dressing lightly with the 2 cups (500 ml) torn-up lettuce. Pile in lettuce-lined bowl, leaving a hollow in the centre. Lift the meat balls out of the dressing they marinated in with a slotted spoon and pile them in the centre of the salad. Serve immediately.

———— SERVES 6 ————

Herb-Garlic Dressing

1/2 cup	olive oil	125 ml
2 tbsp	vinegar	30 ml
2 tbsp	lemon juice	30 ml
1/2 tsp	salt	2 ml
1/4 tsp	dry mustard	1 ml
1/4 tsp	paprika	1 ml
1/2 small clove	garlic, crushed	1/2 small clove
2 tsp	finely chopped parsley	10 ml
1/2 tsp	dried leaf oregano	2 ml
1/4 tsp	dried leaf thyme	1 ml
1/4 cup	mayonnaise	60 ml

Combine all ingredients in a small jar with a tight lid and shake to blend well.

———— MAKES 1 CUP ————

Desserts

Desserts

Cakes, Cookies, Pastries and Desserts

A beautiful cake, a flaky pie or a deliciously rich torte can be the perfect ending to a wonderful meal and can win new laurels for the cook. On the other hand, a simple cookie or cake fresh from the oven may just as easily win applause.

This section includes some very special baking recipes. As well as such old-fashioned favorites as Hermit cookies, you will find Fluffy Sponge Cake, fruit cakes, glorious tortes and party cakes for entertaining. Add to this pies, tarts and turnovers and you are ready to cater to every taste.

And then there are sweets that aren't cookies, pies or cakes. I think the English call them puddings, sweet or colloquially, "afters." That sounds a little ordinary but there is nothing ordinary about the desserts I have assembled here. There are cheesecakes, creams, custards, bavarians, trifles, charlottes and several delicious frozen treats, as well as fine baked and steamed meal-enders. For the occasion that calls for a light finish I have included some of the refreshing fruit desserts that are now so much in demand.

With so many good things to try, is there any wonder that this is the biggest section in the book. I trust that you, like the readers who named them "classics" for this book, will find these recipes, although last in my book, by no means least.

CAKES

Chocolate-Almond Balls

1/2 cup	finely ground blanched almonds	125 ml
1	egg white	1
2 tbsp	brown sugar	30 ml
1 tbsp	water	15 ml
1/2 tsp	almond extract	2 ml
4 oz	milk chocolate	115 g
2 tbsp	milk	30 ml
3/4 cup	soft butter	180 ml
1/4 cup	sugar	60 ml
1 tsp	vanilla	5 ml
2 cups	sifted all-purpose flour	500 ml
1/2 tsp	salt	2 ml
	icing sugar	

Heat oven to 375 °F (190 °C). Have ready lightly greased cookie sheets.

Combine ground almonds, egg white, brown sugar, water and almond extract to make a soft filling for cookies. Set aside.

Combine chocolate and milk in top of double boiler and set over simmering water until chocolate is melted.

Cream butter and sugar. Stir in vanilla and chocolate mixture. Sift flour and salt together into mixture and blend well.

Flatten a rounded teaspoonful of the chocolate dough and put 1/4 tsp (1 ml) of the almond mixture in the centre. Wrap the dough around the almond mixture carefully to make a small ball. Put on cookie sheet. Repeat until all of both mixtures is used.

Bake about 10 minutes or until set. Cool a few minutes then roll in icing sugar. Cool completely and roll in icing sugar again before storing.

———— MAKES 4 TO 5 DOZEN ————

Salted Peanut Jumbos

1 cup	soft shortening (half butter)	250 ml
1 1/2 cups	brown sugar, packed	375 ml
2	eggs	2
3 3/4 cups	sifted all-purpose flour	930 ml
1 1/2 tsp	baking soda	7 ml
1 tsp	baking powder	5 ml
1 tsp	salt	5 ml
1/2 cup	milk	125 ml
2 1/2 cups	bran flakes (ready-to-eat cereal)	625 ml
1 1/2 cups	chopped salted peanuts	375 ml

Beat shortening, sugar and eggs together until fluffy. Sift flour, baking soda, baking powder and salt together and add to first mixture alternately with the milk. Blend in bran flakes and peanuts. Chill until firm, about 1 hour.

Heat oven to 375 °F (190 °C). Grease cookie sheets.

Drop dough by rounded tablespoonfuls about 3 inches (7.5 cm) apart on cookie sheets. Bake 12 to 15 minutes or until nicely browned and set.

———— MAKES ABOUT 3 1/2 DOZEN LARGE COOKIES ————

Hermits

Hermits

1 cup	soft shortening	250 ml
2 cups	brown sugar, packed	500 ml
4	eggs	4
1/4 cup	strong cold coffee	60 ml
2 cups	seedless raisins	500 ml
1 cup	chopped nuts	250 ml
4 cups	sifted all-purpose flour	1 L
1 tsp	salt	5 ml
1 tsp	baking soda	5 ml
1 1/2 tsp	nutmeg	7 ml

Heat oven to 375 °F (190 °C). Grease cookie sheets.

Combine shortening, sugar and eggs and beat until fluffy. Stir in coffee, raisins and nuts. Sift flour, salt, baking soda and nutmeg together into first mixture and stir to blend.

Drop by rounded teaspoonfuls on prepared cookie sheets. Bake 10 to 12 minutes or until set.

——————— MAKES ABOUT 9 DOZEN ———————

Lemon-Cream Cheese Cookies

4-oz pkg	cream cheese (room temperature)	115-g pkg
1/3 cup	soft butter	80 ml
1/2 cup	sugar	125 ml
2 tbsp	grated lemon rind	30 ml
2 tsp	lemon juice	10 ml
1 cup	sifted all-purpose flour	250 ml
2 tsp	baking powder	10 ml
1/4 tsp	salt	1 ml
3/4 cup	crushed corn flakes	180 ml

Blend cream cheese, butter and sugar, creaming until fluffy. Stir in lemon rind and juice.

Sift flour, baking powder and salt together. Add to cream cheese mixture and stir until blended and smooth. Chill about 1 hour.

Heat oven to 350 °F (175 °C).

Shape dough into small balls about 1 inch (2.5 cm) in diameter. Roll each ball in corn flakes. Put on ungreased cookie sheet. Bake 12 to 15 minutes or until set but not brown.

MAKES 2 1/2 TO 3 DOZEN

Dad's Favorite Cookies

1 cup	soft butter	250 ml
3 cups	brown sugar, packed	750 ml
2	eggs	2
1 tsp	vanilla	5 ml
2 cups	sifted all-purpose flour	500 ml
1 tsp	baking powder	5 ml
1/2 tsp	baking soda	2 ml
1/2 tsp	salt	2 ml
1 cup	flaked coconut	250 ml
2 cups	quick-cooking rolled oats	500 ml

Heat oven to 375 °F (190 °C). Grease cookie sheets.

Beat butter, brown sugar, eggs and vanilla together until fluffy.

Sift flour, baking powder, baking soda and salt together into mixture and blend well. Stir in coconut and rolled oats.

Drop by rounded tablespoonfuls 3 inches (7.5 cm) apart on prepared cookie sheets and flatten with a fork. Bake 10 minutes or until nicely browned and set. Cool until firm then lift off sheets and finish cooling on racks.

——— MAKES ABOUT 3 DOZEN LARGE COOKIES ———

Date-Honey Cookies

1 cup	liquid honey	250 ml
1 1/2 cups	peanut butter	375 ml
1/4 cup	soft shortening	60 ml
3	eggs	3
2 tsp	vanilla	10 ml
1 1/2 cups	chopped dates	375 ml
1 cup	quick-cooking rolled oats	250 ml
1 cup	toasted regular wheat germ	250 ml
1 cup	coarsely chopped walnuts	250 ml
1 1/2 cups	sifted all-purpose flour	375 ml
2 tsp	baking powder	10 ml
1 tsp	salt	5 ml
1/2 tsp	cinnamon	2 ml
1/2 tsp	nutmeg	2 ml

dates (optional)

Heat oven to 375 °F (190 °C). Grease large cookie sheets.

Combine honey, peanut butter, shortening, eggs and vanilla in a large bowl and beat until blended and fluffy. Stir in dates, rolled oats, wheat germ and walnuts. Sift flour, baking powder, salt, cinnamon and nutmeg together into first mixture and stir to blend.

Drop by rounded teaspoonfuls on cookie sheets. Cut more dates in half lengthwise and top each cookie with half an date or flatten cookies with the tines of a fork. Bake 18 to 20 minutes.

——— MAKES ABOUT 8 DOZEN MEDIUM-SIZE COOKIES ———

Lemon-Cream Cheese Cookies
and Date-Honey Cookies

Fruit Bars

1 cup	whole-wheat flour	250 ml
1/2 cup	wheat germ	125 ml
1/2 cup	sifted all-purpose flour	125 ml
1 tsp	baking soda	5 ml
1 tsp	salt	5 ml
2 1/2 cups	quick-cooking rolled oats	625 ml
1 cup	liquid honey	250 ml
1 cup	soft shortening, melted (part butter or margarine)	250 ml

Honey-Date Filling
(recipe follows)

Heat oven to 350 °F (175 °C). Grease a 13- x 9- x 2-inch (33- x 23- x 5-cm) oblong cake pan.

Combine whole-wheat flour, wheat germ, all-purpose flour, baking soda, salt and rolled oats together in a bowl, mixing well with a fork. Add honey and melted shortening and blend well. Turn half of mixture into prepared pan and pack it in the bottom evenly. Spread with Honey-Date Filling.

Drop the remaining rolled oats mixture by small spoonfuls all over the top of the filling (don't worry if there are a few small spaces). Bake 30 minutes or until nicely browned. Cool and cut into bars.

——— MAKES 3 TO 4 DOZEN ———

Honey-Date Filling

1 lb	dates, cut up	450 g
3/4 cup	liquid honey	180 ml
1/4 cup	orange juice	60 ml
1 tbsp	orange rind	15 ml
pinch	salt	pinch

Combine all ingredients in saucepan. Bring to a boil, turn down heat and boil gently, stirring, until thick, about 5 minutes.

Butterscotch-Oat Squares

1/4 cup	butter or margarine	60 ml
2/3 cup	brown sugar, packed	160 ml
1/2 tsp	vanilla	2 ml
1 cup	quick-cooking rolled oats	250 ml
1/4 cup	chopped walnuts	60 ml
1/4 cup	sifted all-purpose flour	60 ml
1 tsp	baking powder	5 ml
1/4 tsp	salt	1 ml

→

Heat oven to 300 °F (150 °C). Grease an 8-inch (20.5-cm) square cake pan.

Melt butter or margarine in medium saucepan. Stir in brown sugar, vanilla, rolled oats and nuts. Sift flour, baking powder and salt together into the mixture and mix first with spoon then with fingers until blended.

Turn into prepared pan and press down evenly.

Bake until set, about 25 minutes. Let cool in pan 10 minutes then cut into squares. Finish cooling in pan.

MAKES ABOUT 3 DOZEN

Apricot Bars

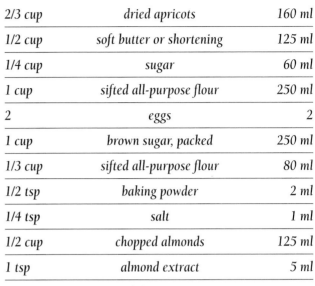

2/3 cup	dried apricots	160 ml
1/2 cup	soft butter or shortening	125 ml
1/4 cup	sugar	60 ml
1 cup	sifted all-purpose flour	250 ml
2	eggs	2
1 cup	brown sugar, packed	250 ml
1/3 cup	sifted all-purpose flour	80 ml
1/2 tsp	baking powder	2 ml
1/4 tsp	salt	1 ml
1/2 cup	chopped almonds	125 ml
1 tsp	almond extract	5 ml
	icing sugar	

Cover apricots with water in small saucepan. Bring to a boil, turn down heat, cover and simmer 10 minutes. Drain, cool and chop finely.

Heat oven to 350 °F (175 °C). Grease an 8- x 8- x 2-inch (20.5- x 20.5- x 5-cm) cake pan.

Mix butter or shortening, sugar and 1 cup (250 ml) flour with a fork, then with fingers until crumbly. Press firmly in an even layer in prepared pan.

Bake 20 to 25 minutes or until set and lightly browned.

Beat eggs well. Beat in brown sugar gradually. Sift 1/3 cup (80 ml) flour, baking powder and salt into egg mixture and blend well. Stir in apricots, almonds and almond extract. Spread over baked bottom crust. Return to oven and bake 30 minutes longer.

Cool to lukewarm and sift icing sugar generously over top. Cool before cutting into bars.

MAKES 2 TO 3 DOZEN

Left: Fruit Bars
Right: Apricot Bars

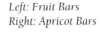

Dutch Squares

3/4 cup	soft butter	180 ml
1 cup	brown sugar, packed	250 ml
3 tbsp	milk	45 ml
2 3/4 cups	sifted all-purpose flour	685 ml
1 tbsp	cinnamon	15 ml
1/2 tsp	mace	2 ml
1/2 tsp	ground anise seed (see note)	2 ml
1/4 tsp	ginger	1 ml
1/4 tsp	nutmeg	1 ml
1/4 tsp	cloves	2 ml
1/4 tsp	baking powder	1 ml
1/8 tsp	salt	0.5 ml
1 lb	blanched almonds, finely ground (see note)	450 g
3 cups	sifted icing sugar	750 ml
2	eggs, lightly beaten	2
2 tbsp	lemon juice	30 ml
1 1/2 tsp	almond extract	7 ml
60	whole blanched almonds	60

Cream butter and brown sugar together until fluffy.. Beat in milk. Sift flour, spices, baking powder and salt together and add to creamed mixture 1/2 cup (125 ml) at a time, beating well after first few additions and then blending well as the dough gets stiffer. Gather the dough into a ball and chill a few minutes so it is easy to handle.

Combine ground almonds and icing sugar while dough is chilling. Add eggs, lemon juice and almond extract, blending very well. Set aside.

Heat oven to 375 °F (190 °C). Grease a 15- x 10- x 1-inch (38- x 25- x 2.5-cm) jelly roll pan thoroughly.

Divide spicy dough into 2 equal parts. Shape 1 part into a slightly flattened rectangle with hands and put it on a long piece of waxed paper and roll the dough into a rectangle about 15 x 10 inches (38 x 25 cm) wide (dampen table top before rolling so waxed paper will stay in place). Strip waxed paper off top of dough and invert the dough on the bottom waxed paper into the prepared pan. Strip off waxed paper and press the dough with fingers into corners and slightly up sides of pan.

Drop the almond mixture by small spoonfuls all over top of dough and spread or pat in gently and evenly almost to the edge of the dough.

Roll other half of spicy dough in the same way as the first half (use new sheets of waxed paper so dough doesn't stick and trim off any rough edges). Invert it over the almond mixture. Patch the corners with the trimmings if necessary and with the edge of a rubber scraper push the top dough down along the sides of the pan to seal the almond mixture inside.

Mark the top dough into squares with the tines of a fork, making 6 lines of fork holes lengthwise and 10 crosswise. Centre each of these squares with a whole almond.

Bake 20 minutes or until nicely browned. Cool for a few minutes in the pan then turn out on large rack to finish cooling. Cut or break into squares to serve.

Note: Grind almonds to very fine through a food chopper or food processor. You should have about 4 cups (1 L). If you can't get ground anise seed, use a mortar and pestle for the seeds or press them firmly with the back of a spoon or the bottom of a small jar until they break up finely.

————— MAKES 60 SQUARES —————

Chocolate Fancies

(unbaked)

1/2 cup	soft butter	125 ml
1/4 cup	sugar	60 ml
3 tbsp	cocoa	45 ml
1	egg	1
1/2 tsp	vanilla	2 ml
1/2 tsp	salt	2 ml
2 cups	graham wafer crumbs	500 ml
1 cup	flaked coconut	250 ml
1/2 cup	chopped toasted almonds	125 ml
2 cups	sifted icing sugar	500 ml
1 tbsp	butter, melted	15 ml
2 tbsp	cream (approx.)	30 ml
1/2 tsp	almond extract	2 ml
1 oz	semi-sweet chocolate (1 square)	30 g
1 1/2 tsp	butter	7 ml

Chocolate Fancies

Combine 1/2 cup (125 ml) butter, sugar, cocoa, egg, vanilla and salt in top of double boiler. Stir to blend well then set over simmering water and cook, stirring constantly, until slightly thickened and smooth, about 5 minutes. (If over-heated, mixture will separate but this won't affect final result.)

Remove from heat and blend in graham wafer crumbs, coconut and almonds. Press firmly into buttered 8-inch (20.5-cm) square pan. Chill while preparing icing.

Mix icing sugar, 1 tbsp (15 ml) butter, cream and almond extract (use just enough cream to make an icing that is easy to spread), blending well. Spread over first layer in pan.

Melt the chocolate and 1 1/2 tsp (7 ml) butter over lowest heat in a small pan. Drizzle it over icing and run the blade of a knife back and forth across the icing to make a design. Chill until shortly before serving.

MAKES 16 SQUARES

Left: Chocolate Bar Brownies
Right: Cookie Treats

Chocolate Bar Brownies

1 cup	butter	250 ml
4 oz	unsweetened chocolate (4 squares)	115 g
2 cups	sugar	500 ml
4	eggs	4
2 tsp	vanilla	10 ml
1 1/2 cups	sifted all-purpose flour	375 ml
1/2 tsp	salt	2 ml
1 1/2 cups	pecan halves	375 ml
	icing sugar	

Heat oven to 375 °F (190 °C). Grease a 13- x 9- x 2-inch (33- x 23- x 5-cm) cake pan.

Put butter and chocolate in top of double boiler and set over simmering water. Heat until butter and chocolate are melted, stirring occasionally.

Put sugar in medium mixing bowl. Pour chocolate mixture over it and stir to blend. Add unbeaten eggs, one at a time, beating with a wooden spoon just enough to blend. Stir in vanilla. Sift flour and salt into chocolate mixture and stir to blend. Stir in pecans.

Spread in prepared pan. Bake 25 to 30 minutes or until sides test done but an impression stays in the middle when touched lightly with finger (brownies are best when slightly underdone).

Sift icing sugar thickly over top and cut in bars while warm.

———— MAKES 3 DOZEN ————

Cookie Treats

1/2 cup	soft butter	125 ml
1/2 cup	soft shortening	125 ml
1 1/4 cups	sugar	300 ml
1	egg	1
1 tsp	vanilla	5 ml
2 1/2 cups	sifted all-purpose flour	625 ml
1 1/2 tsp	baking powder	7 ml
1/2 tsp	salt	2 ml
1 cup	chocolate chips	250 ml
1/2 cup	coarsely broken pecans	125 ml
1/2 cup	flaked coconut	125 ml
1/2 cup	well drained chopped maraschino cherries	125 ml
1 cup	sifted icing sugar	250 ml
1 tbsp	butter	15 ml
1/4 tsp	almond extract	1 ml
2 tbsp	maraschino cherry juice (approx.)	30 ml

Heat oven to 350 °F (175 °C). Grease a 15- x 10- x 1-inch (38- x 25- x 2.5-cm) jelly roll pan.

Beat 1/2 cup (125 ml) butter, shortening, sugar, egg and vanilla together until fluffy. Sift flour, baking powder and salt together into mixture and blend well. Add chocolate chips, nuts, coconut and cherries and blend well (dough should be stiff).

Press dough evenly into prepared pan. Bake 18 to 20 minutes or until brown and centre springs back when touched lightly. Cool to lukewarm in pan.

Combine icing sugar, 1 tbsp (15 ml) butter, almond extract and enough cherry juice to make a rather thin icing. Spread over warm layer. Cut into bars while still warm. Cool.

—————— MAKES 48 BARS ——————

Almond Wafer Rolls

2	egg whites	2
1/2 cup	sugar	125 ml
1/3 cup	sifted all-purpose flour	80 ml
3 tbsp	melted butter or margarine	45 ml
1/3 cup	finely chopped blanched almonds	80 ml
1/4 tsp	almond extract	1 ml
	icing sugar (optional)	

Heat oven to 450 °F (230 °C). Grease small cookie sheets thoroughly.

Beat egg whites until stiff in small bowl. Fold in sugar. Then fold in flour, butter or margarine, almonds and almond extract.

Drop batter by teaspoonfuls 3 inches (7.5 cm) apart on cookie sheets. Spread batter with the back of the spoon into very thin rounds 2 to 3 inches (5 x 7.5 cm) in diameter. (Make and bake only 6 rounds at a time, otherwise they will be cool and hard before you can roll them.)

Bake 3 to 4 minutes or until golden brown. Loosen from sheet immediately and quickly shape each into a loose roll with fingers. Cool on cake rack. Continue baking and shaping cookies until all batter is used, cooling the cookie sheets and greasing between each baking.

Sift icing sugar over cookies when they are cool, if desired. Store in a very tight tin box.

—————— MAKES ABOUT 30 ——————

Brown Sugar Shortbread and Almond Shortbreads

Brown Sugar Shortbread

1 cup	brown sugar, packed	250 ml
1 lb	soft butter	450 g
5 cups	sifted all-purpose flour	1.25 L

Combine all ingredients and squeeze and knead the dough with hands until smooth and satiny, about 20 minutes. Chill overnight.

Heat oven to 300 °F (150 °C).

Work dough, bit by bit, with hands until soft enough to roll. Roll 1/4 inch (0.5 cm) thick (see note) and cut into rounds, squares or any desired shape.

Bake 20 to 25 minutes or until set but only lightly browned on the bottom.

Note: If you have one, use a springerle rolling pin for pretty designs.

——— MAKES 4 1/2 TO 5 DOZEN MEDIUM COOKIES ———

Almond Shortbreads

2 cups	soft butter	500 ml
2/3 cup	sifted icing sugar	160 ml
1/3 cup	light brown sugar, packed	80 ml
1 tsp	almond extract	5 ml
4 1/2 cups	sifted all-purpose flour	1.125 L
1 cup	blanched almonds (approx.)	250 ml
10	candied cherries (approx.)	10
2	egg yolks	2
2 tbsp	milk	30 ml

Put butter, icing sugar, brown sugar and almond extract in large mixing bowl. Beat together until light and fluffy. Add flour and mix, first with a spoon then directly with hands, until dough is very smooth and velvety. Chill several hours.

Split the almonds into their natural halves (see note). Cut each cherry into 6 small pieces.

Heat oven to 300 °F (150 °C). Lightly grease cookie sheets.

Roll dough 1/4 inch (0.5 cm) thick. Cut into 2-inch (5-cm) rounds or stars and put on cookie sheets. Center each cookie with a bit of cherry and surround with almond halves arranged like the petals of a daisy.

Beat egg yolks and milk together with a fork and brush this mixture all over the tops of the cookies.

Bake until set and golden brown on top, 20 to 25 minutes.

Note: If you blanch your own almonds, split them while they are still warm. If you are using commercially blanched almonds they may be quite hard to split, but if you let them soak in boiling water for a few minutes, they will come apart easily.

—— MAKES ABOUT 60 LARGE THICK SHORTBREADS ——

Beat together butter, icing sugar, brown sugar and almond extract in large mixing bowl until light and fluffy.

Add flour and mix, first with a spoon then directly with hands, until dough is very smooth and velvety.

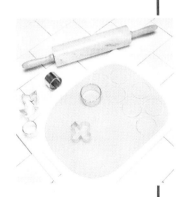

Cut into 2-inch (5-cm) rounds or stars.

Center each cookie with a bit of cherry and surround with almond halves arranged like the petals of a daisy.

Double Chocolate Cake

2 tbsp	shortening	30 ml
2 oz	unsweetened chocolate (2 squares)	60 g
1 cup	sugar	250 ml
1	egg	1
1 1/2 cups	sifted all-purpose flour	375 ml
1 tsp	baking soda	5 ml
1/4 tsp	salt	1 ml
1 cup	buttermilk or soured milk	250 ml
1 tsp	vanilla	5 ml

Creamy Chocolate Icing
(recipe follows)

Heat oven to 350 °F (175 °C). Grease a 9-inch (23-cm) square cake pan.

Combine shortening and chocolate in a small saucepan and set over lowest heat to melt.

Combine sugar, egg and chocolate mixture in mixing bowl and beat well.

Sift flour, baking soda and salt together and add to sugar mixture alternately with mixture of buttermilk or soured milk and vanilla.

Pour into prepared pan and bake about 35 minutes or until top springs back when touched lightly in center. Cool in pan. Ice with Creamy Chocolate Icing.

SERVES 8 TO 10

Creamy Chocolate Icing

2 tbsp	butter	30 ml
1 oz	unsweetened chocolate, cut up (1 square)	30 ml
1 1/2 tbsp	flour	22 ml
1/8 tsp	salt	0.5 ml
1/3 cup	milk	80 ml
2 cups	sifted icing sugar	500 ml
1/2 tsp	vanilla	2 ml
1/4 cup	chopped walnuts	60 ml
1/2 cup	miniature marshmallows	125 ml

Melt butter and chocolate in a small saucepan over lowest heat. Remove from heat and blend in flour and salt. Stir in milk gradually. Return to low heat and cook until very thick and smooth, stirring constantly.

Remove from heat and stir in sugar and vanilla. Set in ice water and continue stirring until of spreading consistency. Stir in nuts and marshmallows and use to ice cake as directed.

Double Chocolate Cake

California Fruitcake

4 cups	sifted all-purpose flour	1 L
2 tsp	cinnamon	10 ml
2 tsp	nutmeg	10 ml
1 tsp	mace	5 ml
1 tsp	cloves	5 ml
1 tsp	allspice	5 ml
1 tsp	salt	5 ml
1 lb	cut up mixed candied fruit	450 g
1 lb	candied cherries, halved	450 g
1 lb	seeded raisins, cut up	450 g
1 lb	seedless raisins	450 g
1 lb	currants	450 g
1 lb	dates, cut up	450 g
1/2 lb	citron, slivered	225 g
1 lb	broken walnuts	450 g
1 lb	butter	450 g
1 lb	brown sugar	450 g
12	egg yolks	12
1 cup	sherry or strong coffee	250 ml
1/2 cup	grape juice	125 ml
1 cup	orange juice	250 ml
2 tbsp	lemon juice	30 ml
	grated rind of 3 oranges	
	grated rind of 1 lemon	
12	egg whites	12

Grease and line with greased brown paper four 9- x 5- x 3-inch (23- x 12.5- x 7.5-cm) loaf pans. Put a pan of hot water in bottom of oven.

Sift flour, spices and salt together onto waxed paper.

Combine fruit and nuts in large bowl. Measure out 1 cup (250 ml) of the flour-spice mixture, add to the fruit and nuts and blend well.

Cream butter and sugar until fluffy. Add egg yolks, one at a time, beating well after each addition. Continue beating until smooth and creamy. Blend in remaining flour mixture alternately with sherry or coffee, grape juice, orange juice and lemon juice, beginning and ending with flour mixture.

Blend in grated orange and lemon rinds and fruit-nut mixture.

Heat oven to 250 °F (120 °C).

Beat egg whites until they hold stiff peaks. Fold into fruit mixture.

Spoon into prepared pans and bake about 3 hours or until a toothpick inserted in the center comes out clean.

Cool for a few minutes in pans then lift out by ends of paper and finish cooling on cake racks. Strip off paper, wrap tightly in aluminum foil and store in a cool dry place for several weeks before using.

— MAKES 4 CAKES —

Two-Tone Fruit Cake

1 cup	seedless raisins	250 ml
1 cup	cut up prunes (see note)	250 ml
2 cups	walnuts, coarsely chopped	500 ml
2 cups	cut up mixed candied peel	500 ml
2 tsp	cinnamon	10 ml
1 tsp	cloves	5 ml
1 tsp	allspice	5 ml
2 tbsp	molasses	30 ml
1 cup	golden raisins	250 ml
1 cup	chopped dried apricots	250 ml
2 cups	chopped blanched almonds	500 ml
1 cup	cup up candied pineapple	250 ml
1 cup	cut up mixed candied peel	250 ml
1/2 tsp	ginger	2 ml
1/2 tsp	mace	2 ml
1 tbsp	lemon juice	15 ml
1 1/2 cups	soft shortening (part butter)	375 ml
2 cups	sugar	500 ml
6	eggs	6
4 cups	sifted all-purpose flour	1 L
2 tsp	baking powder	10 ml
2 tsp	salt	10 ml

Grease and line with greased brown paper three fruit cake pans, 8 x 8 x 3 1/2 inches (20.5 x 20.5 x 8.75 cm), 6 x 6 x 3 3/4 inches (15 x 15 x 9.5 cm) and 4 x 4 x 3 inches (10 x 10 x 7.5 cm).

Combine seedless raisins, prunes, walnuts, 2 cups (500 ml) mixed peel, cinnamon, cloves, allspice and molasses in a large bowl.

Combine golden raisins, apricots, almonds, pineapple, 1 cup (250 ml) mixed peel, ginger, mace and lemon juice in another large bowl.

Cream shortening and sugar together in another large bowl until light and fluffy. Add eggs, one at a time, beating well after each addition.

Sift flour, baking powder and salt together into creamed mixture and stir until blended.

Add half of this batter to each fruit mixture — about 3 1/2 cups (875 ml) and fold each mixture until well blended.

Divide one of the batters among the three prepared pans using 1 cup (250 ml) for the smallest pan, 2 cups (500 ml) for the medium pan and the remainder of the batter for the large pan — about 3 1/2 cups (875 ml). Spread evenly.

Divide other batter in the same way among the three pans and spread it evenly.

Heat oven to 275 °F (135 °C).

Put a pan of hot water in bottom of oven. Bake cakes until a toothpick stuck deep in center comes out clean — about 2 hours for small cake and 2 3/4 hours for medium and large cakes.

Cool for a few minutes in pans then lift out by ends of paper and finish cooling on cake racks. Strip off paper, wrap tightly in aluminum foil and store in a cool dry place for several weeks before using.

Note: Use uncooked prunes. If hard, cover with boiling water and let stand about 5 minutes.

———————— MAKES 3 CAKES ————————

Two-Tone Fruit Cake

Burnt Sugar Cake

1/2 cup	sugar	125 ml
1/2 cup	boiling water	125 ml
3	egg whites	3
1/2 cup	soft butter	125 ml
1 1/2 cups	sugar	375 ml
3	egg yolks	3
1 cup	cold water	250 ml
1 tbsp	cream	15 ml
1 tsp	vanilla	5 ml
2 1/4 cups	sifted all-purpose flour	560 ml
2 tsp	baking powder	10 ml
1/2 tsp	salt	2 ml

Burnt Sugar Fudge Icing (recipe follows)

Heat oven to 350 °F (175 °C). Grease an oblong cake pan, 13 x 9 x 2 inches (33 x 23 x 5 cm).

Put 1/2 cup (125 ml) sugar in heavy skillet. Set over moderate heat and melt, stirring with a wooden spoon. Continue heating until sugar becomes a dark brown syrup (let it get darker than a caramel color but don't let it turn black or it will taste bitter). Stir in boiling water gradually (be careful of steam). Remove from heat. This is the burnt sugar syrup.

Beat egg whites until stiff peaks form. Set aside.

Beat butter, 1 1/2 cups (375 ml) sugar and egg yolks together until fluffy.

Combine cold water, cream, 3 tbsp of the burnt sugar syrup and vanilla.

→

Sift flour, baking powder and salt together. Stir dry ingredients into egg yolk mixture alternately with burnt sugar mixture, beginning and ending with dry ingredients. Fold in egg whites.

Pour into prepared pan and bake about 30 minutes or until top springs back when touched lightly. Cool in pan. Ice with Burnt Sugar Fudge Icing.

————— MAKES 1 CAKE —————

Burnt Sugar Fudge Icing

2 cups	sugar	500 ml
1/2 cup	milk	125 ml
2 tbsp	burnt sugar syrup prepared for cake	30 ml
1 tsp	corn syrup	5 ml
1 tsp	butter	5 ml

Combine ingredients in a heavy saucepan. Stir over moderately high heat until sugar is dissolved then boil without stirring until a few drops in cold water form a soft ball — 234 °F (112 °C) on candy thermometer. Let stand until lukewarm then beat until just beginning to get creamy (watch carefully or icing will get too hard to spread). Spread on Burnt Sugar Cake.

Fluffy Sponge Cake

6	egg yolks	6
1 1/2 cups	sugar	375 ml
1/3 cup	cold water	80 ml
2 tsp	vanilla	10 ml
1 tsp	almond extract	5 ml
1 1/3 cups	sifted all-purpose flour	330 ml
1 1/2 tsp	baking powder	7 ml
1/2 tsp	salt	2 ml
6	egg whites	6
1/2 tsp	cream of tartar	2 ml

Hat oven to 325 °F (160 °C). Have an ungreased 10-inch (25-cm) tube pan ready.

Beat egg yolks in a small bowl with electric mixer until very thick and fluffy, about 5 minutes at high speed. Add sugar gradually, beating well after each addition. Turn mixer speed to low and beat in water, vanilla and almond extract.

Sift flour, baking powder and salt together onto waxed paper and add to egg yolk mixture. Beat on low speed until smooth, scraping down the sides of the bowl often.

Wash beaters very carefully to be sure all egg yolk mixture is removed. Beat egg whites and cream of tartar in large mixer bowl until stiff. Add about 1/2 of the egg white mixture to the egg yolk mixture and fold together with a rubber scraper. Turn the blended mixture into the bowl containing the remaining egg white mixture and fold the two mixtures together gently but quickly.

Pour batter into tube pan. Bake 60 to 65 minutes or until top springs back when touched lightly. Invert immediately on a funnel or the neck of a bottle and let hang upside down until cool. Turn out on cake plate, leaving top side down if you are icing the cake or turning top side up if you are serving it plain.

————— MAKES 1 CAKE —————

Burnt Sugar Cake

Date Loaf Cake

1 tsp	baking soda	5 ml
1 cup	boiling water	250 ml
1 1/2 cups	cut-up dates	375 ml
2/3 cup	brown sugar, packed	160 ml
1	egg	1
1 tbsp	butter	15 ml
1 tsp	vanilla	5 ml
1 cup	seedless raisins	250 ml
1/2 cup	well drained maraschino cherries, halved	125 ml
2 tbsp	maraschino cherry juice	30 ml
2 cups	sifted all-purpose flour	500 ml
1 tsp	baking powder	5 ml
1 tsp	salt	5 ml

Heat oven to 325 °F (160 °C). Grease a 9- x 5- x 3-inch (23- x 12.5- x 7.5-cm) loaf pan.

Add baking soda and boiling water to dates, stir and set aside to cool a little.

Beat brown sugar, egg, butter and vanilla together in a mixing bowl. Stir in date mixture, raisins, maraschino cherries and cherry juice.

Sift flour, baking powder and salt together into the fruit mixture and blend well. Spoon into prepared pan. Bake about 1 hour and 15 minutes.

MAKES 1 LOAF CAKE

Applesauce Cake

1 cup	seedless raisins, cut up	250 ml
1 cup	chopped walnuts	250 ml
2 cups	sifted all-purpose flour	500 ml
1 tsp	salt	5 ml
1 tsp	baking soda	5 ml
1 tsp	cinnamon	5 ml
1/4 tsp	cloves	1 ml
1/2 cup	soft shortening	125 ml
3/4 cup	sugar	180 ml
1	egg	1
1 cup	canned, sweetened applesauce	250 ml

Heat oven to 350 °F (175 °C). Grease and flour a loaf pan, 9 x 5 x 3 inches (23 x 12.5 x 7.5 cm).

Combine raisins and nuts in a bowl. Sift flour, salt, baking soda, cinnamon and cloves together over fruit-nut mixture and toss together.

Beat shortening, sugar and egg together until fluffy. Add flour mixture alternately with applesauce, beating to blend well after each addition.

Spoon into prepared pan.

Bake about 1 hour and 15 minutes or until a toothpick stuck in the centre comes out clean. Cool in pan a few minutes and then turn out on rack to cool.

MAKES 1 LOAF CAKE

Applesauce Cake

Lemon Pound Cake

2/3 cup	soft butter or margarine	160 ml
1 cup	sugar	250 ml
4	eggs	4
1 tsp	grated lemon rind	5 ml
1 1/2 tbsp	lemon juice	22 ml
2 cups	sifted cake flour	500 ml
1/2 tsp	baking powder	2 ml
1/2 tsp	salt	2 ml

Cream butter or margarine until fluffy. Add sugar gradually and beat well after each addition. Continue beating until mixture is fluffy. Add eggs, one at a time, beating well after each addition. Stir in lemon rind and lemon juice.

Sift flour, baking powder and salt together and stir into first mixture, stirring only until blended. Spoon into prepared pan and bake about 1 hour and 15 minutes or until a toothpick stuck in the centre of the cake comes out clean. Turn out and cool on rack.

——————— MAKES 1 LOAF CAKE ———————

Heat oven to 300 °F (150 °C). Grease a 9- x 5- x 3-inch (23- x 12.5- x 7.5-cm) loaf pan.

Grasshopper Cake

2	egg whites	2
1/2 cup	sugar	125 ml
1 3/4 cups	sifted cake flour	430 ml
1 cup	sugar	250 ml
3/4 tsp	baking soda	3 ml
1 tsp	salt	5 ml
1/3 cup	vegetable oil	80 ml
1 cup	buttermilk or soured milk	250 ml
2	egg yolks	2
2 oz	unsweetened chocolate, melted	60 ml

Grasshopper Cream
(recipe follows)

Heat oven to 350 °F (175 °C). Grease and flour two 8-inch (20.5-cm) round layer cake pans at least 1 1/2 inches (3.75 cm) deep.

Beat egg whites until foamy. Add the 1/2 cup (125 ml) sugar, 1 tbsp (15 ml) at a time and beat well after each addition. Continue beating until stiff and glossy.

Sift flour, 1 cup (250 ml) sugar, baking soda and salt into a large mixing bowl. Add oil and half the buttermilk or soured milk. Beat 1 minute (medium speed on the mixer or 150 strokes by hand). Add remaining milk, egg yolks and chocolate and beat 1 minute more. Fold in egg white mixture.

Pour into prepared pans and bake about 30 minutes or until tops spring back when touched lightly. Turn out on racks to cool.

Split each layer into 2 thin layers. Put Grasshopper Cream between the layers and on the top and sides. Chill until serving time. (This can be done several hours ahead of time.) Cut in large wedges to serve.

———— SERVES 12 ————

Grasshopper Cream

1 tbsp	unflavored gelatin (1 envelope)	15 ml
1/4 cup	cold water	60 ml
1/2 cup	green crème de menthe	125 ml
1/3 cup	white crème de cacao	80 ml
1 pt	whipping cream	625 ml

Add gelatin to cold water and let stand 5 minutes. Heat crème de menthe and crème de cacao (do not boil.). Add gelatin and stir until dissolved. Cool (do not chill). Whip cream until stiff. Fold in liqueur mixture (do not beat it in). Chill 15 minutes.

Grasshopper Cake

Yule Cakes

1 1/2 cups	unblanched almonds	375 ml
1 1/2 cups	walnut pieces	375 ml
1 cup	quartered pitted dates	250 ml
1 cup	drained and halved maraschino cherries	250 ml
1 cup	slivered candied orange peel	250 ml
1/2 cup	sultana raisins	125 ml
3/4 cup	sifted all-purpose flour	180 ml
3/4 cup	sugar	180 ml
1/2 tsp	baking powder	2 ml
1/2 tsp	salt	2 ml
3	eggs	3
1 tbsp	maraschino cherry juice	15 ml
1 tsp	almond extract	5 ml

Grease 2 aluminum foil pans, about 7 1/2 x 3 1/2 x 2 1/4 inches (19.25 x 8.75 x 5.5 cm).

Combine nuts, dates, cherries, orange peel and raisins in a large bowl. Sift flour, sugar, baking powder and salt together over fruit and nuts and toss with hands to mix well.

Heat oven to 300 °F (150 °C).

Beat eggs until thick and lemon colored, about 5 minutes at high speed on the mixer. Stir in maraschino cherry juice and almond extract. Pour over first mixture and blend well.

Spoon into prepared pans and press down firmly with back of spoon.

Bake about 1 hour and 45 minutes or until cakes seem firm when touched lightly in the center. Cool in pans for a few minutes then turn out and complete cooling on a rack. Wash pans and return cakes to them when cold. Wrap in foil and store in refrigerator. Or wrap in transparent wrap and tie with a ribbon for gifts. These cakes are ready for eating after 2 or 3 days' storage.

MAKES 2 CAKES

Black Forest Torte

8	egg yolks	8
1	whole egg	1
1 tbsp	water	15 ml
1 cup	sugar	250 ml
3/4 cup	fine dry bread crumbs	180 ml
1/2 cup	finely ground blanched almonds	125 ml
1/2 tsp	almond extract	2 ml
1/3 cup	cocoa	80 ml
1/2 cup	sifted all-purpose flour	125 ml
8	egg whites	8
1 tbsp	unflavored gelatin	15 ml
2 tbsp	cold water	30 ml
2 1/2 cups	whipping cream	625 ml
1/3 cup	sifted icing sugar	80 ml
pinch	salt	pinch
1 tsp	vanilla	5 ml
1/2 tsp	almond extract	2 ml
	Cherry Filling (recipe follows)	
	grated chocolate or chocolate curls	
	candied or maraschino cherries	

Heat oven to 350 °F (175 °C). Grease and flour two 9-inch (23-cm) round layer cake pans, 1 1/2 inches (3.75 cm) deep.

Beat egg yolks, whole egg and 1 tbsp water together until thick and fluffy, about 5 minutes at high speed on the mixer. Add sugar gradually, beating well after each addition. Fold in bread crumbs, almonds and 1/2 tsp (2 ml) almond extract. Sift cocoa and flour together into mixture and fold to blend.

Beat egg whites until just stiff but not dry. Fold into first mixture gently but quickly.

→

Divide evenly between the two prepared pans. Bake 25 minutes or until a toothpick stuck in the center of the cakes comes out clean. Cool for a few minutes then turn out on racks to complete cooling.

Split each layer into 2 thin layers when cool.

Put gelatin in small dish. Add 2 tbsp (30 ml) water and let stand 5 minutes. Set in pan of boiling water and heat until gelatin dissolves. Let cool for about 1 minute.

Beat cream, icing sugar, salt, vanilla and 1/2 tsp (2 ml) almond extract until just beginning to thicken while gelatin is dissolving and cooling. Continue beating cream (turn down speed on mixer if cream starts to get stiff) and add the gelatin in a very thin stream. Beat until stiff peaks form.

Put one of the thin layers of cake on serving plate. Top with Cherry Filling, spreading evenly. Add another layer of cake. Spread with about 1/4 of the whipped cream. Add another layer of cake and another 1/4 of the whipped cream. Top with final layer of cake and ice whole outside of cake with remaining cream.

Sprinkle sides and top of cake generously with grated chocolate or chocolate curls (unsweetened chocolate is best). Cut a few cherries in half and add them to top of cake.

Chill at least and hour before serving. Because of the gelatin in the whipped cream the cake will hold very well and can be made a day in advance of serving if desired.

Black Forest Torte

———————— SERVES 12 ————————

Cherry Filling

14-oz can	red pitted cherries	398-ml can
1 tbsp	cornstarch	15 ml
1/2 tsp	almond extract	2 ml

Drain cherries very well. Measure out 3/4 cup (180 ml) of juice (add a little water if necessary). Add cornstarch to juice in a small saucepan and stir until smooth. Set over high heat and bring to a boil quickly, stirring constantly. Turn heat to low and cook 1 minute, stirring constantly. Remove from heat and stir in almond extract and cherries. Chill until thick and use for filling as directed in recipe.

Strawberry Filled Cake

5 cups	strawberries, washed and hulled	1.25 L
1 cup	water	250 ml
	red food coloring (optional)	
1 1/2 cups	sugar	375 ml
1/3 cup	cornstarch	80 ml
1/2 cup	water	125 ml
	Cooled French Sponge Layers (recipe follows)	
	Boiled Icing (recipe follows)	

Slice enough of the strawberries to measure 2 cups (500 ml). Put them into saucepan and add 1 cup (250 ml) water. Bring to a boil, turn down heat and simmer 3 minutes or until berries are tender. Mash or blend until mixture is smooth. Return to saucepan. Add a few drops of food coloring if desired to make the filling a good bright red. Set over high heat and bring to a boil.

Blend sugar, cornstarch and 1/2 cup (125 ml) water until smooth. Gradually add to boiling mixture and stir constantly until thickened and smooth. Turn down heat and continue cooking and stirring 1 minute. Remove from heat, cover with waxed paper and cool to room temperature. Slice half of remaining berries into thickened berry mixture.

→

Cut each cake layer in half crosswise to make 4 thin layers. Spread 1 layer with about 1/4 of the strawberry mixture, add a second cake layer and another thin layer of strawberry mixture. Repeat once more. Top with remaining cake layer.

Ice whole outside of cake with Boiled Icing, building it up around the sides and leaving a hollow in the center on top. Fill hollow with any remaining strawberry filling and cover filling completely with whole berries.

Chill until serving time. (Cake should be served the day it is made.) Garnish serving plate with more whole berries if desired.

——————— SERVES 12 TO 16 ———————

Heat the large bowl of your mixer under hot tap water. Dry. Break eggs into bowl. Add sugar and vanilla. Beat at high speed on the mixer, scraping the sides of the bowl often, until the mixture stands in stiff peaks (15 to 30 minutes).

Melt butter and cool to lukewarm.

Sprinkle 2 tbsp (30 ml) of the flour over the egg mixture. Fold it in gently but quickly with a rubber scraper. Repeat until all flour is added. Sprinkle butter, 1 tsp (15 ml) at a time, over batter. Fold gently but quickly after each addition.

Pour batter into prepared pans. Bake about 40 minutes or until tops spring back when touched lightly in center.

Loosen cakes carefully all around edges and turn out on cake racks to cool. Peel off paper.

French Sponge Layers

6	eggs	6
1 cup	sugar	250 ml
1 tsp	vanilla	5 ml
1/4 cup	butter	60 ml
1 cup	sifted cake flour	250 ml

Put the unbroken eggs in a bowl and cover with hot tap water. Let them stand until the water is lukewarm, drain and repeat process. (Don't use boiling water — you want the eggs warm but not cooked.)

Heat oven to 350 °F (175 °C). Grease two 9-inch (23-cm) round layer cake pans at least 1 1/2 inches (3.75 cm) deep. Line the bottoms of the pans with heavy brown paper and grease the paper.

Boiled Icing

3/4 cup	sugar	180 ml
3 tbsp	water	45 ml
1/3 cup	corn syrup	80 ml
3	egg whites	3
1 1/2 tsp	vanilla	7 ml

Combine sugar, water and corn syrup in small saucepan. Bring to a boil and boil hard, without stirring to 242 °F (116 °C) (syrup spins 6- to 8-inch (15- to 20.5-cm) thread when dropped from the tines of a fork).

Beat egg whites until stiff. Pour hot syrup in a thin stream into egg whites, beating constantly. Continue beating until stiff peaks form. Blend in vanilla.

Strawberry Filled Cake

Banana-Cream Layer Cake

(party dessert — to serve 24)

	Spice Pound Cake (recipe follows)	
	Bavarian Cream (recipe follows)	
5	firm ripe bananas (approx.)	5
2 cups	whipping cream	500 ml
1/2 cup	sifted icing sugar	125 ml
2 tsp	vanilla	10 ml
	walnut halves (optional)	

Make Spice Pound Cake the day before you want to serve the dessert (or make it well ahead of time and freeze it until the day you want to put the dessert together). Make the Bavarian Cream shortly before you assemble the dessert and keep it at room temperature so it doesn't set.

Split each cake into two equal layers lengthwise and drop the bottom halves back into the baking pans, cut sides up. Spread each cake half with about 1/2 cup (125 ml) Bavarian Cream. Chill until lightly set (I put the cakes in the freezer for a very few minutes). Top each cake layer with two whole bananas running lengthwise down the cake. Fill any space at the ends of the whole bananas with a piece of another banana. Divide the remaining Bavarian Cream evenly between the two pans — about 1 1/2 cups (375 ml) each. Spread it evenly over the bananas and let it run down around the bananas to fill all the spaces. (This layer will nearly fill the pans.) Chill in the refrigerator until lightly set but still a little sticky (so top layers will stick firmly). Add top layers and chill in refrigerator several hours or until Bavarian Cream mixture is very firm.

Unmould cakes on serving plate shortly before serving time. Whip cream until slightly thickened. Beat in icing sugar and vanilla and continue beating until firm. Spread thickly over tops and sides of cakes. Decorate with walnut halves. Chill until serving time. Cut in thick slices to serve.

Note: It is preferable to fill and ice the cakes the day you wish to serve them. However, I find the bananas keep their color well even when the cakes are held overnight so if you wish you can put the cakes together late the day before serving, but do not add the whipped cream icing until shortly before serving time.

———————— EACH CAKE WILL SERVE 12 ————————
→

Banana-Cream Layer Cake

Spice Pound Cake

1 cup	soft butter	250 ml
2 cups	sugar	500 ml
4	eggs	4
1 1/2 tsp	vanilla	7 ml
3 cups	sifted all-purpose flour	750 ml
1/2 tsp	baking soda	2 ml
1/2 tsp	baking powder	2 ml
3/4 tsp	salt	3 ml
1 tsp	cinnamon	5 ml
1 tsp	nutmeg	5 ml
1/2 tsp	allspice	2 ml
1/8 tsp	cloves	0.5 ml
1 cup	buttermilk	250 ml

Heat oven to 350 °F (175 °C). Grease and flour 2 loaf pans, 10 1/2 x 3 3/4 x 2 1/2 inches (25.5 x 8.25 x 6.25 cm).

Cream butter until fluffy. Add sugar gradually and beat until well blended after each addition. Add eggs (not beaten), one at a time, beating well after each addition, stir in vanilla.

Sift flour, baking soda, baking powder, salt and spices together. Add to first mixture alternately with buttermilk, beginning and ending with dry ingredients.

Spoon into prepared pans. Bake about 1 1/4 hours or until a toothpick stuck in the centers of the cakes comes out clean. Turn out on racks to cool.

MAKES 2 LOAF CAKES

Bavarian Cream

1/2 cup	sugar	125 ml
1 tbsp	unflavored gelatin	15 ml
1/4 tsp	salt	1 ml
2 1/4 cups	milk	560 ml
4	egg yolks, slightly beaten	4
1 cup	whipping cream, whipped	250 ml
1 tsp	vanilla	5 ml
1/2 tsp	almond extract	2 ml

Blend sugar, gelatin, salt, milk and egg yolks in medium saucepan. Set over medium heat and cook until mixture comes to a full boil, stirring constantly. Set pan in ice water and chill until mixture mounds slightly when dropped from a spoon. Fold in whipped cream and flavorings. Chill a few minutes just until beginning to thicken slightly (watch carefully — the cream must not set). Keep at room temperature while completing recipe.

Wagon Wheel Apple Pie

Basic Pastry

2 cups	sifted all-purpose flour	500 ml
1 tsp	salt	5 ml
2/3 cup	pure lard	180 ml
	or	
3/4 cup	shortening	160 ml
1/4 cup	ice water	60 ml

Measure flour into bowl. Mix in salt with a fork. Add lard or shortening and cut in coarsely with a pastry blender. Sprinkle in water a tablespoonful (15 ml) at a time and mix lightly with a fork just until all flour is dampened. Gather dough into a ball with fingers and press together firmly. Use as directed in recipes.

MAKES 2 9-INCH (23-CM) CRUSTS
OR 1 DOUBLE CRUST

Wagon Wheel Apple Pie

Basic Pastry (recipe p. 302)

1 tbsp	sugar	15 ml
1 1/2 tsp	flour	7 ml
1 cup	sugar	250 ml
3 tbsp	flour	45 ml
1/4 tsp	salt	1 ml
1/4 tsp	cinnamon	1 ml
1/8 tsp	nutmeg	0.5 ml
2/3 cup	water	160 ml
2/3 cup	raisins	160 ml
2 tbsp	butter	30 ml
5 cups	peeled, sliced apples	1.25 L
	sugar	

Heat oven to 400 °F (205 °C). Line 9-inch (23-cm) pie pan with half of pastry, building up a high fluted edge. Combine 1 tbsp (15 ml) sugar and 1 1/2 tsp (7 ml) flour and sprinkle evenly over bottom of pastry.

Combine 1 cup (250 ml) sugar, 3 tbsp (45 ml) flour, salt, cinnamon and nutmeg in saucepan. Stir in water. Add raisins. Cook over moderate heat until boiling, thickened and smooth, stirring constantly. Remove from heat and stir in butter and apples. Pour into pastry lined pan.

Roll remaining pastry and cut a round with a cookie cutter. Put it in center of pie. Cut strips about 1/2 inch (1.25 cm) wide from remaining pastry and put them on top of pie, running from under the center round to the edge, like the spokes of a wheel. Sprinkle these strips and the center round generously with sugar.

Bake about 40 minutes or until pastry is well browned and apples are tender.

SERVES 6 TO 8

Measure flour into bowl. Mix in salt with a fork. Add lard or shortening and cut in coarsely with a pastry blender.

Sprinkle in water a tablespoonful (15 ml) at a time and mix lightly with a fork just until all flour is dampened.

Roll remaining pastry and cut a round with a cookie cutter. Put it in center of pie. Cut strips about 1/2 inch (1.25 cm) wide from remaining pastry and put them on top of pie, running from under the center round to the edge, like the spokes of a wheel.

Chocolate-Rum Pie

pastry for 1 crust 9-inch (23-cm) pie

1 oz	unsweetened chocolate	30 g
1 tbsp	butter	15 ml
2	eggs	2
1/3 cup	sugar	80 ml
1/2 cup	corn syrup	125 ml
1/2 tsp	vanilla	2 ml
1/2 cup	pecan halves	125 ml
3	egg yolks	3
2/3 cup	sugar	160 ml
1/2 cup	cold water	125 ml
1 tbsp	unflavored gelatin	15 ml
1/3 cup	dark rum	80 ml
1 1/2 cups	whipping cream	375 ml

chocolate curls or pecan halves

Heat oven to 375 °F (190 °C).

Line a 9-inch (23-cm) pie pan with pastry, building up a high fluted edge. Set aside.

Put chocolate and butter in small saucepan and set over lowest heat until melted.

Beat eggs, 1/3 cup (80 ml) sugar, corn syrup, chocolate mixture and vanilla together to blend. Stir in pecans. Pour into pastry-lined pie pan.

Bake 15 to 20 minutes or until filling is just set and pastry is nicely browned. Cool.

Beat egg yolks until foamy. Gradually beat in 2/3 cup (160 ml) sugar.

Combine water and gelatin in small saucepan. Let stand 5 minutes then heat just to the boiling point, stirring. Gradually beat into egg yolk mixture. Beat in rum.

Set bowl in ice water and chill until mixture begins to hold a shape when dropped form a spoon.

Whip cream until stiff and fold into gelatin mixture. Set back in ice water and chill until mixture begins to hold peaks. Spoon over chocolate mixture in pie shell.

Garnish with chocolate curls or pecan halves. Chill until shortly before serving time.

SERVES 6 TO 8

Luscious Lemon Pie

1 1/2 cups	sugar	375 ml
1/3 cup	cornstarch	80 ml
1/8 tsp	salt	0.5 ml
12 oz	plain yogurt	350 g
1/4 cup	lemon juice	60 ml
1/4 cup	orange juice	60 ml
3	egg yolks	3
2 tsp	grated lemon rind	10 ml
	Corn Flake Pie Shell (recipe follows)	
3	egg whites	3
1/4 tsp	cream of tartar	1 ml
1/3 cup	sugar	80 ml

Luscious Lemon Pie

Combine 1 1/2 cups (375 ml) sugar, cornstarch and salt thoroughly in a heavy medium-size saucepan. Add yogurt, lemon juice and orange juice and stir or beat with rotary beater until smooth. Set over high heat and cook until mixture comes to a boil, stirring constantly. Turn heat to low and continue cooking and stirring 2 minutes longer.

Beat egg yolks. Add about half of the hot mixture to the egg yolks gradually, stirring constantly. Return the mixture to the saucepan and cook and stir 2 minutes longer. Remove from heat. Stir in lemon rind. Cool to lukewarm.

Pour into Corn Flake Pie Shell.

Heat oven to 400 °F (205 °C).

Beat egg whites and cream of tartar until foamy. Add 1/3 cup (80 ml) sugar, about 1 tbsp (15 ml) at a time, beating well after each addition. Continue beating until stiff glossy peaks form. Spread over filling in pie, sealing to pie shell all around.

Bake 8 to 10 minutes or until meringue is delicately browned. Cool before serving.

SERVES 6 TO 8

Corn Flake Pie Shell

1 1/2 cups	fine corn flake crumbs	375 ml
1/4 cup	butter, melted	60 ml
2 tbsp	sugar	30 ml

Heat oven to 350 °F (175 °C). Have ready a 9-inch (23-cm) pie pan.

Blend all ingredients. Press the mixture firmly on bottom and up sides of pie pan, building up as high an edge as possible. Bake about 10 minutes. Cool.

Sour Cream-Prune Pie

4-oz pkg	lemon pie filling mix	115-g pkg
1/2 cup	sugar	125 ml
1/4 cup	water	60 ml
2	egg yolks	2
1 3/4 cups	water	425 ml
1/4 tsp	grated lemon rind	1 ml
1 cup	chopped soft prunes	250 ml
1 cup	commercial sour cream	250 ml
1	9-inch (23-cm) baked pie shell	1

Put lemon pie filling in medium saucepan. Stir in sugar and 1/4 cup (60 ml) water. Blend in egg yolks thoroughly. Stir in 1 3/4 cups (425 ml) water, lemon rind and prunes. Set over moderate heat and cook until mixture comes to a full boil and thickens, stirring constantly. Turn down heat and continue cooking 3 minutes more, stirring constantly. Cool. Fold in sour cream.

Spoon mixture into cooled pie shell and chill well.

——————— SERVES 6 TO 8 ———————

Best Raisin Pie

1 cup	sugar	250 ml
3 tbsp	cornstarch	45 ml
1/2 tsp	salt	2 ml
1 cup	orange juice	250 ml
2 tbsp	lemon juice	30 ml
1 cup	water	250 ml
1 tsp	grated orange rind	5 ml
3 tbsp	butter	45 ml
2 cups	seedless raisins	500 ml

Basic Pastry (recipe p. 302)

Combine sugar, cornstarch and salt thoroughly in saucepan. Stir in orange juice, lemon juice and water gradually, stirring until smooth. Add orange rind, butter and raisins. Set over high heat and bring to a boil quickly, stirring constantly. Turn down heat and cook gently 3 minutes more, stirring. Cool.

Heat oven to 450 °F (230 °C).

Line 9-inch (23-cm) pie pan with half of pastry. Pour in filling.

Roll remaining pastry and use to cover pie, fluting edge and cutting vents in the top to let steam escape. Cover edge of pie with a strip of aluminum foil to keep it from getting too brown.

Bake 25 to 30 minutes or until well browned. Serve slightly warm or cold.

—————— SERVES 6 TO 8 ——————

California Raisin Pie

2 cups	seedless raisins	500 ml
2 cups	water	500 ml
1 cup	sugar	250 ml
1/4 cup	butter	60 ml
1/2 cup	water	125 ml
1/4 cup	flour	60 ml
3	egg yolks	3
4 tsp	grated lemon rind	20 ml
1/4 cup	lemon juice	60 ml
1 tsp	cinnamon	5 ml
1/4 tsp	cloves	1 ml
1	9-inch (23-cm) baked pie shell	1
1/2 cup	chopped walnuts	125 ml

Combine raisins, 2 cups (500 ml) water and sugar in medium saucepan. Set over high heat and bring to a boil. Turn heat to moderate and cook gently 10 minutes, stirring often. Add butter. Combine 1/2 cup (125 ml) water and flour, stirring until smooth and stir this mixture gradually into the boiling mixture. Boil 1 minute or until thickened, stirring constantly.

Beat egg yolks lightly and add some of hot liquid from saucepan, a little at a time, beating constantly. Stir egg yolk mixture into boiling liquid gradually along with lemon rind, lemon juice and spices. Simmer 1 minute, stirring. Remove from heat and cool to lukewarm.

Pour mixture into baked pie shell. Sprinkle with walnuts. Serve slightly warm or cold.

—————— SERVES 6 TO 8 ——————

Sour Cream-Prune Pie

Pecan Pie

	pastry for 1 crust 9-inch (23-cm) pie	
4	eggs	4
1 cup	sugar	250 ml
1 cup	corn syrup	250 ml
1/4 cup	melted butter	60 ml
1 1/2 tsp	flour	7 ml
1/4 tsp	salt	1 ml
1 tsp	vanilla	5 ml
1/2 tsp	almond extract	2 ml
2 cups	pecan halves	500 ml

Heat oven to 350 °F (175 °C). Line a 9-inch (23-cm) pie pan with pastry, building up a high fluted edge.

Beat eggs thoroughly. Beat in sugar, corn syrup, butter, flour, salt, vanilla and almond extract. Stir in pecans.

Pour into prepared pastry shell. Cover edge of pastry with a narrow strip of aluminum foil to keep it from browning too much.

Bake 1 hour or until filling is set. Serve slightly warm or cold.

SERVES 6 TO 8

Skillet Pie

2 cups	sifted all-purpose flour	500 ml
3 tbsp	baking powder	45 ml
1 tsp	salt	5 ml
1/3 cup	shortening	80 ml
1 cup	milk (approx.)	250 ml
4 cups	finely chopped rhubarb	1 L
2 cups	chopped apples	500 ml
2 cups	sugar	500 ml
1/3 cup	flour	80 ml
1 tsp	mace	5 ml
1/4 tsp	salt	1 ml
3 tbsp	butter	45 ml
	milk	
	sugar	
	sweetened whipped cream	

→

Skillet Pie

Heat oven to 400 °F (205 °C). Have ready a lightly greased 10-inch (25.5-cm) heavy iron skillet that can go in the oven.

Sift 2 cups (500 ml) flour, baking powder and 1 tsp (5 ml) salt into a bowl. Add shortening and cut in finely with a pastry blender or two knives. Add enough of 1 cup (250 ml) milk to make a soft dough that is easy to handle, mixing lightly with a fork. Turn out on lightly floured board and knead gently about 6 times to smooth and round up. Roll into a circle about 14 inches (36 cm) in diameter. Lift dough into skillet and let excess hang over outside.

Combine rhubarb, apples, 2 cups (500 ml) sugar, 1/3 cup (80 ml) flour, mace and 1/4 tsp (1 ml) salt and pile the mixture into the dough-lined skillet. Dot fruit mixture with butter.

Fold the overhanging dough in over the fruit, leaving centre uncovered.

Brush top of dough lightly with milk and sprinkle generously with sugar.

Bake about 50 minutes or until fruit is tender. Cover loosely with aluminum foil after the first 30 minutes baking to keep the top from browning too much.

Serve warm, cut in wedges. Top with whipped cream.

——— SERVES 6 TO 8 ———

Crêpes à l'Orange

2	eggs	2
1 tsp	sugar	5 ml
1/2 tsp	salt	2 ml
1/2 cup	sifted all-purpose flour	125 ml
1 1/3 cups	milk	330 ml
2 tbsp	melted butter	30 ml
10 oz	whipping cream	300 ml
2 tbsp	icing sugar	30 ml
2 tbsp	Kirsch, Cointreau or Curaçao liqueur	30 ml

*Rich Orange Sauce
(recipe follows)*

Beat eggs until light in a small bowl. Add sugar and salt, beating constantly. Continue beating and add flour alternately with milk and melted butter. Batter will be very thin.

Bake pancakes on lightly greased griddle. Use 3 tbsp (45 ml) or a scant 1/4 cup (60 ml) batter for each pancake and spread the batter as thin as possible. Each cake should be 5 to 6 inches (12.5 to 15 cm) in diameter. Brown on first side and turn carefully to lightly brown second side. Put between the folds of a towel to cool (towel will keep the pancakes from sticking to each other and they will stay soft and flexible). You should have about 12 pancakes.

Whip cream and icing sugar until stiff when pancakes are cool. Fold in liqueur (do not beat it in). Center each pancake with a heaping tablespoonful of the cream and fold all sides of the pancake around the cream so it is completely enclosed in a little roll. Freeze the filled pancakes until shortly before serving time.

Heat Rich Orange Sauce to simmering in a large skillet or in the top pan of a chafing dish over direct heat. Drop in the frozen pancakes and heat, spooning the sauce over constantly, just until heated through, about 2 minutes. (If you heat too long the cream will melt so it's better to have the cream a little firm when you lift the pancakes out of the sauce.) Serve immediately, 2 per person, topped with sauce.

—— SERVES 6 ——

Rich Orange Sauce

1/2 cup	soft butter	125 ml
1 cup	sugar	250 ml
1/2 cup	orange juice	125 ml
1	egg, well beaten	1

grated rind of 1 orange

Combine all ingredients in a small saucepan. Cook over moderate heat just until it comes to a boil, stirring constantly.

Apple Turnovers

1/4 cup	butter	60 ml
6 medium	apples, peeled and cored	6 medium
1/2 cup	brown sugar	125 ml
1 tsp	cinnamon	5 ml
	Cheese Pastry (recipe follows)	
	light cream	
	sugar	

Heat butter in large heavy skillet. Grate apples into skillet, using coarse grater. Cover tightly and cook gently about

3 minutes or until apples are just tender but not mushy. Remove from hat and stir in sugar and cinnamon. If there is a lot of liquid in the pan at this point return to heat and cook quickly, uncovered, until most of the liquid has evaporated. Cool.

Heat oven to 425 °F (220 °C). Have ready ungreased cookie sheets.

Roll pastry thin and cut into 5-inch (12.5-cm) squares. Put a large spoonful of the apple mixture on each square and fold into triangles. Seal edges with a fork. Put turnovers on cookie sheets. Prick tops in 2 places.

Brush tops of pastries with cream and sprinkle generously with sugar. Bake 10 to 12 minutes or until nicely browned.

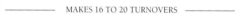

MAKES 16 TO 20 TURNOVERS

Cheese Pastry

3 cups	sifted all-purpose flour	750 ml
1 tsp	salt	5 ml
1 cup	lard	250 ml
1/2 cup	grated old cheddar cheese	125 ml
6 tbsp	ice water	90 ml

Combine flour and salt in a bowl. Add lard and cut in coarsely with a pastry blender. Add cheese and mix in lightly with a fork. Sprinkle in water 1 tbsp (15 ml) at a time, mixing lightly with a fork just until all flour is dampened. Gather dough into a ball and press together firmly with fingers. Divide dough into 2 pieces, roll each piece thin and cut as directed in recipe.

Crêpes à l'Orange

Cherry Tarts

14-oz can	red pitted cherries	398-ml can
1/2 cup	sugar	125 ml
2 tbsp	cornstarch	30 ml
pinch	salt	pinch
1/4 tsp	almond extract	1 ml
	red food coloring	
4-oz pkg	cream cheese (room temperature)	115-g pkg
1 tbsp	light cream	15 ml
1 tsp	sugar	5 ml
8 medium	baked tart shells	8 medium
	sweetened whipped cream (optional)	

Drain cherries well. Measure juice and add enough water, if necessary, to make 1 cup (250 ml) liquid.

Combine 1/2 cup (125 ml) sugar, cornstarch and salt in medium saucepan. Stir in cherry juice gradually, blending until smooth. Set over high heat and bring to a boil, stirring constantly. Turn down heat and cook 1 minute more, stirring. Remove from heat and stir in almond extract and enough coloring to tint a good red. Cool to lukewarm.

Mix cheese, cream and 1 tsp (5 ml) sugar until smooth and blended. Divide this mixture evenly among the baked tart shells. Spread to cover bottom. Top cheese with a few of the cherries, add a little of the thickened juice, then more cherries until both cherries and thickened juice are used up. End with juice so bright red glaze is on top. Chill.

Serve topped with whipped cream.

—————— MAKES 8 ——————

Pineapple-Cheese Tarts

3/4 cup	fine graham wafer crumbs	180 ml
3 tbsp	soft butter	45 ml
1 tbsp	sugar	15 ml
8-oz pkg	cream cheese (room temperature)	225-g pkg
1	egg yolk	1
5 tbsp	sugar	75 ml
1/4 tsp	vanilla	1 ml
1/8 tsp	nutmeg	0.5 ml
1 cup	well-drained crushed pineapple	250 ml
1	egg white	1
1/2 cup	commercial sour cream	125 ml
1 tbsp	sugar	15 ml
1/4 tsp	vanilla	1 ml

Heat oven to 375 °F (190 °C). Butter six 5-oz (150-ml) custard cups.

Measure and set aside 1 tbsp (15 ml) of the graham wafer crumbs. Combine remaining crumbs with butter and 1 tbsp (15 ml) sugar. Press about 2 tbsp (30 ml) of this mixture firmly against bottom and sides of each custard cup with a spoon.

Beat cream cheese until fluffy. Beat in egg yolk, 5 tbsp (75 ml) sugar, 1/4 tsp (1 ml) vanilla and nutmeg. Stir in pineapple. Beat egg white until stiff and fold into pineapple mixture. Spoon equal amounts of mixture into custard cups. Set cups on a shallow pan and bake 20 minutes.

Combine sour cream, 1 tbsp (15 ml) sugar and 1/4 tsp (1 ml) vanilla. Spread this mixture evenly over baked tarts. Sprinkle with the saved graham water crumbs — 1/2 tsp (2 ml) for each tart. Return to oven and bake 5 minutes more. Serve slightly warm or cold, unmoulded on serving plates.

—————— SERVES 6 ——————

Holiday Tarts

Basic Pastry (recipe p. 302)

2	eggs	2
2/3 cup	brown sugar, packed	160 ml
2/3 cup	corn syrup	160 ml
3 tbsp	soft butter	45 ml
1/4 tsp	salt	1 ml
1/4 tsp	nutmeg	1 ml
1/4 tsp	cinnamon	1 ml
1/4 tsp	almond extract	1 ml
1/4 tsp	vanilla	1 ml
1/2 cup	chopped mixed candied fruit	125 ml
1/4 cup	currants	60 ml
1/4 cup	chopped walnuts	60 ml

Have ready pans for 32 tiny tarts — 2 inches (5 cm) in diameter.

Roll pastry very thin and cut 32 rounds 3 inches (7.5 cm) in diameter with a cookie cutter. Line tart pans with these rounds.

Heat oven to 450 °F (220 °C).

Beat eggs lightly. Beat in sugar, corn syrup, butter, salt, nutmeg, cinnamon, almond extract and vanilla. Stir in fruit and nuts.

Spoon this mixture into pastry-lined tart pans filling each about 2/3 full.

Bake 10 minutes at 450 °F (220 °C), then reduce oven temperature to 325 °F (160 °C) and continue baking about 10 minutes more or until filling is set and pastry browned.

Loosen tarts where filling has bubbled up over crust so that they don't stick and then allow tarts to cool to lukewarm in pans. Invert pans on tea towel and let tarts drop out. Finish cooling on racks.

———— MAKES 32 SMALL TARTS ————

Holiday Tarts

Cottage Cheese Cake

1 cup	*fine rusk crumbs*	250 ml
3 tbsp	*melted butter*	45 ml
3 tbsp	*sugar*	45 ml
3/4 tsp	*cinnamon*	3 ml
2 lb	*cottage cheese*	900 g
5	*eggs*	5
1/2 cup	*sifted all-purpose flour*	125 ml
1 cup	*sugar*	250 ml
2 tsp	*grated lemon rind*	10 ml
2 tbsp	*lemon juice*	30 ml

1/2 tsp	*vanilla*	2 ml
1 cup	*whipping cream*	250 ml

Strawberry Topping
(recipe follows)

Heat oven to 350 °F (175 °C). Lightly butter a 9-inch (23-cm) spring-form pan.

Combine rusk crumbs, melted butter, 3 tbsp (45 ml) sugar and cinnamon. Press evenly in bottom of prepared pan. Bake 10 minutes.

Press cottage cheese through a sieve into mixer bowl. Add eggs, one at a time, and beat well after each addition. Mix

→

flour and 1 cup (250 ml) sugar and beat into cheese mixture. Stir in lemon rind, lemon juice and vanilla. Whip cream and fold in. Pour on crust in the spring-form pan.

Bake about 1 hour and 10 minutes or until set. Cool in pan, then chill. Top with Strawberry Topping. Chill again.

——————— SERVES 8 TO 12 ———————

Strawberry Topping

2 cups	strawberries	500 ml
1/4 cup	cornstarch	60 ml
1 cup	sugar	250 ml
1/4 cup	orange juice	60 ml
2 tbsp	grated orange rind	30 ml
3 cups	whole strawberries	750 ml

Whirl the 2 cups (500 ml) strawberries in the blender or press through a sieve to make a purée. Combine cornstarch and sugar in saucepan. Stir in strawberry purée, orange juice and orange rind. Set over high heat and cook until thick and clear, stirring constantly. Turn down heat and cook and stir 1 minute. Cool slightly.

Top cheesecake with whole berries. Spoon warm mixture over berries.

Combine rusk crumbs, melted butter, 3 tbsp (45 ml) sugar and cinnamon. Press evenly in bottom of prepared pan. Bake 10 minutes.

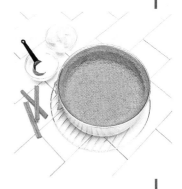

Press cottage cheese through a sieve into mixer bowl. Add eggs, one at a time, and beat well after each addition.

Mix flour and 1 cup (250 ml) sugar and beat into cheese mixture. Stir in lemon rind, lemon juice and vanilla. Whip cream and fold in.

Top cheesecake with whole berries. Spoon warm mixture over berries.

Cottage Cheese Cake

Lemon Snow

1 cup	sugar	250 ml
3 tbsp	cornstarch	45 ml
2 cups	boiling water	500 ml
	rind and juice of 2 lemons	
2	egg whites	2
	Custard Sauce (recipe follows)	

Mix sugar and cornstarch thoroughly in saucepan. Stir in water gradually. Add lemon juice and rind. Set over high heat and bring to a boil, stirring constantly. Turn down heat and cook 2 minutes, stirring. Cool to lukewarm.

Beat egg whites until stiff but not dry. Slowly add lemon mixture, beating with a rotary beater.

Pour into bowl or serving dishes and chill several hours or overnight until set. Serve with Custard Sauce.

—— SERVES 4 ——

Custard Sauce

3/4 cup	milk	180 ml
2	egg yolks	2
2 tbsp	sugar	30 ml
1/8 tsp	salt	0.5 ml
1 tsp	vanilla	5 ml

Scald milk in top of double boiler over direct heat.

Beat egg yolks in small bowl. Blend in sugar and salt and gradually stir in hot milk. Return mixture to top of double boiler and set over simmering water. Cook, stirring constantly, until mixture coats a metal spoon (about 10 minutes). Cool. Stir in vanilla.

Creamy Orange Tapioca with Pears

1	egg	1
1/3 cup	sugar	80 ml
1/8 tsp	salt	0.5 ml
1 1/2 cups	milk	375 ml
3 tbsp	quick-cooking tapioca	45 ml
2 tbsp	grated orange rind	30 ml
1 cup	whipping cream, whipped	250 ml
1 tsp	vanilla	5 ml
	Poached Pears (recipe follows)	
	toasted slivered almonds (optional)	

Combine egg, sugar and salt in a saucepan. Beat them together with a wooden spoon until blended. Stir in milk, tapioca and orange rind. Let stand 5 minutes. Set over moderate heat and cook until mixture comes to a full rolling boil, stirring constantly. Turn down heat and continue cooking and stirring 1 minute more. Remove from heat and cool.

Whip cream and fold into tapioca mixture along with vanilla. Pour into bowl and chill well. Spoon chilled mixture into sherbet glasses at serving time. Top each serving with a poached pear half and sprinkle with toasted almonds.

—— SERVES 6 ——

→

Creamy Orange Tapioca with Pears

Poached Pears

1 cup	sugar	250 ml
1 cup	water	250 ml
2 tbsp	lemon juice	30 ml
1	2-inch (5-cm) piece vanilla bean	1
	or	
2 tsp	vanilla	10 ml
3 large	ripe pears	3 large

Combine sugar and water in saucepan and bring to a boil. Add lemon juice and vanilla.

Peel pears and cut in half. Remove stems and seeds. Drop into the boiling sugar syrup and simmer 3 minutes or until just beginning to get tender. Cool in syrup and chill well. Lift out of syrup with a slotted spoon and use as directed.

Chilled Strawberry Soufflé

1 pt	strawberries	625 ml
1 tbsp	unflavored gelatin	15 ml
1/4 cup	cold water	60 ml
4	egg yolks, beaten	4
1/2 cup	sugar	125 ml
1 tbsp	lemon juice	15 ml
	red food coloring (optional)	
4	egg whites	4
pinch	salt	pinch
1/4 cup	sugar	60 ml
1 cup	whipping cream	250 ml
1/4 cup	toasted slivered almonds	60 ml

Wash and hull strawberries. Set aside 4 large berries for decorating soufflé later. Put remaining berries in the blender and blend into a purée.

Combine gelatin and cold water in small dish. Let stand 5 minutes. Set in boiling water and heat until gelatin is dissolved. Beat egg yolks and 1/2 cup (125 ml) sugar with rotary beater in top of double boiler until thick and lemon-colored. Stir in lemon juice. Set over simmering water and cook, stirring constantly, until thickened, about 5 minutes. Stir in gelatin. Remove from heat and cool (do not chill).

Stir in strawberry purée. Add a few drops of coloring to tint a pretty pink.

→

Beat egg whites and salt until foamy. Gradually beat in 1/4 cup (60 ml) sugar. Continue beating until stiff peaks form. Beat cream until stiff.

Fold egg white mixture then cream into strawberry mixture. Fold as little as possible.

Put a collar of waxed paper — extending about 3 inches (7.5 cm) above the dish — around a 6-cup (1.5-L) soufflé dish. Pour in the strawberry mixture. Chill until firm.

Carefully strip off waxed paper collar. Decorate soufflé with slices of the strawberries you set aside and the slivered almonds.

—————— SERVES 6 ——————

Peach-Banana Whip

1 cup	sugar	250 ml
1 1/2 cups	water	375 ml
3 large	ripe peaches	3 large
1 tbsp	unflavored gelatin	15 ml
1/4 cup	cold water	60 ml
1/4 cup	lemon juice	60 ml
pinch	salt	pinch
1 large	ripe banana	1 large
1/2 cup	whipping cream	125 ml

Combine sugar and water in medium saucepan. Bring to a boil and boil 5 minutes. Peel peaches and chop coarsely. Add to boiling syrup. Bring back to a boil, turn down heat and simmer 5 minutes or until peaches are just tender.

Drain, measuring out 1 1/2 cups (375 ml) of the liquid. Return this liquid to saucepan and bring to a boil. Cool peach pieces.

Add gelatin to cold water and let stand 5 minutes. Add to boiling peach liquid and stir until dissolved. Stir in lemon juice and salt. Chill by setting in ice water until beginning to thicken. Stir often.

Mash banana with a fork and stir into gelatin mixture. Fold in peach pieces. Chill again for a few minutes if necessary until mixture begins to mound when dropped from a spoon. Whip cream and fold in. Spoon into sherbet glasses and chill until set.

—————— SERVES 6 ——————

Chilled Strawberry Soufflé

Crème Caramel

1/2 cup	sugar	125 ml
4	egg yolks	4
1/3 cup	sugar	80 ml
1/4 tsp	salt	1 ml
2 cups	milk	500 ml
1 tsp	vanilla	5 ml

Heat 1/2 cup (125 ml) sugar in a heavy skillet over low heat until sugar is completely melted and golden brown, stirring constantly with a wooden spoon.

Pour a little of the sugar syrup into each of six oven-proof moulds or custard cups. Tip the cups immediately to coat the bottom and sides as much as possible with the syrup. If the cups are heated with boiling water and dried just before adding the syrup the sugar won't harden quite as quickly and you will have a little more time to spread it around the moulds. Don't worry if they aren't completely coated.

Heat oven to 350 °F (175 °C). Put a pan of hot water — have water 1/2 inch (1.25 cm) deep — large enough to hold moulds or cups in oven to heat.

Beat egg yolks, 1/3 cup (80 ml) sugar and salt together. Scald milk and stir into egg mixture gradually. Add vanilla.

Pour into caramel-coated moulds or custard cups and set in pan of hot water in oven.

Bake 45 to 50 minutes or until a metal knife inserted in center of custards comes out clean. Remove from hot water immediately. Cool and chill. Unmould at serving time so caramel runs down custards forming a sauce.

SERVES 6

Rum-Pineapple Dessert

4	egg yolks	4
1/2 cup	sugar	125 ml
1 1/2 cups	milk	300 ml
1/2 cup	pineapple juice (drained from sliced pineapple)	125 ml
2 tbsp	unflavored gelatin	30 ml
1/4 cup	cold water	60 ml
1/4 cup	golden rum	60 ml
1 cup	whipping cream	250 ml
	Sponge Layer (recipe follows)	
1 tbsp	rum	15 ml
6 slices	canned pineapple	6 slices
	maraschino cherries	
	sweetened whipped cream (optional)	

Beat egg yolks and sugar together with a wooden spoon in the top of a double boiler. Stir in milk and pineapple juice. Set over simmering water and cook until hot and slightly thickened, about 10 minutes. Stir constantly.

Add gelatin to cold water and let stand 5 minutes. Add to hot egg yolk mixture, stirring until gelatin is dissolved. Set top of double boiler in a bowl of ice water and stir constantly just until mixture is cool and beginning to thicken a little (be careful not to chill it so it sets at this point). Remove from ice water and stir in 1/4 cup (60 ml) rum.

Whip cream and fold into gelatin mixture. Pour into 8-inch (20-cm) round layer cake pan and chill until firm.

Put Sponge Layer on flat serving plate. Drizzle 1 tbsp (15 ml) rum over cake. Turn out gelatin layer on top of cake. Decorate top of gelatin layer with half slices of pineapple and maraschino cherries. Chill until serving time. Pipe sweetened whipped cream around bottom of dessert at serving time if desired.

Note: This dessert can be made successfully by substituting 1 envelope dessert topping mix prepared according to package directions, for the whipped cream in the jellied cream layer.

SERVES 6

→

Rum-Pineapple Dessert

Sponge Layer

1	egg	1
1/3 cup	sugar	80 ml
1 1/2 tbsp	water	22 ml
1/4 tsp	vanilla	1 ml
1/3 cup	sifted all-purpose flour	80 ml
1/4 tsp	baking powder	1 ml
pinch	salt	pinch

Heat oven to 375 °F (190 °C). Line the bottom of a 9-inch (23-cm) round layer cake pan with waxed paper and grease sides of pan.

Beat egg until thick and lemon-colored in small mixer bowl (about 5 minutes at high speed on the mixer). Beat in sugar gradually. Stir in water and vanilla. Sift flour, baking powder and salt together into mixture and beat until smooth. Pour into prepared pan.

Bake about 12 minutes or until top springs back when touched lightly. Turn out on rack and strip off waxed paper. (This should be a very thin layer of cake.) Cool.

Raspberry Bavarian

1 lb	frozen raspberries, thawed	450 g
2/3 cup	evaporated milk	160 ml
1 tbsp	unflavored gelatin	15 ml
1/4 cup	sugar	60 ml
1/8 tsp	salt	0.5 ml
2	egg yolks	2
1/4 cup	water	60 ml
1 tsp	lemon rind	5 ml
2	egg whites	2
2 tbsp	sugar	30 ml
1 tbsp	lemon juice	15 ml

Press raspberries through a sieve to make a purée, discarding seeds.

Pour evaporated milk into a metal pan and chill in freezer until ice crystals form around edge.

Combine gelatin, 1/4 cup (60 ml) sugar and salt thoroughly in a saucepan. beat egg yolks and water together and stir into gelatin mixture along with raspberry purée. Set over moderate heat and cook until mixture just comes to the boiling point, stirring constantly. Remove from heat and stir in lemon rind. Chill by setting in ice water just until mixture begins to thicken.

Beat egg whites until foamy. Add 2 tbsp (30 ml) sugar gradually and beat until stiff and glossy. Fold into gelatin mixture. Put chilled evaporated milk in a bowl and beat until stiff peaks form. Add lemon juice and continue beating until very stiff. Fold into gelatin mixture.

Spoon mixture into six 6-oz (180-ml) custard cups and chill until firm.

Note: If desired, partly thaw a second package of frozen raspberries and use them to garnish the desserts. If there are still ice crystals in the berries, they will hold their shape and look almost like fresh berries.

—————————— SERVES 6 ——————————

Raspberry Bavarian

Holiday Tipsy Pudding

2/3 cup	cold milk	180 ml
3-oz pkg	instant vanilla pudding mix	85-g pkg
2 cups	cold commercial eggnog	500 ml
1/2 tsp	almond extract	2 ml
1/2 cup	whipping cream	125 ml
2	layers baker's sponge cake — about 7 inches (18 cm) in diameter	2
1/2 cup	sweet sherry	125 ml
8-oz jar	raspberry jam	227-ml jar
1 cup	whipping cream	250 ml
2 tbsp	sifted icing sugar	30 ml
1/2 tsp	vanilla	2 ml
	cherries	
	angelica or green candied pineapple	

Put cold milk in small mixer bowl. Add pudding mix and beat at low speed until blended. Gradually beat in eggnog. Stir in almond extract. Whip 1/2 cup (125 ml) cream until stiff peaks form and fold into eggnog mixture. Set aside.

Split each layer of cake crosswise to make 2 thin layers. Put one of these layers, cut side up, in a deep bowl. Sprinkle with 2 tbsp (30 ml) of the sherry and spread with 1/3 of the jam. Pour about 1/4 of the eggnog mixture over. Add another layer of cake and repeat additions of sherry, jam and eggnog mixture. Repeat once again. Top with remaining layer of cake, sprinkle with 2 tbsp (30 ml) sherry and pour remaining eggnog mixture over all. Chill several hours or overnight.

Whip 1 cup (250 ml) cream, sugar and vanilla until stiff peaks form at serving time. Press through a pastry bag or cookie press to make rosettes all over the top of the dessert. Decorate edge with holly made with a cherry half for the berries and leaves cut from angelica or pineapple.

SERVES 8

Split each layer of cake crosswise to make 2 thin layers.

Put one of these layers, cut side up, in a deep bowl. Sprinkle with 2 tbsp (30 ml) of the sherry and spread with 1/3 of the jam.

Top with remaining layer of cake, sprinkle with 2 tbsp (30 ml) sherry and pour remaining eggnog mixture over all. Chill several hours.

Press whipping cream through a pastry bag or cookie to make rosettes all over the top of the dessert. Decorate edge with holly made with a cherry half for the berries and leaves cut from angelica or pineapple.

Dancing Ladies Charlotte

3/4 cup	mixed candied fruit	180 ml
1/2 cup	chopped maraschino cherries	125 ml
1/4 cup	maraschino cherry juice	60 ml
4	egg yolks	4
1/3 cup	sugar	80 ml
pinch	salt	pinch
1 1/2 cups	milk	375 ml
2 tbsp	unflavored gelatin	30 ml
3/4 cup	water	180 ml
1 tsp	almond extract	5 ml
1/2 cup	chopped lightly toasted pecans	125 ml
1 1/2 cups	whipping cream	375 ml

Ladyfingers
(store-bought or from recipe which follows)

sweetened whipped cream

maraschino cherries

Combine candied fruit and chopped cherries in small dish. Add maraschino cherry juice and let stand at room temperature 1 hour, stirring often.

Beat egg yolks in top of double boiler. Beat in sugar. Add salt and milk and stir to blend. Set over simmering water and cook, stirring, until mixture coats a metal spoon, about 20 minutes.

Add gelatin to water and let stand 5 minutes. Add to hot egg yolk mixture and stir until gelatin is dissolved. Remove from heat. Stir in soaked fruit and almond extract. Set in ice water and chill until beginning to hold shape. Fold in pecans.

Whip cream until stiff peaks form and fold into gelatin mixture.

Line bottom and sides of charlotte mould or 8-cup (2-L) casserole or bowl completely with ladyfingers (cut the ladyfingers to fit). Pour in gelatin mixture.

Chill several hours until set. Unmould on serving plate and decorate base and top with rosettes of whipped cream and maraschino cherries.

SERVES 8 TO 10

→

Dancing Ladies Charlotte

Ladyfingers

3	egg whites	3
pinch	salt	pinch
1/3 cup	sugar	80 ml
3	egg yolks	3
1 tsp	vanilla	5 ml
2/3 cup	sifted cake flour	160 ml

Heat oven to 350 °F (175 °C). Grease and flour a large cookie sheet.

Beat egg whites and salt until soft peaks form. Add sugar gradually, beating well after each addition. Beat until stiff and glossy.

Beat egg yolks and vanilla until thick and lemon colored. Add to egg whites and fold in gently but quickly. Fold in flour.

Press through a pastry tube or cookie press with a large plain tip into strips 2 1/2 inches (6.25 cm) long onto prepared cookie sheet. (If you don't have a pastry tube or cookie press, shape rounded teaspoonfuls of batter into strips.)

Bake 8 to 10 minutes or until set and very lightly browned on the bottom. Remove from sheets and cool on racks. Store in tightly closed tin box.

MAKES 3 DOZEN

Beat egg whites and salt until soft peaks form.

Add egg yolk-vanilla mixture to egg whites and fold in gently but quickly. Fold in flour.

Press through a pastry tube or cookie press with a large plain tip into strips 2 1/2 inches (6.25 cm) long onto prepared cookie sheet.

Coconut Ice Cream Dessert

3/4 cup	*flaked coconut*	180 ml
5 cups	*coffee ice cream* (see note)	1.25 L
3/4 cup	*coffee liqueur (approx.)*	180 ml

Heat oven to 350 °F (175 °C). Spread coconut on a shallow pan and toast in oven until golden, about 10 minutes. Cool.

Spoon ice cream into 6 serving dishes. Spoon some of the coffee liqueur over each serving. Sprinkle each with 2 tbsp (30 ml) of the coconut. Serve immediately.

Note: If you can't get coffee ice cream, vanilla is good for this dessert, too. Or you can soften vanilla ice cream by creaming with a wooden spoon or beating with electric mixer in a chilled bowl (work quickly so ice cream softens but doesn't melt) and stirring in 2 tsp (10 ml) powdered instant coffee. Freeze the ice cream again until firm before making dessert.

——————— SERVES 6 ———————

Peach-Orange Frost

1 cup	*well drained canned peach slices*	250 ml
1 tsp	*unflavored gelatin*	5 ml
1 tbsp	*lemon juice*	15 ml
1/2 cup	*syrup from canned peaches*	125 ml
1	*egg yolk*	1
1/2 cup	*orange juice*	125 ml
1/2 tsp	*grated orange rind*	2 ml
1/4 cup	*sugar*	60 ml
pinch	*salt*	pinch
1 cup	*light cream*	250 ml
1	*egg white*	1

drained canned peach slices (optional)

Mash 1 cup (250 ml) peach slices thoroughly with a fork or blend until smooth. Add gelatin to lemon juice and let stand 5 minutes. Heat peach syrup and add softened gelatin. Stir until gelatin is dissolved. Cool (do not chill).

Beat egg yolk slightly. Stir it into gelatin mixture along with orange juice and rind, sugar, salt, cream and mashed peaches. Pour into a metal pan and freeze until firm.

Beat egg white until stiff. Scrape the frozen mixture into a chilled bowl and beat with rotary beater or electric mixer until smooth. Fold in egg white and return to metal pan. Freeze until firm.

Spoon into sherbet glasses at serving time and garnish with extra peach slices.

——————— SERVES 6 TO 9 ———————

Left: Peach-Orange Frost
Right: Creamy Maple Mousse

Creamy Maple Mousse

1 cup	maple syrup	250 ml
1 1/2 tsp	unflavored gelatin	7 ml
2 tbsp	cold water	30 ml
2	egg yolks, lightly beaten	2
1 pt	vanilla ice cream, softened	625 ml

Put maple syrup in a small saucepan and bring to a boil. Boil hard until reduced to 1/2 cup (125 ml), about 15 minutes.

Add gelatin to cold water and let stand 5 minutes. Add to hot maple syrup and stir until dissolved. Pour this hot mixture gradually into egg yolks, beating constantly. Add softened ice cream and blend well.

Pour into four custard cups or 4-oz (125-ml) moulds. Freeze until firm. Unmould to serve.

———————— SERVES 4 ————————

Orange-Apricot Sherbet

1 cup	light cream	250 ml
1 cup	sugar	250 ml
3/4 cup	corn syrup	180 ml
1 cup	canned apricot nectar	250 ml
1 cup	fresh orange juice	250 ml
1/4 cup	fresh lemon juice	60 ml
2 tsp	grated orange rind	10 ml
1 tsp	grated lemon rind	5 ml
2	egg whites	2

Combine cream, sugar and corn syrup in saucepan. Heat to scalding. Remove from heat and cool. Stir in apricot nectar, orange juice, lemon juice, orange and lemon rind. Pour into a metal pan and freeze until firm.

Beat egg whites until stiff. Put frozen sherbet in chilled bowl and beat until fluffy (work quickly so sherbet doesn't melt). Fold in egg whites. Return to pan and freeze until firm.

Note: As a special treat try layering this refreshing sherbet in parfait glasses with coffee liqueur between the layers.

MAKES ABOUT 1 QT (1.25 L)

Chocolate-Eggnog Tortoni

3/4 cup	cold milk	180 ml
4-oz pkg	instant chocolate pudding mix	115-g pkg
1 1/4 cups	commercial eggnog	300 ml
1/2 tsp	vanilla	2 ml
1/2 tsp	almond extract	2 ml
1/2 cup	whipping cream	125 ml
2/3 cup	finely crushed vanilla wafers	160 ml
1/2 cup	finely chopped blanched almonds, toasted	125 ml
1/2 cup	flaked coconut, toasted	125 ml
	whole toasted almonds	
	maraschino cherries	

Put milk in small mixer bowl. Add pudding mix and mix on low speed until blended. Gradually beat in eggnog. Stir in vanilla and almond extract.

Whip cream until stiff peaks form and fold into chocolate mixture. Fold in vanilla wafer crumbs, chopped almonds and coconut.

Line 12 muffin cups with large-size paper baking cups. Spoon the mixture into cups, filling right to top. Cover muffin pan with aluminum foil and freeze chocolate mixture until firm, 4 hours or overnight. Garnish top of each little dessert with whole toasted almonds and a maraschino cherry and set each cup on a doily on serving plate.

MAKES 12 SMALL DESSERTS

Chocolate-Eggnog Tortoni

Red Fruit Cup

16-oz pkg	frozen raspberries, thawed	450-g pkg
1/2 cup	sugar	125 ml
1/4 cup	water	60 ml
2 cups	fresh cherries, stemmed and pitted	500 ml
2 cups	small watermelon balls	500 ml
3/4 cup	chilled sparkling rosé wine (approx.)	180 ml

Drain raspberries into a saucepan. Set fruit aside. Add sugar and water to raspberry syrup and bring to a boil. Boil hard 10 minutes or until reduced to about half. Cool and chill.

Combine raspberries, cherries and watermelon, tossing lightly with a fork. Spoon into 6 large sherbet glasses or goblets. Spoon the sugar syrup over the fruit, dividing it evenly. Add wine to nearly fill glasses. Serve immediately.

———————— SERVES 6 ————————

Apple-Lemon Crumb Pudding

2 tbsp	cornstarch	30 ml
1 cup	sugar	250 ml
1 tsp	grated lemon rind	5 ml
3 tbsp	lemon juice	45 ml
2	eggs	2
1 cup	boiling water	250 ml
3/4 cup	sifted all-purpose flour	180 ml
1 tsp	baking powder	5 ml
1/4 tsp	salt	1 ml
3/4 cup	brown sugar, packed	180 ml
2/3 cup	fine dry bread crumbs	160 ml
1/2 cup	flaked coconut	125 ml
1/2 cup	soft butter	125 ml
2	apples	2

cream, ice cream or whipped cream

Heat oven to 350 °F (175 °C). Butter a baking dish about 9 x 6 x 1 1/2 inches (23 x 15 x 3.75 cm).

Combine cornstarch and sugar thoroughly in top of double boiler. Stir in lemon rind and juice. Add eggs and beat well. Stir in boiling water gradually. Set over simmering water and cook until thick and smooth, stirring constantly. Cool.

Sift flour, baking powder and salt into a bowl. Add brown sugar, bread crumbs and coconut. Add butter and mix, first with a fork then with fingers, until a crumbly mixture is formed. Put a little more than half of this mixture in the prepared pan. Pack down firmly.

Peel, core and slice apples thin, spreading them evenly over the mixture in the baking pan. Spread lemon mixture over the apples. Sprinkle top with remaining crumb mixture.

Bake 40 to 45 minutes. Serve warm with cream or ice cream or cold with whipped cream.

——————— SERVES 6 TO 8 ———————

Apple-Marmalade Pudding

6 medium	cooking apples	6 medium
3/4 cup	brown sugar, packed	180 ml
1 2/3 cups	sifted all-purpose flour	410 ml
3 tsp	baking powder	15 ml
1/2 tsp	salt	2 ml
1/2 cup	sugar	125 ml
1/3 cup	shortening	80 ml
1	egg	1
1/3 cup	orange marmalade	80 ml
1/2 cup	milk	125 ml
1 tsp	cinnamon	5 ml
2 tbsp	sugar	30 ml

Butterscotch Sauce
(recipe follows)

Heat oven to 400 °F (205 °C). Butter a shallow baking dish about 13 x 9 x 2 inches (33 x 23 x 5 cm).

Peel and core apples. Slice very thin and spread in prepared baking dish. Sprinkle with brown sugar. Put dish in hot oven while making topping.

Sift flour, baking powder, salt and 1/2 cup (125 ml) sugar into bowl. Add shortening and cut in finely. Beat egg. Stir in marmalade and milk. Add to dry ingredients and mix until blended.

Remove apples from oven and spread batter over them. Combine cinnamon and 2 tbsp (30 ml) sugar and sprinkle over batter. Bake 20 to 25 minutes or until batter is cooked through and apples are tender. Serve, cut in large squares and top with Butterscotch Sauce.

——————— SERVES 8 TO 12 ———————

→

Left: Apple-Lemon Crumb Pudding
Right: Apple-Marmalade Pudding

Butterscotch Sauce

3 tbsp	cornstarch	45 ml
1 cup	brown sugar, packed	250 ml
pinch	salt	pinch
1 cup	cold water	250 ml
1 cup	boiling water	250 ml
1/4 cup	butter	60 ml
2 tsp	vanilla	10 ml

Mix cornstarch, sugar and salt thoroughly in saucepan. Stir in cold water, blending until smooth.

Stir in boiling water. Bring to a boil over high heat, stirring constantly. Boil 1 minute. Remove form heat. Stir in butter and vanilla. Serve hot.

——— MAKES ABOUT 2 1/2 CUPS (625 ML) ———

Honey-Peach Crisp

6	peaches, peeled and sliced	6
1/2 cup	broken walnuts	125 ml
1 tbsp	lemon juice	15 ml
1/3 cup	liquid honey	80 ml
1/2 cup	all-purpose flour	125 ml
1/2 cup	rolled oats	125 ml
3/4 tsp	cinnamon	3 ml
1/3 cup	soft butter	80 ml
	cream or ice cream	

Heat oven to 375 °F (190 °C). Butter an 8-cup (2-L) casserole.

Put peaches in prepared casserole. Sprinkle with walnuts. Combine lemon juice and honey and pour over.

Blend flour, rolled oats, cinnamon and butter until crumbly. Spread over peaches.

Bake 30 to 35 minutes or until peaches are tender and topping is browned. Serve warm with cream or ice cream.

 SERVES 6

Cherry Crunch

1 cup	quick-cooking rolled oats	250 ml
1/2 cup	chopped blanched almonds	125 ml
1/2 cup	sifted all-purpose flour	125 ml
1 cup	sugar	250 ml
1/2 cup	butter	125 ml
1/2 tsp	almond extract	2 ml
19-oz can	cherry pie filling	540-ml can
	cream or ice cream	

Heat oven to 375 °F (190 °C). Have ready an 8-inch (20.5-cm) square cake pan.

Combine rolled oats, almonds, flour and sugar. Add butter and mix, first with a fork then with fingers, to make a crumbly mixture.

Sprinkle half of crumbly mixture into cake pan, spreading it evenly and packing it down lightly. Drop cherry pie filling by small spoonfuls over crumbly mixture and spread it evenly to within 1/2 inch (1.25 cm) of sides of pan. Sprinkle remaining crumbly mixture over top of cherry pie filling.

Bake about 40 minutes or until well browned on top and bottom. Serve warm, spooned into fruit dishes and topped with cream or ice cream.

SERVES 6

Rhubarb Crisp

4 cups	cut up rhubarb	1 L
1 cup	sugar	250 ml
1/4 cup	all-purpose flour	60 ml
1/2 tsp	cinnamon	2 ml
1/2 cup	water	125 ml
1 cup	sifted all-purpose flour	250 ml
1/2 cup	quick-cooking rolled oats	125 ml
1 cup	brown sugar, packed	250 ml
1/2 cup	butter, melted	125 ml
	cream	

Heat oven to 375 °F (190 °C). Butter a square baking dish about 8 x 8 x 2 inches (20.5 x 20.5 x 5 cm).

Combine rhubarb, sugar, 1/4 cup (60 ml) flour and cinnamon and put in prepared baking dish. Pour water over all.

Combine 1 cup (250 ml) flour, rolled oats, brown sugar and melted butter, mixing with a fork to make a crumbly mixture. Sprinkle over rhubarb.

Bake 35 minutes or until rhubarb is tender. Serve warm with cream.

SERVES 6

Left: Honey-Peach Crisp
Right: Rhubarb Crisp

Cottage Pudding

1 3/4 cups	sifted all-purpose flour	425 ml
2 tsp	baking powder	10 ml
1/2 tsp	salt	2 ml
3/4 cup	sugar	180 ml
1/4 cup	soft shortening	60 ml
1	egg	1
3/4 cup	milk	180 ml
1 tsp	vanilla	5 ml

Blueberry Sauce or Golden Citrus Sauce
(recipes follow)

Heat oven to 375 °F (190 °C). Grease a 9-inch (23-cm) square pan.

Sift flour, baking powder, salt and sugar into a bowl. Add shortening, egg, milk and vanilla and beat hard until batter is smooth. Pour into prepared pan and bake 25 to 30 minutes or until top springs back when touched lightly in the center. Cut in large squares and serve warm with hot Blueberry Sauce or Golden Citrus Sauce.

———————— SERVES 6 TO 9 ————————

Blueberry Sauce

1/2 cup	sugar	125 ml
2 tbsp	cornstarch	30 ml
1/2 tsp	cinnamon	2 ml
pinch	salt	pinch
1 cup	water	250 ml
11-oz pkg	frozen blueberries	310-ml pkg

Combine sugar, cornstarch, cinnamon and salt thoroughly in saucepan. Stir in water gradually, stirring until smooth after each addition. Add blueberries. Set over high heat and bring to a boil, stirring constantly. Turn heat to low and continue boiling and stirring 1 minute more. Keep hot until serving time.

———————— MAKES ABOUT 2 CUPS (500 ML) ————————

Golden Citrus Sauce

2 tbsp	cornstarch	30 ml
1/4 cup	sugar	60 ml
1 cup	orange juice	250 ml
2 tbsp	lemon juice	30 ml
1 cup	crushed pineapple with juice (see note)	250 ml
3 large	oranges, peeled, sectioned and cut in small pieces	3 large

Mix cornstarch and sugar thoroughly in medium saucepan. Add orange juice gradually, stirring until smooth. Add lemon juice and pineapple. Stir to blend. Set over high heat and heat to boiling, stirring constantly. Turn down heat and continue boiling and stirring 5 minutes. Stir in orange pieces. Keep hot until serving time.

Note: Stir pineapple before measuring, then spoon both fruit and juice into measuring cup.

———————— MAKES ABOUT 3 CUPS (750 ML) ————————

Left: Cottage Pudding
Right: Rice Custard

Rice Custard

6	eggs	6
3 cups	milk	750 ml
1 cup	sugar	250 ml
2 tsp	vanilla	10 ml
1/2 tsp	salt	2 ml
1 1/2 cups	cooked rice	375 ml
1 cup	seeded raisins	250 ml
	nutmeg	

Heat oven to 350 °F (175 °C). Butter a 10-cup (2.5-L) casserole. Put a pan of hot water — 1 inch (2.5 cm) deep — large enough to hold casserole in oven.

Break eggs into prepared casserole and beat to blend with a fork. Stir in milk, sugar, vanilla and salt, blending well. Add rice and raisins and stir. Sprinkle generously with nutmeg.

Set casserole in pan of hot water in oven and bake until set, about 1 hours and 25 minutes. Stir with a fork after first 30 minutes baking. Serve warm or cold.

SERVES 8

Apricot Upside-Down Cake

20-oz can	apricot halves	568-ml can
1/4 cup	butter, melted	60 ml
1/2 cup	brown sugar, packed	125 ml
1/4 cup	coconut	60 ml
	maraschino cherries (optional)	
1/3 cup	soft shortening	80 ml
1	egg	1
1 cup	sugar	250 ml
1 1/3 cups	sifted all-purpose flour	330 ml
2 tsp	baking powder	10 ml
1/2 tsp	salt	2 ml
2/3 cup	milk	160 ml
1/2 tsp	almond extract	2 ml
1/2 cup	flaked coconut	125 ml
	Apricot Sauce (recipe follows)	

Heat oven to 350 °F (175 °C). Have ready a 9-inch (23-cm) square cake pan.

Drain apricots well, saving juice for sauce. Stir butter, brown sugar and 1/4 cup (60 ml) coconut together in cake pan. Lay apricot halves, some cut side up and others cut side down with a cherry tucked underneath, in the butter-sugar mixture.

Combine shortening, egg and sugar in small mixing bowl. Beat at high speed until fluffy. Sift flour, baking powder and salt together. Combine milk and almond extract. Add sifted dry ingredients to shortening mixture alternately with milk mixture, beginning and ending with dry ingredients. Stir until smooth after each addition. Stir in 1/2 cup (125 ml) coconut.

Spread over apricots. Bake 55 to 60 minutes or until center springs back when touched lightly.

Invert on serving plate and let pan stand over cake a minute to be sure all the apricot mixture drops out. Serve warm, cut in squares and topped with a little Apricot Sauce.

SERVES 6 OR 9 →

Apple Topped Gingerbread

Apricot Sauce

	apricot juice	
2 tbsp	cornstarch	30 ml

Measure apricot juice and add water to make 2 cups (500 ml) liquid. Put about 1/4 cup (60 ml) of this liquid in a small dish. Add cornstarch and stir until smooth. Heat rest of apricot juice to boiling and stir in cornstarch mixture gradually. Bring back to a boil over high heat and boil 1 minute. Serve warm.

1/2 cup	soft butter	125 ml
2/3 cup	sugar	180 ml
2	eggs	2
1/4 cup	molasses	60 ml
2 cups	sifted all-purpose flour	500 ml
1 tsp	soda	5 ml
1/2 tsp	salt	2 ml
1 tsp	ginger	5 ml
1 tsp	cinnamon	5 ml
1/4 tsp	allspice	1 ml
1 cup	milk	250 ml
	hot applesauce	

Heat oven to 350 °F (175 °C). Grease a 9- x 9- x 2-inch (23- x 23- x 5-cm) square pan.

Cream butter. Add sugar and beat together until fluffy. Add eggs and beat again until well-blended and fluffy. Beat in molasses.

Sift flour, soda, salt, ginger, cinnamon and allspice together. Add to first mixture alternately with milk, mixing to blend after each addition.

Pour into prepared pan and bake 35 minutes or until top springs back when touched lightly in the center. Serve warm cut in large pieces. Spoon hot applesauce over each serving.

——— SERVES 6 ———

Left: Apricot Upside-Down Cake
Right: Apple Topped Gingerbread

Baked Orange Soufflé

	sugar	
1/4 cup	butter	60 ml
1/3 cup	flour	80 ml
pinch	salt	pinch
1 cup	milk	250 ml
1 tbsp	grated orange rind	15 ml
1/2 cup	orange juice	125 ml
6	egg yolks	6
6	egg whites	6
1/4 cup	sugar	60 ml

Orange Sauce
(recipe follows)

Fasten a double strip of aluminum foil tightly around a 10-cup (2.5 L) soufflé dish letting the foil extend about 2 inches (5 cm) above the top of the dish. Butter the dish and the inside of the foil. Sprinkle about 2 tbsp (30 ml) sugar into dish and shake it around to coat the dish and the foil.

Heat oven to 325 °F (160 °C).

Melt butter in medium saucepan. Sprinkle in flour and salt and stir to blend. Remove from heat and add milk all at once. Stir to blend. Return to moderate heat and cook until boiling, thickened and smooth, stirring. Remove from heat. Stir in orange rind and juice.

Beat egg yolks until thick and lemon-colored (5 minutes at high speed on mixer). Stir in orange mixture gradually (use low speed on mixer if desired).

Beat egg whites until foamy. Add sugar gradually, beating well after each addition. Continue beating until stiff. Fold in egg yolk mixture. Pour into prepared soufflé dish.

Bake about 1 hour and 15 minutes or until well browned and set. Serve immediately with warm Orange Sauce spooned over.

Note: This soufflé is delicious but not sweet. It is perfect when the sweet Orange Sauce is added.

—————— SERVES 8 ——————

Orange Sauce

1/2 cup	sugar	125 ml
2 tbsp	cornstarch	30 ml
pinch	salt	pinch
1 1/2 cups	orange juice	375 ml
1 tbsp	butter	15 ml
1	orange, peeled, sectioned and diced	1

Combine sugar, cornstarch and salt thoroughly in medium saucepan. Stir in orange juice gradually, stirring until smooth. Set over high heat and bring to a boil, stirring 1 minute. Stir in butter. Keep warm. Stir in orange bits at serving time.

Strawberry-Pineapple Delight

Strawberry-Pineapple Delight

1/4 cup	sugar	60 ml
2 cups	sliced fresh strawberries	500 ml
1/2 cup	canned pineapple pieces with juice	125 ml
3-oz pkg	strawberry gelatin crystals	90-g pkg
2 tbsp	lemon juice	30 ml
1 pinch	salt	1 pinch
1 cup	strained pineapple	250 ml

Add sugar to strawberries and stir lightly. Let stand for 30 minutes at room temperature. Measure and strain strawberry juice and add water to make 1 cup of liquid.

Mix this liquid with the pineapple juice in a small saucepan and bring to a boil. Put gelatin powder in a bowl and pour over boiling liquid. Mix until gelatin powder is dissolved. Add lemon juice and salt while mixing. Cool in ice water stirring occasionally until gelatin begins to thicken. Stir in strawberries and pineapple bits. Pour into sherbet cups and refrigerate until firm.

6 PORTIONS

Mixed Fruit Cocktail

2/3 cup	orange juice	160 ml
2 tbsp	lemon juice	30 ml
1/3 cup	sugar	80 ml
2 tsp	grated orange rind	10 ml
1 tsp	grated lemon rind	5 ml
1/8 tsp	salt	0.5 ml
3	peaches	3
3	pears	3
1 cup	blueberries (fresh or frozen)	250 ml
	mint sprigs	

Combine orange juice, lemon juice, sugar, orange rind, lemon rind and salt in a small saucepan. Bring to a boil, turn down heat, simmer 5 minutes. Pour into a shallow metal pan and cool. Put in freezer and chill until a few ice crystals form around the edges.

Peel and slice peaches. Peel and cube pears. Mix these fruits with the blueberries and spoon some of the mixture into each of 6 sherbet glasses. Spoon a little of the icy orange juice mixture over each. Garnish with sprigs of mint and serve immediately.

SERVES 6

Chocolate Soufflé

	butter	
	sugar	
3 oz	unsweetened chocolate	90 g
2 tbsp	butter	30 ml
3/4 cup	sifted all-purpose flour	180 ml
3/4 cup	sugar	180 ml
1/3 tsp	salt	0.5 ml
2 cups	milk	500 ml
6	egg yolks	6
1/2 tsp	vanilla	2 ml
8	egg whites	8
1/4 tsp	cream of tartar	1 ml
	Liqueur Sauce (recipe follows)	

Butter a 10-cup (2.5-L) soufflé dish well. Sprinkle in about 2 tbsp (30 ml) sugar and shake it around to coat bottom and sides. Make a collar of doubled aluminum foil that will just fit around the top of the dish. Butter it and sprinkle with sugar. Fasten it tightly around the soufflé dish, sugared side in.

Put chocolate and butter in a small bowl and set in pan of simmering water to melt.

Combine flour, sugar and salt in large heavy saucepan. Stir in milk gradually. Set over moderate heat and cook until mixture is very thick and beginning to bubble, stirring constantly. Remove from heat.

Beat egg yolks well with a wooden spoon. Beat in a little of the hot mixture. Gradually stir egg yolk mixture into mixture in saucepan. Cook just until mixture bubbles, stirring. Remove from heat. Add chocolate mixture and vanilla and beat to blend well. Cool 10 minutes.

Heat oven to 350 °F (175 °C).

Combine egg whites and cream of tartar in a large mixer bowl. Beat until egg whites are stiff but not dry. Add about 1/3 of the egg whites to the chocolate mixture and fold to blend very well. Add remaining egg whites and fold as little as possible just until blended.

Pour into prepared soufflé dish. Bake 55 to 60 minutes or until just set. Serve immediately with Liqueur Sauce spooned over.

———— SERVES 8 ————

Liqueur Sauce

4	egg yolks	4
2 tbsp	sugar	30 ml
1/4 cup	coffee liqueur	60 ml
1/3 cup	whipping cream, whipped	80 ml

Beat egg yolks in top of double boiler until thick. Beat in sugar gradually and continue beating until very thick and lemon-colored. Set over simmering water and beat in coffee liqueur slowly. Beat until mixture is fluffy, about 5 minutes. Set in ice water and beat until cold. Fold in cream. Chill until serving time.

Individual Fruit Puddings

2/3 cup	chopped mixed candied fruit	160 ml
3/4 cup	cut up dates	180 ml
2/3 cup	golden raisins	160 ml
2 tsp	grated orange rind	10 ml
1/2 cup	coarsely chopped walnuts	125 ml
2 tbsp	all-purpose flour	30 ml
1/4 cup	soft shortening	60 ml
1/4 cup	sugar	60 ml
1	egg	1
1 tbsp	orange juice	15 ml
1/2 cup	sifted all-purpose flour	125 ml
1/2 tsp	baking powder	2 ml
1/4 tsp	salt	1 ml

sweetened whipped cream
or Brandy Butter Sauce
(recipe follows)

Grease six 6-oz (180-ml) custard cups.

Mix candied fruit, dates, raisins, orange rind and nuts in a bowl. Add the 2 tbsp (30 ml) flour and toss together until fruit is coated with flour.

Beat shortening, sugar and egg together until well blended. Stir in orange juice.

Sift flour, baking powder and salt together into shortening mixture and stir to blend well. Add to fruit mixture and mix well.

Spoon into prepared custard cups. Cover each with a square of aluminum foil. Put on rack in large saucepan or kettle. Add boiling water to just cover bottoms of custard cups. Cover pan tightly and steam puddings 1 hour and 15 minutes or until tops spring back when touched lightly.

Unmould and serve topped with whipped cream or Brandy Butter Sauce.

———— SERVES 6 ————

Brandy Butter Sauce

1 cup	brown sugar, packed	250 ml
1 cup	light cream	250 ml
1/4 cup	butter	60 ml
1/4 cup	brandy	60 ml

Stir sugar and cream together in a small saucepan until sugar is dissolved. Set over low heat. Add butter and cook until mixture comes to a boil, stirring often.

Remove from heat, stir in brandy and serve hot.

———— MAKES ABOUT 1 3/4 CUPS (430 ML) ————

Steamed Apple-Raisin Pudding

1/4 cup	butter	60 ml
1/2 cup	brown sugar, packed	125 ml
1	egg	1
1/2 cup	molasses	125 ml
1 tbsp	grated orange rind	15 ml
2 cups	finely ground quick-cooking rolled oats (see note)	500 ml
1/2 tsp	salt	2 ml
1/2 tsp	baking soda	2 ml
1 tsp	baking powder	5 ml
1 tsp	ginger	5 ml
1 tsp	cinnamon	5 ml
1/2 cup	buttermilk or soured milk	125 ml
1 cup	chopped peeled apples	250 ml
1/2 cup	seedless raisins	125 ml
	Lemon Sauce (recipe follows)	

Steamed Apple-Raisin Pudding

Grease thoroughly and sugar an 8-cup (2-L) mould with a tube in the center.

Cream butter and sugar to blend. Beat in egg, molasses and orange rind.

Mix ground rolled oats, salt, soda, baking powder and spices well and add to first mixture alternately with buttermilk or soured milk. Stir in apples and raisins. Spoon into prepared mould. Cover tightly with aluminum foil and set on rack in a large kettle. Add boiling water to halfway up the side of the mould, cover the pan tightly and steam 1 1/2 hours.

Unmould and serve hot cut in wedges.

Note: Grind rolled oats through the fine blade of the food chopper or use the blender.

SERVES 8

Lemon Sauce

1 cup	sugar	250 ml
1/4 tsp	salt	1 ml
2 tbsp	cornstarch	30 ml
1/4 cup	lemon juice	60 ml
1 1/2 cups	boiling water	300 ml
2 tsp	grated lemon rind	10 ml
1 tsp	grated orange rind	5 ml
1 tbsp	butter	15 ml

Combine sugar, salt and cornstarch thoroughly in saucepan. Stir in lemon juice and boiling water gradually. Set over high heat and bring to a boil, stirring constantly. Turn down heat and boil gently 1 minute. Remove from heat and stir in lemon rind, orange rind and butter. Serve hot.

Fruit Cocktail

1 large	ripe avocado, cubed	1 large
1/2 cup	cubed canned peaches	125 ml
1 cup	halved seeded grapes	250 ml
1/2 cup	frozen strawberries, thawed just enough to break apart	125 ml
1/4 cup	canned peach syrup	60 ml
2 tbsp	lime juice	30 ml
2 tbsp	honey	30 ml

Combine fruits in a bowl. Combine peach syrup, lime juice and honey and pour over fruit. Cover with transparent wrap and chill well, stirring occasionally. Spoon into sherbet glasses to serve.

SERVES 4 TO 6

Fruit in Jelly

28-oz can	pineapple tidbits	796-ml can
28-oz can	sliced peaches	796-ml can
14-oz can	red pitted cherries	398-ml can
4	oranges, peeled and sectioned	4
6-oz pkg	lemon jelly powder	165-g pkg
2 cups	Sauternes wine	500 ml
4	bananas, sliced thick	4
3 cups	seedless green grapes or halved, seeded red grapes	750 ml

Drain pineapple tidbits and peaches and measure out 1 cup (250 ml) of each kind of juice. (Refrigerate any remaining juice for some other use.) Drain cherries. Dry pineapple, peaches, cherries and orange sections on paper towelling.

Heat the 2 cups (500 ml) fruit juice to boiling. Put jelly powder in a bowl and add hot fruit juice. Stir until jelly powder is dissolved. Stir in Sauternes. Set jelly mixture in a bowl of ice water and chill just until beginning to thicken, stirring often.

Layer fruit in a large glass bowl — 14-cup (3.5-L) size is just right — in this order while jelly is chilling: peach slices, banana slices, half of grapes, cherries, pineapple tidbits, orange sections, remaining grapes. Pour jelly over fruit. Cover and chill several hours. (The jelly will not be rubbery stiff but will just be stiff enough to cling to the fruit.) Serve in large sherbet glasses.

SERVES 12

Fruit Cocktail

Crusty Baked Apples

1/3 cup	soft butter or margarine	80 ml
3/4 cup	brown sugar, packed	180 ml
3/4 cup	sifted all-purpose flour	180 ml
1 1/2 tsp	cinnamon	7 ml
3/4 tsp	ginger	3 ml
1/4 tsp	nutmeg	1 ml
1/8 tsp	salt	0.5 ml
6 medium	baking apples	6 medium
2 tbsp	brown sugar	30 ml

whipped cream or light cream

Heat oven to 350 °F (175 °C). Have ready a baking dish that will just hold the apples with a little space between.

Cream butter or margarine and 3/4 cup (180 ml) brown sugar together until well blended. Stir in flour, cinnamon, ginger, nutmeg and salt and blend well.

Peel and core apples. Score the outside of each apple deeply all over with the tines of a fork. Press sugar mixture all over outside of each apple with hands (if you press quite firmly the sugar mixture will stick well). Set apples in baking dish. Put 1 tsp (5 ml) brown sugar in the middle of each.

Bake about 40 minutes or until apples are tender and outsides are crisp. Serve warm with cream.

MAKES 6

Cream butter or margarine and brown sugar together until well blended. Stir in flour, cinnamon, ginger, nutmeg and salt and blend well.

Peel and core apples. Score the outside of each apple deeply all over with the tines of a fork.

Press sugar mixture all over outside of each apple with hands.

Set apples in baking dish. Put 1 tsp (5 ml) brown sugar in the middle of each.

Bake about 40 minutes or until apples are tender and outsides are crisp.

Whole-Wheat Nut Bread

3 cups	whole-wheat flour	750 ml
2 tbsp	sugar	30 ml
3 tsp	baking soda	15 ml
1 tsp	salt	5 ml
1/2 tsp	nutmeg	2 ml
1/2 cup	molasses	125 ml
2 cups	buttermilk or soured milk	500 ml
1/2 cup	chopped pecans	125 ml
1 tbsp	molasses	15 ml
1 tbsp	melted butter	15 ml
1/4 cup	finely chopped pecans	60 ml

Heat oven to 350 °F (175 °C). Grease a 9- x 5- x 3-inch (23- x 12.5 x 7.5-cm) loaf pan.

Measure whole-wheat flour into mixing bowl. Add sugar, soda, salt and nutmeg and mix together lightly with a fork. Beat 1/2 cup (125 ml) molasses and milk together with fork and add to dry ingredients. Stir just to blend. Add 1/2 cup (125 ml) nuts and blend very lightly. Spoon into prepared pan.

Bake 45 minutes or until a toothpick stuck in the center comes out clean. Combine 1 tbsp (15 ml) molasses, melted butter and 1/4 cup (60 ml) nuts and spread over top of loaf. Return to oven for 5 minutes. Turn out on rack to cool.

MAKES 1 LOAF

Cornmeal Loaf

1/2 cup	warm water	125 ml
1 tsp	sugar	5 ml
1 pkg	dry yeast	1 pkg
3/4 cup	boiling water	180 ml
1/2 cup	cornmeal	125 ml
1 tbsp	grated orange rind	15 ml
3 tbsp	soft shortening	45 ml
1/4 cup	molasses	60 ml
2 tsp	salt	10 ml
1	egg	1
2 3/4 cups	sifted all-purpose flour	685 ml

Grease a 9- x 5- x 3-inch (23- x 12.5- x 7.5-cm) loaf pan.

Measure warm water. Add sugar and stir until sugar is dissolved. Sprinkle yeast over and let stand 10 minutes. Stir well.

Combine boiling water, cornmeal, orange rind, shortening, molasses and salt in large mixer bowl, beating at low speed until blended. Cool to lukewarm. Add yeast mixture, egg and half the flour. Beat at low speed to blend, then continue beating 2 minutes at medium speed. Stir in remaining flour with a wooden spoon.

Spoon into prepared pan and flatten top with lightly floured hand. Let rise in a warm place until dough is 1 inch (2.5 cm) below top of pan, about 50 minutes.

Heat oven to 375 °F (190 °C). Bake loaf about 35 minutes or until it sounds hollow when tapped on top.

——— MAKES 1 LOAF ———

Applesauce Bread

2	eggs	2
2/3 cup	brown sugar, packed	160 ml
1/3 cup	cooking oil	80 ml
1 cup	canned sweetened applesauce	250 ml
1 1/2 cups	sifted all-purpose flour	375 ml
1 tsp	baking powder	5 ml
1 tsp	baking soda	5 ml
1 tsp	salt	5 ml
1 tsp	cinnamon	5 ml
1/2 tsp	nutmeg	2 ml
1 1/2 cups	rolled oats	375 ml
3/4 cup	cut-up dried prunes	180 ml
1/2 cup	chopped walnuts	125 ml

Heat oven to 350 °F (175 °C). Grease a loaf pan, 9 x 5 x 3 inches (23 x 12.5 x 7.5 cm).

Beat eggs, brown sugar and oil together well. Stir in apple-sauce.

Sift flour, baking powder, soda, salt and spices together into first mixture. Add rolled oats, prunes and nuts and blend well.

Spoon into prepared pan and bake 45 to 50 minutes or until a toothpick stuck in the center comes out clean.

——— MAKES 1 LOAF ———

Left: Whole-Wheat Nut Bread
Right: Cornmeal Loaf

347

Index